THE FRANCHISE

PITTSBURGH PENGUINS

A Curated History of the Pens

BOB GROVE

TRIUMPH BOOKS

Library of Congress Cataloging-in-Publication Data available upon request.

This book is available in quantity at special discounts for your group or organization. For further information, contact:

Triumph Books LLC
814 North Franklin Street
Chicago, Illinois 60610
(312) 337-0747
www.triumphbooks.com

Printed in U.S.A.
ISBN: 978-1-63727-895-6
Design by Preston Pisellini
Page production by Patricia Frey

For Claire, Suzanne and Brent

CONTENTS

PART 4 The Cup Seasons

PART 5 The Builders

Foreword

In 1982, I drove my mom's 1978 Mercury Cougar through the Squirrel Hill Tunnel into Pittsburgh, not knowing a thing about the city, the people, the dialect or how rabid a fan base it had for its sports teams. Something told me I belonged here and I was determined to plant my roots in this city even though I had zero guarantees that I would be here more than a week. As a walk-on free agent with the Penguins, I was offered a couple of nights in a hotel, some meal money and, most importantly, an opportunity.

"The City of Champions" was a slogan that was proudly saluted as the Steelers had won their fourth championship in six years in 1979—the same year the Pirates won the World Series. Unfortunately, the Penguins were a bit of a mess in the late 1970s and early 1980s—until, of course, Mario Lemieux arrived and ignited hope and excitement that meant being a Penguins fan was cool again.

Since the Penguins came into the NHL in 1967, only the Montreal Canadiens (10) and Edmonton Oilers (five) have as many Stanley Cups as the Penguins, who earned five in a 26-year span. Those playoff runs brought more joy to this city than words can express, and I was so proud to have played a part on the ice for those first two Cups. No other organization has had one generational player in Mario pass the torch to another in Sidney Crosby and in such a short time period continue to win championships. The winning atmosphere around Pittsburgh was in the air, like the aroma of the blooming white flowers of the dogwood trees.

I kid around sometimes on the air now as a radio and TV analyst for the team that we are the "Penguinies," which means we are an organization that does nothing easy, from dealing with the wins and losses to the hurdles we have had to overcome; from bankruptcy and car accidents to several players, including Mario, battling through cancer diagnoses to Sidney Crosby's career-threatening concussion. That is what makes being a Penguins fan so great: we as a city and as an organization have had some greatness in Mario and Sid dropped in our lap, but almost every great achievement has come on the heels of heart-wrenching moments.

On and off the ice, the Penguins have experienced incredible highs and lows. Nothing has come easy, and I guess that is what makes it all worth it to have five Stanley Cup championships associated with that crest. I've been incredibly lucky and blessed to be here to see almost all of it unfold.

One other person has also had a seat at the front of the roller coaster: Bob Grove. Nobody, and I mean nobody, knows this organization like Bob does and can recall in great detail the dates and details of some of the most significant moments that have been memorable mile markers for a ride that I hope never ends. Bob is so much more than a historian. He has a passion for the game, the team and the city that makes me proud to call him a dear friend, and I hope you thoroughly enjoy this book.

—Phil Bourque

PART 1

THE EARLY YEARS

1

Owners' Carousel

Since the National Hockey League formed in 1917, the stark reality is that not every team survives in its original market. Pittsburgh hockey fans discovered this the hard way in 1930, losing the NHL's Pirates after just five seasons. It took the league 37 years to return to the city, although that return often threatened to be only temporary. The geographic fate of the Pittsburgh Penguins, indeed, has withstood more rumors, speculation and close calls than any NHL franchise that has remained in its original home for six decades.

Along the way, across the continent, newspaper coverage running the gamut from one sentence to one paragraph to entire stories has introduced, mentioned, amplified, questioned or denied rumors of the Penguins moving to Seattle, Hamilton, Ont., Atlanta, Kansas City, Denver, Cleveland, Edmonton, Alta., Miami, Long Island, San Francisco and New Jersey.

Much of this uncertainty traced its origins back to the franchise's birth in 1967, when the idea of the Penguins lasting long enough in Pittsburgh to be five-time Stanley Cup champions would have been deemed the most improbable kind of dream.

As the Penguins poured onto their home ice for their first NHL game against the famed Montreal Canadiens on Oct. 11, 1967, it was a moment of understandable civic pride. A group of 20 local investors had produced the $2 million expansion fee that made Pittsburgh one of six new cities doubling the league's size. It was a well-known hockey market sporting a 26-year association with and three championships in the NHL's development league, the American Hockey League (AHL), and had beaten bids from Vancouver, Buffalo, Cleveland and Baltimore to land in the world's top hockey league.

What fans at the Civic Arena, Pittsburgh's six-year-old architectural wonder with a domed, retractable roof in the city's Lower Hill District, didn't know that night was team ownership was already in need of investment capital. Four weeks later—just a dozen games into the team's existence—it was announced baseball's Atlanta Braves had withdrawn their bid to purchase 40 percent of the Penguins, and a Pittsburgh newspaper headline put the odds at 60-40 the team would be staying in the city.

Thus was born the financial environment in which the team lived for much of its formative years, a "here today, possibly gone tomorrow" existence. In the Penguins' first 11 seasons, the absence of owners with deep and stable financial resources directly affected their ability to compete. Among the 1967 expansion franchises, only the Oakland Seals, known as the California Golden Seals when they moved to Cleveland in 1976, played fewer or won fewer playoff games than the Penguins in those first 11 seasons.

It had all started with such promise. As a youth growing up in Pittsburgh's Squirrel Hill neighborhood and attending

Allderdice High School, Peter Block listened to *Hockey Night in Canada* radio broadcasts and attended Pittsburgh Hornets' AHL games at Duquesne Garden. When he found out the NHL was expanding, he began trying to raise money to submit a franchise application. "The idea that all those guys who I used to listen to on the radio could be coming to Pittsburgh... the idea was fantastic to me," Block said. But he was getting nowhere and mentioned it one day during a business trip to Harrisburg with Pitt Law School classmate and State Senator Jack McGregor.

"He was more or less complaining about the opportunity that was there and seemed to be slipping away," McGregor said. "I told him I might be able to develop some investor interest." McGregor was only a casual hockey fan and more interested in baseball and football, but he was better connected. "I got lucky, or I guess Pittsburgh got lucky," he said, "and the first four or five calls I made were to some people who were very sympathetic in support of the project."

McGregor and Block weren't the first group to propose putting a team in Pittsburgh. Chicago banker John Gleason, a Notre Dame graduate, had already assembled a group that included local promoter John McGreevey as part of what NHL President Clarence Campbell called "a very strong Pittsburgh representation." The only thing standing in the city's way, he said, was the need to add at least 1,800 seats to the Civic Arena to get capacity up to 12,500, a process for which the city Auditorium Authority had already been given approval.

McGregor's list of investors read like a roll call of Pittsburgh's best-known families. In addition to McGregor and Block, the original group of investors included H.J. Heinz III, Henry Hillman and Richard Mellon Scaife. Art Rooney Sr., owner of the Pittsburgh Steelers, was approached but did not think it was proper to own two teams in the same city. Yet he contributed in a different way as he successfully lobbied half-brothers Bruce and Jim Norris, owners of the Detroit Red Wings and Chicago Black Hawks, respectively, to support Pittsburgh's inclusion in the 1967 expansion, having known Jim Norris through his horse racing interests. "Art was really the unsung hero of the whole saga," McGregor said.

Pittsburgh was announced on Feb. 9, 1966, as one of the league's six new teams, with the franchise going to McGregor and Block. Campbell noted that "Pittsburgh's list of men involved all are fine, worthy gentlemen representative of the kind that any league would be proud of."

It was an outstanding group, to be sure, but Block said later the NHL "never knew how little all these people actually had in the deal." Block said the group, which included former Yale University hockey captain Clint Childs, had contributed about $700,000 toward the expansion fee and borrowed the rest from Mellon Bank. The group's purpose had been to raise the expansion fee and win Pittsburgh a place in the NHL, not necessarily to bankroll the team's operation for years going forward, and initially only McGregor and Block were actively involved in the team's business.

By the time the team hit the ice, Hockey Club of Pittsburgh, Inc. had been dealing with a quick escalation in NHL salaries and its unexpectedly larger share of NHL settlements with the Western Hockey League and American Hockey League whose markets had been taken. It was looking for investment outside the city because efforts to find more local capital had been unsuccessful.

Just eight months after the Penguins' franchise was granted, two-thirds of the Penguins' owners also invested in the formation of the Pittsburgh Phantoms, a team in the new National Professional Soccer League. This turned out to be a major mistake. The last-place Phantoms lasted one season, losing a reported $750,000, employing four coaches and contributing to the NPSL's sketchy existence by playing an infamous game in Toronto in which the referee instructed players to go down with feigned injuries to ensure the national CBS telecast had time to insert commercials.

The soccer losses—Campbell called them "a tragedy"—were incurred before the Penguins' inaugural season and were weighing on the minds of affected Penguins' investors eager to find new capital sources, like the one from Atlanta. Braves' president Bill Bartholomay told the *Atlanta Journal* "there was a great deal of infighting and much turmoil" among the Penguins' owners when his group decided to back off its verbal agreement with the team.

Block later described the ownership group as "completely fragmented." Given the soccer disaster, he said, "the result was that guys wanted to get out of hockey. Every nickel we put in, we lost."

Four months after the Braves pulled out, but still one week before the Penguins' first season was completed, 80 percent interest in the team was purchased by nine Michigan businessmen, a group headed by Donald Parsons. Parsons, who grew up in the Philadelphia area, was board chairman of the Bank of the Commonwealth in Detroit and head of The Parsons Group, which controlled a stable of 19 U.S. banks.

Parsons watched average attendance in the second season fall to a still-franchise low 6,008 in 1968–69, and while it increased the following season with a team good enough to win a playoff round, attendance remained below levels the team had achieved in its inaugural season. By then, Parsons had bigger banking challenges and had been borrowing heavily, attracting the scrutiny of regulators and the U.S. Treasury. By late summer, 1970, Parsons resigned his Bank of the Commonwealth position and was selling the team, and by December the NHL assumed operation of the Penguins.

Campbell had no shortage of potential buyers but made it clear the league's first choice was to keep the team in Pittsburgh. He told reporters Atlanta Hawks' owner Tom Cousins, looking for a hockey team to join his NBA team in the soon-to-open Omni Coliseum, "tried to move the Penguins to Atlanta but we don't believe in carpetbagging franchises." Campbell instead cut a deal, giving Cousins first right of refusal on the NHL's next expansion franchise (Cousins' Atlanta Flames began play in 1972) in return for Cousins helping to fund a group headed by William Blair of East Liverpool, Ohio, that wanted to buy the Penguins and keep them in town.

But it was a Pittsburgh group which purchased the team for $7 million in April 1971. Block, who had resigned his position with the Penguins prior to Parsons' purchase of the team, was back as an owner along with Elmore Keener, Peter Burchfield III and 38-year-old Tad Potter, a marketing executive with Peoples Natural Gas Co. and grandson of Rockwell International founder Willard Rockwell.

Like Block, Potter had grown up a hockey fan "back to the days of Duquesne Gardens, where I sold popcorn while I was in high school," he said. "I can still remember I took the 64 streetcar from Edgewood and got off on Craig Street, me and three other kids. We loved hockey."

As the team's chief executive officer, Potter was taking over 18 months before the 1972 debut of the rival World Hockey Association, which increased NHL salaries and competition for players, and just before the U.S. economy was hit by double-digit inflation and high unemployment. Despite these challenges and the team's failure to qualify for the playoffs in two of its first three seasons under Potter's ownership, attendance grew to a franchise-record average of 11,224 in 1974–75, when the team recorded a 20-game home unbeaten streak—still the franchise record—and opened the playoffs with five straight victories.

All of it amid obvious financial difficulties.

"We had two towels per player, we couldn't get sticks, weren't paying hotel bills on road, you could see something was going on," remembers center Pierre Larouche, who was drafted in 1974. "My junior team was treated better than we were here at the time. But you play hockey, that's your job, you don't pay attention to what's going on. We knew things were tight, but to what level, I don't think anybody knew."

Center Syl Apps Jr., who had joined the team in 1971, was already used to it. "We always seemed to be in financial trouble," Apps said. "It was kind of an interesting time for Pittsburgh. The Steelers were winning, the Pirates were winning, and we were the poor cousins. If you were just playing the game, it didn't rub guys too much. Where it did hurt a little...at one point we had six or seven players with one pair of skates. If you had a dozen sticks, 'You better use them, cause we're not sending them back.' Things were pretty sparse, let's put it that way."

Then the bottom fell out, both on and off the ice.

In a cruel twist for fans, in the second round of the 1975 playoffs, the Penguins became just the second team in NHL history to blow a 3–0 series lead and lost to the New York Islanders. Seven weeks later, the IRS padlocked the Penguins' offices, citing the team's failure to pay more than $527,000 in employee withholding taxes. The following day, Equibank filed suit against the team to recover almost $5 million in loans. One more victory over the Islanders would have brought at least two and perhaps more home playoff dates with revenue that would have helped considerably.

Potter had been keeping the NHL apprised of his efforts to find new capital for the team and said he had been negotiating a payment plan with the IRS. "They got a new district director, and this new guy came in and decided he was going to make a name for himself," recalled Potter. "An agent who was working down there told me later—and I can still remember him saying this to me—the new guy said, 'Shut them down now. Make some noise.' So they came into my office and said, 'Don't touch a thing. Just get up from your desk and leave.'"

The team was $6.5 million in debt, including about $1 million owed to the league, and was placed in receivership. General manager Jack Button had been named receiver by the U.S. District Court and was accountable for the team's daily operation and finances, while Potter continued looking for new investors. Frank Fuhrer, local owner of the Pittsburgh Triangles of World Team Tennis, said his family talked him out of buying the Penguins. Potter had a brief discussion with New York Yankees' owner George Steinbrenner, who Potter said wanted the ability to move the team.

When Larouche went to the Civic Arena to grab his equipment, he was told "not to do anything, not to buy anything. The team is going to Seattle." A Seattle group which had been closely monitoring the Penguins' situation said it had been asked to submit a bid by the NHL, which refused to operate the Penguins for a second time in five years. "We're full of good sentiments," Campbell said, "but we're out of money."

But in early July 1975, the league accepted a better bid of $3.8 million from a group headed by Albert Savill of Columbus,

Ohio, a native of England and owner of the Columbus Owls of the International Hockey League. The group, which included Otto Frenzel III and Wren Blair, who owned the Saginaw Gears of the IHL and had spent the previous seven seasons as general manager of the NHL's Minnesota North Stars, rescued the team from a likely move to Seattle.

Blair served as the Penguins' president and general manager and had just 20 percent interest in the team, but by December 1976, he had been phased out of his day-to-day role, telling reporters he had other business interests and the Penguins were not the most prominent among them. Four months later, businessman Edward DeBartolo Sr. of Youngstown, Ohio, took Blair's stock and more, becoming one-third owner of the team, which as always was in search of investors.

One year later, in April 1978, DeBartolo took full control of the team, which had now featured six different ownership groups in 11 seasons. "I initially got involved to help out two friends," DeBartolo told the *Pittsburgh Press*. "But sometimes you get drawn into something you don't want."

DeBartolo became a billionaire as owner of the world's biggest mall development company and by the time of his death in 1994 was still ranked among the 100 richest people in America by *Forbes* magazine. While all of the Penguins' previous owners had included principals with some ties or affinity for hockey, DeBartolo had none, though he also purchased the San Francisco 49ers of the NFL and several racetracks.

But the hard-working DeBartolo, who had graduated from Notre Dame with a degree in civil engineering, was an investor with a financial profile unlike any of those who had previously owned the team. His 13-and-a-half-year tenure as Penguins' principal owner ended the days of looking for capital infusions into the team, and the stability DeBartolo brought to the

Penguins allowed them to preserve a future in the city despite falling to the bottom of the NHL standings in 1983 and 1984.

DeBartolo understood from the start the massive challenge on his hands, as the *Pittsburgh Post-Gazette* had written in the summer of 1978 that Pittsburgh "is not regarded as an Eden by NHL players, either as a place to live or work, the latter because of past tendencies by Penguin management to keep such a firm hold on club funds that George Washington grimaced."

Having just completed his first season with the Penguins at the time DeBartolo took full control of the team, NHL bad boy Dave Schultz said, "This is no knock against Pittsburgh, but it has a bad name. Players aren't excited about coming here. My first few months, I was very disheartened, but now I love it."

DeBartolo didn't simply shrug off the money he was losing in his early years in the NHL, and he was losing a lot. By the summer of 1985, he had folded his Pittsburgh Maulers team in the United States Football League but also owned the Pittsburgh Spirit of the Major Indoor Soccer League, and he was tired of losing money with his Pittsburgh sports franchises—losses he said totaled $38 million, including $19 million with the Penguins.

So he challenged the Penguins and Spirit to sell an average of 10,000 season tickets each for their upcoming seasons—while he also sought tax and other concessions from city and county governments—in a campaign known as Action for the Spirit and Penguins (ASAP), after which he would decide the teams' futures with him in Pittsburgh. DeBartolo received some concessions and kept both teams for the next season, although the Spirit folded the following spring after a last-place finish.

"There was a lot of strife in the office about the viability of the Penguins and whether Edward J. DeBartolo had had enough," remembers Paul Steigerwald, then the team's director of marketing, adding that employees were closely monitoring reports of a possible move to Hamilton, Ont.

The Penguins would suffer later ownership drama, including a bankruptcy in 1998 under co-owners Roger Marino and Howard Baldwin and a tentative sale in 2006 to Canadian billionaire Jim Balsillie, who never shook the perception that he preferred to move the team to Hamilton, Ont., and later withdrew his bid. But there was no denying the Penguins had paid a high price in performance for the instability and chronic lack of funding displayed by their owners through those first 11 seasons.

2

A Radio Lifeline

IF MANY NHL PLAYERS VIEWED PITTSBURGH AS A PLACE to avoid in the 1970s, play-by-play man Mike Lange came to know it as the home of his dreams.

"I'll be very honest with you. When I came to Pittsburgh I thought I'd be here one year. I thought, the way my career was going to go, that I'd have to move around a few more times before I was able to accomplish what I wanted to accomplish. And lo and behold, he we are," Lange said in 2000, just past the halfway point of a 46-year Hall of Fame career calling Penguins' games on radio and television.

"It turned out to be a perfect fit for me. I walked into a situation that was tailor-made for me. With Bob Prince here and the uniqueness of the city and the broadcasters, which I didn't have any clue about when I first came here, it just seemed to be the thing that happened here. You can call it fate from above, and I really have a firm belief in fate, and I think that's what happened. I was destined to come here."

And destined to be loved by his fans in Pittsburgh and beyond. The city had already responded positively to the incomparable broadcast styles and personalities of two local legends: Prince, the Pirates' play-by-play man, and Myron Cope, the Steelers' radio color voice. Pittsburgh embraced Lange with the same fervor, and long before he retired in 2021 and passed away in 2025, he had cemented his legacy as a man who grew hockey's popularity, provided the soundtrack to a thousand memories and acted as the fans' lifeline to the team.

Lange grew up in Sacramento, California, earned his broadcasting degree at Sacramento State University and cut his professional teeth in Phoenix and San Diego. Pittsburgh was not even on his radar until the Western Hockey League folded in 1974, ending his play-by-play role for the San Diego Gulls, to which he had graduated after beginning his career with the WHL's Phoenix Roadrunners. Gulls' general manager Max McNab contacted Penguins' general manager and friend Jack Button, and Lange sent Button his résumé with two pennies taped to it. It began, "I'd like to put my two cents in..."

Lange was nothing if not creative. He had used similar approaches in previous job searches, sending Oakland A's owner Charlie Finley a résumé wrapped around a baseball bat and ABC Sports' Roone Arledge a résumé inside a baseball glove. Baseball was Lange's first love; he didn't attend his first hockey game until his college days. Lange had sent Phoenix broadcasting legend Al McCoy, then the play-by-play man for the Roadrunners, a résumé wrapped around a stuffed Roadrunner while looking for a job with the team. When the Roadrunners' PR man quit, Lange was hired and within weeks was providing color on the broadcasts before taking over for McCoy when he left for the Phoenix Suns.

Lange debuted with the Penguins on Oct. 9, 1974, but with the Penguins' future up in the air after being placed into receivership just after the conclusion of that season, he returned to San Diego and called San Diego Jaws' games in the North American Soccer League. Lange had applied for a Pirates' play-by-play position that year but lost it to Lanny Frattare, and when Gary Morrell left the Penguins' job after just one season, general manager Wren Blair offered it to Joe Starkey, whom Lange had replaced in 1974. Starkey turned it down and Lange was rehired for the 1976–77 season.

Fate again.

"I didn't mind being the second choice," said Lange, who also called Washington Diplomats soccer in the late 1970s and wound up calling some Pirates games on television in the late 1980s. "This is where I should have been all along. This is my place...my kind of people, my way of life."

Lange had asked for and was granted permission from his mentor McCoy to use McCoy's "Great Balls of Fire" catchphrase to follow the call of an important play on the ice, but Lange was about to create a vast inventory of his own. Following Prince's advice to get out in the community and interact with fans, Lange did that whenever possible at blues' clubs, community events, bars and restaurants. It was in those environments or while running errands or shopping, for example, that Lange would note quirky things he heard people say.

As Lange wrote on The Players Tribune in 2017, "One night I happened to be sitting at a bar, minding my own business, when everything changed. This guy walks in, and I could just tell he was a real character. As he strides in, he points to another gentleman sitting at the bar and calls out to the bartender, 'Buy Sam a drink, and get his dog one, too.' I heard it, and my ears perked up.

"There was something about it. Something uniquely Pittsburgh. And I thought...OK, you got something here. I wrote it down on a bar napkin. A few nights later the Penguins scored a big goal and the building exploded—and it just came out of me. 'Ohhhhh, buy Sam a drink, and get his dog one, too!' And you know what? At first, it didn't hit. It flopped. Nobody knew what to make of it. But I kept my ears open, and I kept absorbing these sayings."

Pittsburgh fans quickly grew to love his catchphrases, often getting both the drama of a goal call and then the anticipation of what Lange might say next. Lange characterized them as "expressions of disbelief" after he couldn't process what he had just seen on the ice. Soon fans who bumped into him began suggesting their own catchphrases for his use, and to ensure he had them right, he would ask each one to write it down, and soon he had a shoebox full of scraps of paper.

A goaltender beaten by Jaromír Jágr "doesn't know whether to cry or wind his watch." An early Pittsburgh goal might bring, "Get in the fast lane, grandma, the bingo game is ready to roll" or "Lookout, Loretta!" He exhorted fans to "call Arnold Slick from Turtle Creek," (which Pittsburghers rhyme) or suggested, "Let's go hunt moose on a Harley." When the Penguins scored a goal that put a game out of reach, Lange informed fans that "Elvis has just left the building," which became a particular favorite of Mario Lemieux's mother.

Said McCoy after Lange had established his reputation for the catchphrases, "You have to report the game, but you also have to hold an audience for three hours, so you have to give them something more than just the game. Mike's not afraid to have fun with it, and that's what separates him from the rest of the broadcasters."

Paul Steigerwald, who has done play-by-play and color for the Penguins on both radio and TV in his 46-year career as a Penguins' employee or broadcaster, spent years working with Lange and still marvels at how the California boy fit the city.

"He tapped into the ethos of Western Pennsylvania," Steigerwald said. "He was a folk hero in the true sense. Using the phrases given to him by the fans, he literally made the fans part of the process. That's a touch very few broadcasters accomplish in their careers."

Lange also involved the fans by opening The Night Owl Club, which they could join by listening to a Penguins' broadcast that hit the midnight mark. Steve Mears, who grew up in Pittsburgh, said Lange was "the number one reason" he pursued a broadcast career that now includes calling games for the Islanders, Penguins and Blue Jackets. He remembers as a kid looking forward to Lange beginning each broadcast with "It's a Hockey Night in Pittsburgh."

Mears called Lange's catchphrases "the icing on the cake. It was our entrance into his world with all these different characters like Arnold Slick and Loretta. He created this little world and we were all invited in. And that took his popularity to a completely different stratosphere."

While players and coaches came and went, sometimes at a dizzying pace, Lange could be counted upon to be there game after game and year after year, and fans especially seemed to lean on his presence for support when the Penguins were near the bottom of the standings. His calls began to be simulcast on television in 1979, although radio, to which he returned in 2006, was his favorite medium.

"I love to create the story on my own," said Lange, who was inducted into the Hockey Hall of Fame media wing in 2001 as winner of the Foster Hewitt Award. The Penguins named their press box the "Mike Lange Media Level" in 2019.

"Mike was the heart and soul of the franchise," said Matt McConnell, who had graduated from suburban Mt. Lebanon High School and later briefly took over the Penguins' radio calls shortly after Lange had moved exclusively to television in 1993.

Some fans were simply enamored with Lange's catchphrases, but most understood they were listening to a consummate pro who knew the game and his role while displaying an uncanny sense of anticipation. "He had that sixth sense of just knowing when something big was about to happen in any given game, he knew when those moments were, and he could build that anticipation, and that's what kept you on the edge of your seat as a hockey fan," Mears said.

Lange also developed a unique take on hockey's traditional "he shoots and scores" broadcast call by dragging out the pronunciation of "he," and thus fans understood the Penguins had scored before Lange actually finished telling them so.

"He was succinct, he was on the puck, you knew what was happening," said McConnell, whose long career in hockey also includes calling NHL games for the Ducks, Thrashers, Wild, Coyotes and Mammoth. "He was almost a reflection of the city. Pittsburgh is one of the hardest-working places on earth. He was no-nonsense, he was hard work, the way he called games was almost a blue-collar way of calling the games. He knew what the fans wanted, and that's why he was so successful."

As the Penguins evolved into a high-scoring team after the drafting of Lemieux in 1984, keeping up with the pace of their game was not always an easy exercise. But Lange mastered it, remembers Jack Michaels, who listened to Lange while growing up in Meadville, Pa., about 100 miles north of Pittsburgh, and went on to call games for the Edmonton Oilers.

"The Penguins played a breakneck style and they were elite. I was absolutely fascinated by Mike's ability to go 10 minutes of absolute chances at both ends, non-stop action, tons of different twists and turns, without one stumble or even a hesitation in connecting sentences," Michaels said, "amazed by his vocal ability to rattle though 10 minutes of uninterrupted play-by-play with unbelievable energy and clarity. My dad was an English professor, and he was impressed by how fluid and intelligent Mike sounded in the midst of total chaos. I love all the catchphrases like everybody else. But what I remember is in terms of raw play-by-play at that pace and level of intelligence...no one's ever done it better."

Similarly, Steigerwald pointed to the way Lange delivered the game as the skill that set him apart from his peers.

"He made people excited about hockey when they heard his voice and the way he called a game," he said. "There was a certain intonation in his voice, I call it the sound of urgency, that made it sound like it's more of an important event, like 'this matters.' The sayings were phenomenal, but it was the calling of the game and the way he could convey the excitement of the game using his voice as an instrument that, to me, made him great.

"Mike called it letting the game come to you. Mike's voice was unique in that he had a deep resonance but also a sharp treble sound. He had it all, his voice was literally an instrument, and I think his love of the blues and music really helped him develop that ability to use his voice to convey the different levels of excitement or importance in a hockey game. He was a master in every sense of the word."

Underlying Lange's style was a very strong work ethic. He chatted with players after practices, scribbled observations at morning skates and prepared notes on a legal pad for every game—pieces of information he might want or need to call upon, although he never allowed a broadcast to be overwhelmed with them. That legal pad always included a random handful of his catchphrases that would be checked off as he employed them. He was particularly diligent about watching the pre-game warmups of both teams and often remarked during games about the feelings a player or team had evoked for him as he watched them in that warmup.

"He had a great story about being in the media room at Three Rivers Stadium," Mears remembers. "He had numerous sheets of paper out getting ready for a Pirates-Cubs game, notes everywhere, and Harry Caray came in and said, 'What's all this about?'

"I've always kept that in mind, all that things he would do to prepare. He was talking to all the players, had great relationships with them, and they would divulge information. They would trust him and give him the true pulse of the team that only they would know. So he would always have some kind of unique thing to share that only he seemed to know among the media contingent because of those relationships."

One player with whom Lange had a special relationship was Jágr, a Czechoslovakian drafted by the Penguins in 1990. Lange sat on the team bus with Jágr in his early seasons, and Jágr promised to come up with a catchphrase for him. Jágr, of course, had to write it down, and it turned out to be "He smoked him like a bad cigar!" Lange used it numerous times to follow goals scored by Jágr over his 11-year career in Pittsburgh.

More than two decades later, Lange wrote Jágr's suggestion "will always be my favorite of the bunch. It's still in my shoebox."

3

Expansion Struggles

PITTSBURGH HAD A CHAMPIONSHIP HOCKEY TEAM LONG BEFORE the Penguins, as the American Hockey League's Hornets won titles in three of their final 11 seasons in the city, two as the farm team of the Toronto Maple Leafs in 1952 and 1955 and one as the Detroit Red Wings' affiliate in 1967. The 1967 Calder Cup Final victory against Rochester concluded just five and a half months before the Penguins made their NHL debut, and that market environment influenced the thinking of the Penguins' owners.

For starters, the team avoided lifting the Hornets' nickname as they left the market. "There was some (support) for it, but I basically said I wouldn't allow it," said Peter Block, then executive vice president. "The Hornets were a minor-league team. I knew we were going to get some bad players (in the Expansion Draft), and I didn't want to be called just another minor-league team."

Instead, team president Jack McGregor's wife, the former Carol Dangerfield of nearby Edgewood, had already found one she liked. "When Jack got the franchise, he was so thrilled," she remembered. "Then he said, 'Oh my gosh, we've got to name it.' I said, 'I love to think of things like that.' I was thinking of something with a 'P.' And I said to Jack, 'What do they call the Civic Arena?' And he said, 'The Big Igloo.' So I thought ice... Pittsburgh...Penguins. We talked about other names, but we kept coming back to the Penguins."

Ownership made clear to general manager Jack Riley, who had previously served as president of the AHL, that his teams needed to win right from the start as the Penguins began competing for fans and for one of the four playoff spots that would fall to expansion teams as they were all grouped together in the NHL's Western Division. Veterans would immediately make them competitive. Drafting and developing younger players was important but not as big a priority.

Philadelphia (Quebec) and Los Angeles (Springfield) both had the capital to purchase AHL teams to supplement their rosters, and both used several players that first season who had been acquired in those sales—most of them in their mid-to-late 20s. Perhaps not surprisingly, those two teams finished first and second, respectively, in the West Division that first season. The Penguins, already looking for additional investors as their first season began, had no such luxury either financially or philosophically.

The league's new teams each selected 20 players in the Expansion Draft, which made available predominantly aging stars and journeymen. But younger players with long NHL careers ahead of them were available, although the Penguins got only Keith McCreary. Philadelphia picked Bernie Parent, Gary Dornhoefer and Joe Watson, all three of whom helped them win the Stanley Cup in 1974; the Kings landed Mike Corrigan, Lowell MacDonald and Bill Flett; the Blues took

Darryl Edestrand, Ron Schock and Rod Seiling; and the Seals grabbed Bryan Hextall Jr. and J.P. Parise.

Riley had moved the previous summer to sign four players and loan them out until the Penguins made their debut, but it was the oldest of those who wound up having the biggest impact. During Pittsburgh's inaugural season, 33-year-old goaltender Les Binkley earned six shutouts, the second-highest total in the NHL and a team record that stood for 30 years. He played five seasons in Pittsburgh before leaving for the WHA, where he played until the age of 41.

That first Penguins team had an average age of more than 30 years, including eight players aged 32 or older, but the team's experience didn't translate into playoff berths in either of their first two seasons. Their oldest player in 1967–68, future Hall of Famer Andy Bathgate, 35, led them in scoring. Another Expansion Draft pick, 35-year-old Ken Schinkel, led the Penguins in scoring in their second season. When Schinkel retired in 1973 to coach the team, he was the Penguins' all-time leader in games played and points, and he eventually had a 22-year career with the team, also serving as a scout, assistant general manager and director of player personnel.

The 1968–69 season gained infamy in Pittsburgh when new mascot Penguin Pete, who had appeared on the Civic Arena ice on a few occasions, contracted pneumonia and died in late November.

The hiring of Hall of Famer Red Kelly, who had won eight Stanley Cups with Detroit and Toronto, to coach the team helped push Pittsburgh into the playoffs for the first time in 1969–1970. The Penguins swept Oakland in the first round (they wouldn't win another best-of-seven playoff series until 19 years later) and came within two victories of playing for the Stanley Cup when they suffered a second-round loss to St.

Louis. It was as close to the Cup as the Penguins would get for another two decades, and Kelly pulled out all the stops. After losing the first two games of the series in St. Louis, Kelly replicated a ploy he witnessed as a player under the legendary Punch Imlach in Toronto, dumping $7,250 in small bills—the equivalent of a Cup winner's share—on the dressing room floor before Game 3. The Penguins won the next two games.

The most notable roster development that season was the emergence of center Michel Brière, from Shawinigan Falls, Que., as the team's first young star. The 5-10, 165-pound center had recorded an eye-popping 320 points in 100 games over two seasons with Shawinigan of the Quebec Junior Hockey League before being selected by Pittsburgh in the third round of the 1969 draft, and he promptly led the Penguins with 32 assists—the second-best total among NHL rookies in 1969–70. His 44 points were third among rookies, two behind Philadelphia's Bobby Clarke.

Riley had offered Brière a $13,000 contract and a $4,000 signing bonus before that season, but Brière wanted $5,000. Remembered Riley, "I said, 'Why do you think you'll be worth it?' And he said, 'Because I'll play hockey for the Pittsburgh Penguins for the next 20 years.' Well, I agreed and told him I'd have the contract drawn up in a couple days. But Brière said, 'I've got to sign the contract today. My father worked in the mines all his life, and he worked hard, and this is his birthday.' I wrote it out long-hand."

The Penguins were concerned about whether Brière, 20, could withstand the certain physical pounding he was about to get from bigger, older players in the NHL, but Brière was undeterred. "The biggest question," Kelly said midway through Brière's first season, "was whether he could take the gaff in this league, but I've never seen him stopped yet." Years later,

Sullivan remembered Brière as a player with "a heart as big as a house." Added Riley, "A lot of teams tried to run him, but he was like a ghost."

The fiery Brière scored the overtime goal that gave the Penguins their first playoff series win in the sweep over the Seals, and he led all NHL rookies in playoff scoring with eight points in 10 games. Teammate Glen Sather, who went on to coach Wayne Gretzky and the Edmonton Oilers to four Stanley Cups, noted Brière's elusiveness. "He played like Gretzky in a lot of ways," he said.

Remembered Clarke, who developed into a Hall of Famer, "He was a better player than I was the first year. He was tough, he was quick and he really competed hard. He looked like he was going to be an outstanding player in the league."

But Brière's first NHL season was also his last. Two weeks after the Penguins were eliminated from the playoffs, Brière's sports car failed to negotiate a curve north of Malartic, Que., and he was thrown from the vehicle. He sustained a coma from which he never recovered, passing away 11 months later in Montreal.

"You asked yourself what life was all about," said teammate Jean Pronovost, another Shawinigan Falls native, who frequently visited Brière in the hospital. "He was very coachable, not big, but very tough mentally. He was willing to do anything to win. Those are the guys who have a tendency to shine in the playoffs. They know everything's on the table. We all had great expectations for him."

Midway through the following season, the Penguins traded with the New York Rangers for center Syl Apps Jr., whose Hall of Fame father had helped Toronto to three Cup titles, and he turned out to be an important addition. A superb playmaker, Apps piled up 349 assists with Pittsburgh before being traded in 1977 and by that time had become the team's all-time assists leader—a distinction he held until 1989. Today, the only Penguins who have averaged more assists per game than Apps are all in or about to join the Hockey Hall of Fame—Mario Lemieux, Paul Coffey, Ron Francis, Jaromír Jágr and Sidney Crosby.

"He had good hockey sense and was a competitive son of a gun," remembers linemate Lowell MacDonald. "His competitive nature was such that...he wanted the team to play perfectly, we needed to play perfectly as a line. He was worried about our plus-minus situation, about our backchecking. He was really driven by the idea that we should win and play well."

But Apps alone couldn't get them into the playoffs in 1971. By then the Penguins' roster included nine players aged 32 or older—even more than they featured in their first season—and six players who were 36 or older. The NHL was a much, much older league then than it is today, but four years into their NHL journey the Penguins had little to show for their predisposition toward veterans.

It took a near-miracle for the Penguins to qualify for the post-season in 1972. Pittsburgh trailed Philadelphia by two points for the final playoff spot with two games to play, and the Penguins visited Philadelphia on April 1 needing at least a tie to stay alive. The Penguins pulled goaltender Jim Rutherford, and after missing a breakaway moments earlier, Greg Polis scored with 46 seconds left to forge a 4–4 tie. The next night, the Penguins needed a home win over St. Louis and a Buffalo home victory over the Flyers to reach the post-season, and while Pittsburgh was beating the Blues, 6–2, Gerry Meehan scored with four seconds left to give the Sabres an improbable 3–2 win over Philadelphia. Pittsburgh was competitive but nonetheless was swept in the first-round series against heavily favored Chicago.

The Penguins missed the playoffs again in 1973 and 1974, which meant fans had gone four consecutive years without witnessing a single playoff victory. But the 1970s still wound up being a decade in which they managed to have some fun at the Igloo.

Polish cousins Tom Niemiec and Ken Rusnak formed Bob Woytowich's Polish Army after taking a liking to the Penguins' defenseman upon his acquisition from Minnesota at the start of the 1968–69 season for a first-round draft pick—just one of a number of ill-advised Penguins trades involving their first-round picks over the first 15 years of the modern NHL draft. Woytowich played parts of four seasons in Pittsburgh, and his Army was always there for him in Section D-24 of the Civic Arena with their ever-present big sign.

In a 1977 trade that sent Apps to the Kings, Pittsburgh acquired forward Gene Carr, who spent only 70 games in a Penguins uniform. But longtime Civic Arena organist Vince Lascheid often greeted Carr by playing the mashup of Count Basie's "Jumpin' at the Woodside" and "One O'Clock Jump" that served as the theme music for Gene, Gene the Dancing Machine on NBC's *The Gong Show*. This prompted fan Harry "The Whale" Melani to mimic the dance routine.

Lascheid was a treasure, an organist who did multiple stints at the Civic Arena over the years and was seemingly capable of conjuring a thousand songs in a heartbeat, often laced with humor and sometimes cynicism. Paul Coffey was greeted with the Maxwell House coffee jingle, Lowell MacDonald with the jingle from McDonald's "You Deserve a Break Today" campaign, the Blues' Bob Gassoff with the Alka-Seltzer "Plop, Plop, Fizz, Fizz" jingle. When fans ignored pleas to stop throwing things on the ice, Lascheid played "What Kind of Fool Am I?" When the Penguins' power play began terrorizing the NHL in the early 1990s, a penalty to opponents brought the theme from *Jaws* in the moments before the power play began.

Also performing for the Pirates, Triangles, Steelers and Spirit, Lascheid elicited reactions from outside the seats, too. During a November 1990 game, referee Paul Stewart had one of the off-ice officials call up to Lascheid to tell him to stop playing songs that belittled his work. The next time Stewart did a game in Pittsburgh, a month later, he and his linesmen skated onto the ice to the theme from The Three Stooges.

Lascheid, who played with bandleader Tex Beneke when he toured the U.S. after World War II, began working with the Penguins in 1970. He wrote "Here Come the Penguins," complete with lyrics, as the music to which the team would take the ice for the start of games. In 2003, he was inducted into the Penguins Hall of Fame.

Games against the Blues, who had reached the Cup Final in each of their first three seasons, provided plenty of material for Lascheid in the early 1970s, as they had become the Penguins' biggest rivals. The loud St. Louis crowds concerned coach Red Kelly enough that he had his players briefly wear earmuffs on the bench at St. Louis Arena in a January 1970 game. The rivalry was fueled by more than the 1970 playoff series, however, and had much to do with a Blues' lineup that featured a progression of players whose physical antics set the Penguins and their fans on edge, including Gasoff, Noël Picard, André Dupont, Steve Durbano and especially defenseman Barclay Plager.

Barclay Plager and brothers Bob and Bill briefly played together in the Blues' lineup between 1968 and 1972, but Barclay was a regular for St. Louis' first nine seasons and racked up 159 penalty minutes in just 47 career games against Pittsburgh. If there was trouble on the ice, he was usually in the middle of it, and Penguins' fans often serenaded him with chants of "BARRRRR-clee" at games in Pittsburgh.

"I think it was two things," hard-nosed defenseman Bryan Watson said of the St. Louis rivalry, which had produced 26 victories for the Blues and just 16 for the Penguins while they were division rivals. "One, we had to get past them to get to the Cup Finals, and two, we just did not like them. And they did not like us. It was a fabulous rivalry."

It was at home against St. Louis that the Penguins set a still-standing NHL record by scoring the fastest five goals in a game in 2:07 on Nov. 22, 1972, driving Pittsburgh's rally from a 4–3 third-period deficit to a 10–4 victory. The rivalry went to another level in January 1974, when new general manager Jack Button's first trade for the Penguins dealt Polis and Watson to the Blues for tough guys Durbano and Bob "Battleship" Kelly in an effort to return to the playoffs.

In his first game with the team, Durbano broke the nose of Vancouver's Dave Dunn in a fight, and he and Kelly both earned fighting majors in their first home game with the Penguins—against the Blues just one week after the trade. A record Pittsburgh crowd of 13,324 watched the Penguins' 4–1 victory, which Kelly and Durbano celebrated afterward by joining triumphant hands on the ice, which turned into an iconic Penguins' photo. Kelly said later, "The Blues won't be bothering us too much anymore."

The 1973–74 season was the seventh and last in which Pittsburgh and St. Louis played in the same division, and the rivalry subsequently began to fade away. But it was the second of four consecutive seasons, primarily under coaches Ken Schinkel and Marc Boileau, in which the Penguins began to get noticed for their offensive firepower. This was a little glimpse of what the franchise would one day come to base its entire reputation upon.

In 1972–73, the Penguins featured seven 20-goal scorers; only Boston (9) had more that season. Pittsburgh got a team-record 35 goals from right winger Al McDonough, who had been acquired the previous season from the Kings in exchange for Woytowich. Apps added 29, and left winger MacDonald, whose career had previously been hampered by knee injuries, scored 34. At the conclusion of that season, MacDonald became the first Pittsburgh player to receive an NHL trophy when he was named winner of the Bill Masterton Trophy for dedication to the game.

The day after McDonough was traded in January 1974, Schinkel replaced him with Pronovost on a line that included Apps and MacDonald. While the team's offensive depth was not the same this season, these three right-handed shots bordered on unstoppable together. MacDonald scored a team-record and career-high 43 goals, while Pronovost scored 40 and Apps 24. Thus combining for 107 goals, the second-highest total of any NHL trio, publicist Terry Schiffhauer dubbed them "The Century Line." Sixty-three of those goals, nearly 60 percent, came after they were put together.

"We played more of a European style," MacDonald said. "We had three guys who could anticipate what the other person was going to do, and that made the line work. It functioned. It was dangerous."

Apps had 39 assists in 38 games after the line was formed that season. "We knew where everybody was," he said. "My wingers knew I very rarely shot the puck. Even when I should have shot the puck, I was always looking to set them up because I didn't have a very good shot. We started to trust each other. I told Pronie, 'What are you coming to the corner for? If I get the puck, I won't have anyone to pass it to.'"

Said Pronovost, "The chemistry was there. We had some good qualities, and our little weaknesses complemented each other. The biggest thing was Syl was very unselfish. He didn't care who scored a goal as long as we scored a goal."

Undrafted out of his junior team in Niagara Falls, Pronovost was an incredible success story for the Penguins. He had played two seasons with Oklahoma City of the Central Professional Hockey League when Riley sent the fourth overall pick in the 1969 draft to Boston for the 23-year-old Pronovost. The Bruins were about to win their first Stanley Cup in 29 years and worried about losing Pronovost in future expansion or intra-league drafts, and it wound up being one of the rare instances when Pittsburgh traded a first-round pick and won the trade by a landslide. The Bruins used the pick to draft Frank Spring, who played 61 NHL games.

Pronovost was an honest hockey player, played both sides of the puck, worked hard and eventually turned himself into a 50-goal scorer in the NHL.

"Pronie was a very steady hockey player, not a flashy performer but a good, steady performer," remembered Boileau. "You could count on him day in and day out, whether you were playing in Pittsburgh or on the road. He did everything in a quiet way, not boastful. He just did his job."

Said Watson, "He could score and he could check, and he was a great team player. In those days, he would have been considered one of the top five two-way players in the game. He wouldn't just skate up the ice; he was involved with the defensive part of it. I know, because he played my side. He took more pride in his goals against than his goals for. He was a defenseman's dream, because you knew he was going to be there."

When he was traded to Atlanta in 1978, Pronovost was the Penguins' all-time leader in games played (753), goals

(316), points (603), power-play goals (70) and game-winning goals (42).

The line, of course, stayed together for the 1974–75 season, when the Penguins moved to the newly formed Norris Division and Button continued his makeover of the team with three more major additions. He traded Nick Beverly to the New York Rangers for veteran Vic Hadfield; he traded forward Blaine Stoughton and a first-round pick in the 1977 draft (still three years away at that point) to Toronto for 23-year-old right wing Rick Kehoe, who had already put up a 33-goal season for the Leafs as a 21-year-old; and he used the eighth pick in the 1974 draft to select center Pierre Larouche, who had just scored 94 goals in 67 games for his junior team in Sorel, Que.

Larouche, who had never watched an NHL game in person before playing in one, scored a goal in his NHL debut and wound up leading all league rookies in scoring in his first season, recording 31 goals and 68 points. He often played on a line with Chuck Arnason and "Battleship" Kelly, who was cementing his reputation as a feared fighter and a winger who could score, delivering a career-high 27 goals. Kehoe scored 32 goals with his new team, Hadfield added 31 and Pronovost 43, while center Ron Schock, who had never before registered 50 points in a season, had a career-high 86. Suddenly the Penguins had nine 20-goal scorers, a feat that has never been matched in team history. Only Montreal (10) had more that season.

Despite ongoing and serious financial problems, the Penguins had their best season ever, finishing sixth overall in the 18-team league, a height they would not surpass until 1993. Undrafted rookie Gary Inness was a surprise in goal, and Pittsburgh swept its preliminary round, best-of-three playoff series against the Blues, a team that featured not only nemesis Barclay Plager but two men who would later serve the

Penguins as both coach and general manager in Eddie Johnston and Craig Patrick.

After beating the Blues, the Penguins next faced the New York Islanders and promptly won the first three games, knocking future Hall of Famer Billy Smith—who would later develop a reputation as a "money" goalie—out of the New York net. "Battleship" Kelly had four goals in those three games, and defenseman Ron Stackhouse, another Button acquisition the previous season who in the mid-1970s was among the top scoring defensemen in the NHL, had assists in each game. Pittsburgh, which had won a total of six playoff games in its history prior to this season, had now won five in the span of 10 days.

"We were on the edge of becoming a top team that year," remembered defenseman Colin Campbell, who had been drafted by Pittsburgh in 1973 but elected to play in the World Hockey Association for one season before signing with the Penguins. He later went on to a long career as an NHL executive, most recently as vice president and director of hockey operations. Said Larouche, "You go down the lineup, look at the team, it was a great team."

Islanders' coach Al Arbour had an extra day off to consider his options after Game 3, as a John Denver concert forced the teams to take a two-day break before Game 4 on Long Island. Arbour pinned his hopes on backup goaltender Glenn Resch, who had allowed six goals on just 14 shots in his last start, an 8–3 loss in the preliminary round to the Rangers. But Resch stopped 27 shots in a 3–1 Islanders' win in Game 4.

New York won Game 5 in Pittsburgh, 4–2, handing the Penguins just their second home loss in five months as Resch made 36 more saves. A convincing 4–1 home win by the Islanders in Game 6 tied the series and put them on the precipice of history for Game 7 in Pittsburgh, a chance to become the second team in NHL history—and first in 33 years—to win a series after losing the first three games.

On April 26, Resch and Inness were perfect through two periods, and the Islanders' Ed Westfall then stunned a capacity crowd at the Civic Arena by scoring with 5:18 left in the game for a 1–0 victory. Resch finished with 30 saves and his first career playoff shutout, and he finished the series by stopping 124 of 128 Pittsburgh shots, an unheard of .969 save percentage. The Penguins came tantalizingly close to getting the first goal several times, but it was the Islanders who advanced to face the defending Cup champion Flyers in the next round.

"We were hitting the post left, right and center," remembers Apps, whose father had played on the Toronto team that was the first to rally from a 3–0 playoff deficit, against Detroit in the 1942 Cup Final. "It's one of those 'what ifs.' What if we had scored the one goal in the last game instead of Westfall? Would that have changed things going forward?"

Another "what if": had Brière been in the Penguins' lineup in 1975, he would have been in the prime of his career and likely would have made a difference in a series so close.

Resch went on to play 12 more NHL seasons, but that Game 7 performance always stayed with him. "I'll never forget how the Penguins came out flying," he said. "Jean Pronovost came down, took a shot, hit the goal post. Syl Apps picked it up, walked out, hit the other goal post. I kissed (the posts) in that seventh game after two rang off there. I thought, hey, if there's somebody that's been more influential in my life recently, I don't know who it is."

Said Block, "It was like the gods of hockey were saying, 'Not you guys.'"

Westfall did so many interviews after the game that by the time he was showered and dressed, his teammates had all left the arena. Walking out, he spotted Apps, who he knew through the NHL Players Association, among a group of Penguins and their wives. "We stood and talked for a while," Westfall remembered. "Then I said, 'Where are you guys going? Can I go?' I ended up spending the whole night with most of the rest of the Penguins team at a place called the Pleasure Bar. It was as strange as the series."

There was speculation after the series the Penguins had erred in sitting around Long Island for two days given the break between Games 3 and 4. "I would have sooner been home," remembered defenseman Dave Burrows. "Management thinks players can stay together and bond even more, but it gives you more time to think about the series and maybe you get nervous about it."

The Penguins simply couldn't afford to fly back home and return for Game 4, which didn't surprise Kehoe. "If we get out of New York, we're up 3–0, and keep our focus, they don't get back in the series," he said. "I remember I was out of sticks, and they didn't order any, so Jude Drouin (of the Islanders) gave me a half-dozen sticks to use. I know they weren't the good ones, but it was nice of him."

Boileau agreed. "Had we come home to Pittsburgh and relaxed a little bit and then flown back to New York on Saturday night, that could have made a difference," he said, but ultimately he didn't believe that was an important factor in the Penguins losing the series. "There was a big reason for it, but I've never discussed it and I don't want to discuss it."

Campbell, on the other hand, didn't mind discussing his own theory.

"We just weren't tough enough," Campbell said. "I don't think we got beat by the Islanders more than we got beat by the fact that...the impending series was going to be with the Flyers. A lot of our guys didn't have the character, the (guts), to play Philly and they knew it. I knew it. We just died. We had some good people and some guys who disappeared, and that was the problem. They were team tough and we weren't."

A change in ownership in the months following the loss meant the end of Button's tenure as Penguins' GM, which was unfortunate as he had proven to be an astute judge of talent. New part-owner Wren Blair took over the general manager's spot, having worked for years in that role with the North Stars. Before the 1975–76 season was over, Inness, Durbano, Arnason and dependable defenseman Bob Paradise had all been traded. The Penguins kept right on producing goals, however, finishing the season as the NHL's second-highest-scoring team behind Philadelphia before losing in the preliminary round to Toronto. In a March home game against Boston, Pronovost became the first player in Pittsburgh history to record 50 goals and Larouche the first Penguins' player to reach 100 points.

Just four months past his 20th birthday, Larouche was the youngest NHL player ever to record 100 points in a season, breaking Bobby Orr's record by more than 18 months. The dynamic native of Taschereau, Que., who had taken on the nicknames "The King" and "Lucky Pierre," had it all. He was a smooth skater with terrific vision, a good shot and the ability to read plays and execute off them. He finished the season with a team-record 53 goals; later in his career with the New York Rangers, only a wrist injury prevented Larouche from becoming the first player in NHL history to score 50 goals for three different teams.

But in the mid-1970s, he was still growing up, learning a new language and testing his barriers, and Larouche was temperamental and cocky, sometimes showing up late for practice.

"He just had talent oozing out of him," Burrows said. "The cockiness part helped his game. He would do things, try things, that no other rookie would try. He was so confident in himself. There's such a fine line between doing something great and really blowing it. I'm the type of personality that wouldn't try a lot of things because I'd be afraid of blowing it. He was the type of guy who would try everything because he wanted to do something great."

Larouche had been the talk of the town in his first seasons with the Penguins, even prompting the team to stage a "Win a Date with Pierre" contest. But he told reporters he was unhappy with his ice time early in the 1976–77 season and, after arriving late and missing a November practice, he was assigned to the team's AHL affiliate in Hershey. Larouche refused to report and was suspended, missing two games before rejoining the team and quickly scoring in eight of the next 10 games.

By early January 1977, however, he asked general manager Baz Bastien to trade him to "a team that's going somewhere," although that trade didn't materialize for another 10 months and after the Penguins had been beaten again by Toronto in the 1977 preliminary round. On the morning of Pittsburgh's Nov. 29, 1977, game in Montreal, Bastien traded Larouche to the Canadiens, who were in the middle of a run of four consecutive Stanley Cups. He had three assists in a 9–1 Montreal win over Pittsburgh that night and later went on to score 50 goals and win two Cups with the Canadiens. Larouche had averaged 1.05 points per game in his Pittsburgh career, a team record at the time of his trade.

Bastien, a former All-Star goaltender in the AHL before losing an eye in the Maple Leafs' training camp in 1949, had been hired the previous summer from the Kansas City Scouts as assistant general manager and eventually replaced Blair in December 1976. He was hardly new to Pittsburgh, having been a player, coach and general manager with the AHL Hornets, coaching them to the 1967 Calder Cup. Bastien wasn't shy about trying to reshape the Penguins, and in the span of 12 months beginning in September 1977, traded four of the team's top five all-time scorers in Pronovost, Apps, Schock and Larouche, as well as defensemen Denis Owchar and Burrows. It didn't help in 1978, when Pittsburgh missed the playoffs.

Fan favorite Burrows, claimed in the 1971 intra-league draft from Chicago on a suggestion from then assistant general manager Button, was sent to his hometown of Toronto. He was the definition of a defensive defenseman with Pittsburgh, often paying the toll for the Penguins' offensive disposition or inattention to defense. Burrows was a strong one-on-one defender and a masterful shot-blocker, and he was rarely caught out of position.

Pittsburgh gave him a chance to break into the NHL and, for the 1971–72 season, to play with Hall of Famer Tim Horton, whom he had watched as a kid growing up in Toronto. Pittsburgh also gave him the anonymity he needed away from the rink.

"I wanted to be a Penguin forever," Burrows said. "When I got traded to Toronto, I would have preferred to stay in Pittsburgh. You would get noticed everywhere you went in Toronto. I wanted to play the game and go home. Pittsburgh was at that time more of a low-key city. I loved to play there. I'd do anything I could to do my best in Pittsburgh, and that's where I wanted to stay."

When Bastien wasn't trading players, he was often trading draft picks—26 of them over six drafts as general manager, including four first-round picks and a pair of second-round picks. He traded his last five picks in the 1977 draft to the Flyers as part of the Inness deal, and sold seven late-round picks to the Blues for cash in 1978. Thus this was a period that took Pittsburgh's poor drafting history to new lows.

From the start of the modern NHL draft in 1969 through the 1983 draft, the Kings (14) were the only NHL team to trade a first-round pick more often than the Penguins (8). These included Pittsburgh trading the sixth overall pick in 1978, the 10th overall pick in 1979, the seventh overall pick in 1981 and then swapping first-round picks with Minnesota in 1983, moving from the first overall pick to the 15th. Pittsburgh's trades of 1969 and 1977 first-round picks were actually sound transactions, bringing them Pronovost and Kehoe, respectively, but with the benefit of historic hindsight, had the Penguins held onto every first-round choice they had between 1969 and 1983, they could have drafted Terry O'Reilly, Mike Bossy, Al Secord, Michel Goulet, Grant Fuhr and Steve Yzerman.

Every NHL team's draft history includes several historic misses that look bad in retrospect, but the Penguins' return for many of their first-round deals was simply not commensurate with the value surrendered. Those returns included Woytowich, Orest Kindrachuk, Ross Lonsberry, Tom Bladon, Hartland Monahan, and Rod Schutt—none of whom moved the needle for Pittsburgh. The trading of the 10th pick in 1979—considered by many the best draft class in NHL history—for the journeyman Monahan was particularly curious, as the Penguins traded Monahan 16 days after acquiring him.

With the exception of the Oakland Seals franchise, which ceased to exist after moving to Cleveland and then being merged with the Minnesota North Stars franchise, the Penguins made fewer draft picks than any other 1967 expansion team through the 1983 draft. In that same time period, the Penguins got less than half as many games out of their first-round picks than did the North Stars and Flyers, the latter clearly the most initially successful of the NHL's 1967 expansion franchises.

Through the first two decades of post-expansion life for the 1967 teams, the Flyers were everything their in-state rival Penguins were not. They reached the Cup Final six times and won twice, and they missed the playoffs only twice to Pittsburgh's 11 times. The Penguins won just 27 of 120 regular-season games against Philadelphia in those first 20 seasons, and despite competing in the same division for much of their early existence, the teams did not meet in the playoffs until 1989.

Once they began to bump into each other in the post-season, there were of course some special memories for both teams. The Flyers won a Game 7 at Pittsburgh in the opening round of the 1989 playoffs, then rallied from a 2–0 deficit to win a second-round series in 2000 that included a five-overtime Game 4 road victory courtesy of a Keith Primeau goal. The Penguins answered by bumping the Flyers out in both 2008 and 2009 on their way to the Stanley Cup Final, and the Flyers responded with a first-round victory in 2012 in a crazy series filled with emotion and goals.

But in the early days, their natural geographic rivalry didn't subsist on the memories of bitter playoff battles or a semblance of competitive balance in regular-season games. It maintained itself through the sheer number of games they played as division rivals—especially when they played at the Spectrum in Philadelphia. Beginning in February 1974, the Penguins went 0–39–3 over 42 games played there, which remains the longest road winless streak by a team against one opponent in NHL history. It helped to create for the Penguins and their fans a hatred they couldn't match for any other team.

"Every interview you got from the first day of training camp was, 'How are you going to beat the Flyers?' It almost was more important to win a game in Philadelphia than it was to win the Stanley Cup when I first got to Pittsburgh," recalled winger Rob Brown, drafted by Pittsburgh in 1986. "I grew up with Calgary and Edmonton, all their wars, the Battle of Alberta, so I had seen what rivalry was like. Then I got to Pittsburgh-Philadelphia and it was very, very similar. I very quickly understood the importance of beating Philadelphia."

During their Spectrum Jinx, almost one out of every three losses the Penguins suffered was by a margin of four or more goals, including defeats of 11–0, 13–4 and 11–4. Beginning in October 1976, they suffered three consecutive shutouts there by a combined score of 18–0. Even their rare ties there sometimes felt like losses, as was the case on Dec. 20, 1979. The Flyers were on a 27-game unbeaten streak, one shy of Montreal's NHL record, and the Penguins took a 1–0 lead deep into the night, thanks to a goal from Stackhouse and superb goaltending from Greg Millen. But Flyers' defenseman Behn Wilson—whom the Flyers had drafted sixth overall in 1978 with a pick they got from the Penguins—scored with 4:08 left and the Flyers earned a 1–1 tie. Referee Dave Newell ignored Pittsburgh's howls that Wilson had kicked the puck into the net.

"We had them, we had the streak broken for sure," remembered Millen, who made 34 saves. "I can still see it...I thought it was kicked in. You left that game thinking maybe we deserved a better fate."

Pittsburgh finally ended the streak on February 2, 1989, 15 years after it began, with a 5–3 victory in which Brown scored the game-winning goal and former Flyers' goaltender Wendell Young made 39 saves for the Penguins. The win came just hours after disc jockeys Scott Paulsen and Jim Krenn from Pittsburgh station WDVE dressed as witch doctors and broadcast live from the Spectrum in an effort to break the jinx. "I think it's a monkey off the whole city's back," Penguins' coach Gene Ubriaco told the *Pittsburgh Press.*

The Penguins were only four years into their Spectrum Jinx in 1978 when Bastien traded the Flyers the first-round pick that turned into Wilson for Kindrachuk, Lonsberry and Bladon. Wilson lasted five seasons in Philadelphia, but none of the three players arriving in Pittsburgh lasted more than three seasons. All three, however, were in the lineup in 1979 when the Penguins beat the Sabres in the preliminary round in dramatic fashion, winger George Ferguson scoring in the opening minute of overtime in the third and decisive game in Buffalo. But they were swept by Boston in the second round, and the Sabres series turned out to be the only playoff round won by the Penguins over a 13-season span.

Pittsburgh took the favored Bruins to a fifth and deciding game before losing in the first round in 1980, the same season the Penguins added Team USA Olympic hero Mark Johnson to their lineup and switched their sweater colors from blue and white to black and gold to match those of the Pirates and Steelers. Their playoff losses continued under new coach Eddie Johnston, but at least they brought some drama.

The Blues finished with the NHL's second-best record in 1980–81 but needed a goal from winger Mike Crombeen in double overtime to beat the underdog Penguins in the decisive Game 5 of the first round in 1981 at St. Louis, and the Penguins' 1982 first-round loss to the Islanders was even more painful.

After his team was blown out in successive road games to start the series against the two-time defending Cup champs, owner Edward DeBartolo Jr. offered Pittsburgh fans who had purchased tickets for Games 3 and 4 a refund if they wanted it—hardly standard procedure in professional sports. The Penguins responded with a pair of victories, right winger Kehoe scoring in overtime of Game 3 behind a strong performance from goaltender Michel Dion, and former Islander André St. Laurent then delivering two goals in Game 4. The Game 3 victory had been especially satisfying for Kehoe, who delivered the first game-winning goal of his playoff career and then added another in Game 4.

Kehoe became a prolific scorer in Pittsburgh, recording a team-record 55 goals in 1980–81, when he also won the NHL's Lady Byng Trophy for sportsmanship and playing excellence. He finished tied for fourth in the NHL in both goals and power-play goals that season and only twice went more than three games without scoring. Kehoe eight times scored 29 or more goals in a season and finished among the Penguins' top three goal-scorers in eight of his first nine seasons with the team.

When he retired in 1984 due to a neck injury, Kehoe was Pittsburgh's all-time scoring leader with 636 points and ranked second in games played (722), goals (312) and assists (324). His tenure with the team lasted 32 years and included posts as head coach, assistant coach and pro scout. He is one of just five former Pittsburgh players to also coach the team, joining Schinkel, Lou Angotti, Gene Ubriaco and Eddie Olczyk.

Back on Long Island for Game 5, the Penguins forged an improbable 3–1 lead by scoring three unanswered goals in the span of 7:30 late in the second period. "All of a sudden," remembered Islanders' captain Bryan Trottier, "they had us on our heels." But the Islanders responded with two goals in the final five and a half minutes of regulation to force overtime, survived a scare when Mike Bullard's early overtime shot grazed the goal post and completed their comeback five minutes later when John Tonelli scored in a 4–3 win. Dion, who was spectacular in stopping 43 shots, said after the game Tonelli's goal "shattered my heart into a thousand pieces."

For the first time in their history, the Penguins finished with the NHL's worst record in 1982–83, but they didn't benefit from having the first choice in the draft—they had swapped first-round picks with Minnesota in a trade eight months earlier, falling from No. 1 to No. 15 in a draft that saw five of the first nine selections wind up in the Hockey Hall of Fame. The Penguins also sent Ferguson to the North Stars in that trade, getting in return winger Anders Håkansson—the first European-trained player to skate for the Penguins, putting them firmly behind the curve of teams broadening their scouting horizons—and defenseman Ron Meighan, who played 41 games in Pittsburgh and retired at the age of 21.

Tragedy struck in March when Bastien was killed in an automobile accident after attending an event sponsored by the Pittsburgh chapter of the Professional Hockey Writers' Association, and Johnston was named GM two months later. He hired an alumnus of the 1968–69 team, Angotti, as coach.

Angotti had his hands more than full. He inherited a team that was the NHL's second-worst defensive squad, had lost rugged defenseman Paul Baxter and veteran winger Peter Lee to free agency, had traded away veterans St. Laurent and Greg Malone, a dependable center, and was about to use 48 players over the course of the season—still a team record. Twenty-six of those players, more than half the roster, had never before played for the Penguins, and almost half of those were younger than 23 at the time of their team debut.

The dizzying number of faces coming in and out of the lineup reflected the lack of mature talent and experience the team had under contract, and the results in the standings were inevitable. The Penguins lost eight of their first nine games, later endured three 13-game stretches in which they won only once and then finished the season with eight straight losses. "I can honestly say right now we were a minor-league team," Bullard told TSN years later, remembering the season in which he scored 51 goals for Pittsburgh. "A minor-league team playing in the NHL."

Johnston that season made the first two trades in team history that brought a first-round pick to the Penguins without having to surrender one. The first came in October, sending to Philadelphia former first-round pick Rich Sutter, who hadn't recorded a single point in nine games with the team and wanted the reunion he got with twin brother, Ron, a Flyers' center. The second came the day before the NHL trade deadline in early March and sent Carlyle to Winnipeg while also bringing the Penguins future considerations that turned out to be defenseman Moe Mantha, whom the Penguins didn't want to join them until after the season—for reasons that soon became clear.

Acquired from Toronto in the 1978 trade that sent Burrows to the Leafs, Carlyle in 1981 won the Norris Trophy as the league's best defenseman and remains the only Pittsburgh defenseman to do so. He set single-season team records for goals, assists and points by a defenseman, was a gifted point man on the power play and also killed penalties while soaking up huge amounts of ice time as the Penguins' top defenseman during his tenure with them. But like the team, Carlyle struggled during the 1983–84 season and became a sensible target for the Jets, who lost defenseman Dave Babych to injury just before the trade.

But by the time Carlyle was dealt on March 5, it was evident the Penguins were focused on preserving their narrow lead over New Jersey for last place in the league. At stake was the resulting first overall choice in the 1984 draft, which some team was going to use on 6-4 center Mario Lemieux, who in 1983–84 was finishing his junior career with Laval of the Quebec Major Junior Hockey League by scoring 133 goals and 282 points in 70 games—numbers so gaudy they read like fiction. Lemieux looked less like a once-in-a-generation talent and more like a once-in-a-lifetime talent.

The Devils were giving the Penguins a run for their money in this race to the bottom and sat alone in last place on Feb. 27 with 17 games to play. But New Jersey then went unbeaten in its next three games to put the Penguins back at the bottom by themselves by a margin of two points going into the last meeting between the teams on March 6 in New Jersey.

Two days before the low-down showdown, New Jersey team president Bob Butera told the *Newark Star-Ledger,* "We're trying to win every game and I hope Pittsburgh is, too. I think they're a better team than they're showing...I hope they're doing the same thing we're doing. I mean, there's no way we're going to start teaching our players how to lose."

The Penguins 10 days earlier had demoted goaltender Roberto Romano, who shut out Minnesota while winning three of his last seven NHL starts, to their Baltimore farm team, which was putting the finishing touches on the AHL's best record despite two-thirds of its roster having spent time with the Penguins. So that start against New Jersey went to goaltender Vincent Tremblay, who had been acquired from Toronto the previous summer and had spent the entire season in Baltimore before being promoted to the NHL just days before the game.

The Devils broke a 3–3 tie with three goals in the third period for a 6–5 victory, and Tremblay lost all four starts he made for Pittsburgh down the stretch that season while compiling a 6.02 goals-against average as part of the NHL's worst defensive team. They were the last four starts of his NHL career. The Penguins had won each of their first three games against the Devils that season, but they lost three of their last four against them.

When the Penguins returned home from New Jersey to play their next game against Quebec, they drew their second consecutive sub-4,000 crowd and wound up averaging just over 6,800 fans per home game in 1983–84, the second-lowest total in team history. Interest in the team rose barely above apathy. The Penguins were being outdrawn by the Pittsburgh Spirit, playing its fifth season in the Major Indoor Soccer League, and in mid-March the Penguins' radio flagship station KQV preempted a Penguins' game to carry an important Spirit game in Cleveland. That's how far the Penguins had fallen, and how much seemed to be at stake for them in the 1984 draft.

TSN's 2014 documentary *Playing to Lose* closely examined the Penguins' 1983–84 season, and Johnston told the network "we just didn't have the talent...we got completely out of a playoff (spot) and we had no place to go. I think what you got to do, you got to look out for your franchise then. I think that's more important." Added Angotti, "Eddie Johnston and I did what we thought we had to do to save a franchise. We were coaching not to win."

The Penguins won just 16 games and finished three points below New Jersey, last overall in the NHL for the second consecutive season. The players who skated for the 1983–84 Penguins, however, never questioned the effort put forth by those in the lineup. "We always wanted to win every game," said center Dave Hannan, who later won Stanley Cups with Edmonton and Colorado, "but we were missing a lot of talent."

By the summer of 1984, the Penguins had won the fewest regular-season games, won the fewest playoff games, won the fewest playoff rounds and joined the Kings in drafting the fewest players of the five remaining 1967 expansion teams. Even worse, Buffalo, which entered the league three years after the Penguins, and the New York Islanders, who entered five years later, had also surpassed them in all those categories. The Islanders had won four Stanley Cups and the Flyers two, while St. Louis (three times), Minnesota (once) and Buffalo (once) had reached the Cup Final.

It painted a depressing picture for Pittsburgh hockey fans, whose team seemed to be betting its future existence in the market on the ability of one 18-year-old from Montreal to turn it all around. "I can't blame the franchise, because they were dying," Bullard told TSN. "You look back at it now, Eddie Johnston looks like a genius."

PART 2

THE LEGENDS

4

Le Magnifique

WHEN MARIO LEMIEUX PLAYED THE FINAL REGULAR-SEASON game of his junior career for Laval of the Quebec Major Junior Hockey League in mid-March 1984, there was nothing at stake for the Voisins. They had long ago clinched the league's best record and were on their way to the league playoff championship. But there was something at stake for Lemieux, who had already broken Pierre Larouche's single-season league record for points but remained three shy of his boyhood idol Guy Lafleur's single-season record for goals.

Lemieux scored six goals that night to finish with 133, adding five assists in a 16–4 win over Longueuil to delight a home crowd that included Edmonton star Wayne Gretzky, watching Lemieux for the first time the night before the Oilers played in Montreal. "After watching him for one period," Gretzky told the *Montreal Gazette*, "I can tell you that he's going to be a good pro."

Fast forward seven months, to Oct. 11, 1984. Making his NHL debut with the Penguins in Boston, Lemieux scored unassisted on his first shift and first shot—taking the puck from the Bruins' First Team All-Star defenseman Ray Bourque and then sliding it past Pete Peeters, who two seasons earlier had won the Vezina Trophy as the league's best goaltender. The kid soon to be known as "Le Magnifique" had officially arrived 2:59 into his first NHL game.

The Lemieux goal helped the Penguins to a 2–0 lead after the first period that night, and Penguins' general manager Eddie Johnston remembered that Bruins' GM Harry Sinden "came down to me after the period and said, 'Why didn't you trade that damn pick to us?' His second words were, 'This guy might be the best player in hockey.'"

The symbolism of Lemieux beginning his career in Boston was not lost on Johnston, who had won two Stanley Cups with the Bruins as a goaltender in the early 1970s and in 11 seasons there saw first-hand what the signing of defenseman Bobby Orr had meant to a Boston franchise that had missed the playoffs for seven consecutive seasons before Orr joined them in 1966. Johnston envisioned Lemieux having the same impact on the Penguins, which is why the unusual trade proposals he received from his peers before the 1984 draft had zero chance of succeeding.

All three Stastny brothers from Quebec, including future Hall of Famer Peter? All 12 of the Minnesota North Stars' 1984 draft picks? A guarantee by the Canadiens to better any potential deal offered by the rival Nordiques? Years later, Johnston said of the Penguins' future in Pittsburgh had he traded his No. 1 pick, "We'd have been out of there." So at the Montreal Forum, Johnston began the draft by announcing his choice, appropriately, in French.

When Lemieux made his home debut against Vancouver, the game attracted 15,741 fans, about 9,000 more than the Penguins averaged the previous season. The "Lemieux Debut" had certainly captured Pittsburgh's interest, and 18 seconds into the game Lemieux set up a goal by Doug Shedden to start the Penguins toward their first victory of the season.

Thus Lemieux was already displaying a talent for the exceptional as a teenager, an innate ability to meet the moment. Given a bright spotlight, he would produce a brighter performance. Given high expectations, he would exceed them. Given a challenge, he would accomplish it and likely in a memorable way. The Penguins had had some stars along the way, but never a player remotely like the one they drafted at the Montreal Forum on June 9, 1984—the day their fortunes as a franchise changed forever.

"We had reason to buy into the concept of this guy being another cut above any other player the Penguins had ever had," said Paul Steigerwald, then the Penguins' director of marketing. "We were so sick of losing. And there were all these things that were fueling our hope and belief this guy was really going to lead us to somewhere great, right from the beginning."

The very start of Lemieux's relationship with the Penguins included a little acrimony over his rookie contract being negotiated by powerful agent Gus Badali, who also represented Gretzky and seemed intent on including an attendance clause to benefit Lemieux. Badali suggested to Lemieux that he not approach the Penguins' draft table after being selected to underscore his dissatisfaction with the negotiations, and Lemieux did not. But he agreed to his contract five days later, and the Penguins began sewing onto a black and gold sweater his number 66—a flip of the 99 worn by Gretzky, suggested years earlier by Bob Perno, who worked with Badali.

Lemieux amassed 100 points in his first season to earn the Calder Trophy as NHL Rookie of the Year despite the team finishing next-to-last overall, and he also became the first rookie named MVP of the NHL All-Star Game. Soon comparisons with Gretzky would follow. Gretzky was nearly five years older and had entered the NHL when the league absorbed the Oilers and three other former WHA teams in 1979, and by his third NHL season was surrounded by six future Hall of Fame players in Grant Fuhr, Paul Coffey, Kevin Lowe, Jari Kurri, Glenn Anderson and Mark Messier—a group that won four Stanley Cups between 1984 and 1988.

Lemieux's supporting cast with the rebuilding Penguins was not remotely comparable even after three seasons, but Johnston had ended the trading of valuable draft picks and was stockpiling young players who would later prove invaluable in the trade market. The team improved but narrowly missed the playoffs by two points in 1986, four points in 1987 and one point in 1988.

Nevertheless, Lemieux kept right on creating offense despite being the focal point of every opponent's game plan and the subject of high levels of defensive chicanery. He located shots with precision, could score from anywhere, drew untold amounts of penalties and made breathtaking passes a matter of course. His skillset, combined with an off-the-charts hockey IQ and his large frame and incredible reach, allowed him to excel in any situation and especially in one-on-one opportunities, where he routinely deked defensemen and goaltenders with an ease that was rarely seen even in the NHL.

One breathtaking example of this entire package came in late March 1988 in Quebec against the Nordiques. Killing a penalty, the 6-4, 215-pound Lemieux burst out toward Nordiques' rookie forward Marc Fortier, who had momentarily lost the puck in his skates at the right point. Feeling the pressure, Fortier tried a hurried forehand pass toward the slot that Lemieux read and stretched out to block with his stick, taking off with the puck toward the Quebec goal. The 6-0, 190-pound Fortier hooked Lemieux repeatedly through the neutral zone, knocking Lemieux's left hand off his stick as the Penguins' center advanced the puck with one hand until finally using his left hand to hold Fortier off. Fortier then wrapped his arms around Lemieux, who returned his left hand to his stick, faked a forehand wrist shot and beat goaltender Mario Gosselin on the backhand.

Throughout these frustrating early seasons without playoff payoffs, Lemieux made everyone around him better—especially his linemates.

In Lemieux's rookie season, he played with big left wing Warren Young, a 28-year-old rookie who had scored two goals in 20 previous NHL games with Minnesota and Pittsburgh. Young scored two goals on opening night in Boston, two more in the Penguins' home opener against Vancouver and finished the season with a career-high 40 goals, more than all but 21 players in the league.

Young signed a big contract with Detroit the following summer, opening a spot on Lemieux's left for free agent Terry Ruskowski, who responded with a career-high 26 goals—three more than he had scored in his previous two seasons combined in Los Angeles. During the 1986–87 and 1987–88 seasons, Randy Cunneyworth sometimes played on Lemieux's left and delivered his two best goal-scoring seasons in the NHL, netting 26 and then 35 goals.

"I'd see him turn up the ice, he'd have two or three guys on him and he'd be shaking them off, and sometimes the goalie would somehow miraculously make a save and I would follow him in and tap in an empty-netter or a rebound," said Cunneyworth. "I had nobody on me and he had the three guys trying to tackle him. Everyone asks me how I scored my goals, and I do remember a lot of them like that after he did all the work and I'd get all the glory of the goal. It's a half joke, but it's half true.

"I can't say I was that smart of a player to read everything Mario did, because his game was so complex. That's probably why I wasn't a mainstay on his line. I kind of stuck to my own game a lot and that might have been a weakness of mine. If I had figured out more of Mario's game, I might have been a linemate for longer. Part of my role was trying to protect him. He would get hooked, held and punched and run, and part of my role was to run them before they ran him."

The 1987–88 season was a particularly memorable portrait of contrasts for Lemieux, who began it by joining Team Canada for the 1987 Canada Cup and taking advantage of his first opportunity to deliver under intense pressure on hockey's international stage. He scored twice in 1:43 to help Canada rally from a 2–0 deficit and defeat Czechoslovakia in the semifinals, then scored the double-overtime winner in Game 2 of the best-of-three final against the Soviet Union before winning the series by scoring on a laser-perfect wrist shot with 1:26 left in Game 3 off a Gretzky drop pass, a goal Canadians will never forget.

He finished with a tournament-best 11 goals, four of them game-winners, and 18 points in nine games as he and Gretzky as linemates proved unstoppable. "I always knew he was a great hockey player and he was going to be one of the best," said defenseman Paul Coffey, "but what I witnessed in the '87 Canada Cup was special."

Lemieux was already a confident player, but that tournament took his confidence to new levels. When he returned to the Penguins, said teammate Dave Hannan, "he was possessed." Lemieux had 12 points in the first four games and finished the season with career highs in goals (70), assists (98) and points (168), winning his first Art Ross Trophy as the NHL's leading scorer, breaking Gretzky's seven-year hold on the award. But the Penguins won only two of the first 11 games that season and midway through it endured a 10-game winless streak under new coach Pierre Creamer, who had never coached in the NHL and was in over his head.

Pittsburgh needed a victory at Washington in the penultimate game of the season to keep its playoff hopes alive, but multiple players said later Creamer didn't understand the stakes and had to be convinced of the necessity for preparing to pull goaltender Steve Guenette for an extra attacker as the overtime clocked ticked down. Guenette was just heading off the ice when Lemieux went wide to beat Capitals' defenseman Larry Murphy, who took down Lemieux only to have the falling Lemieux chip a backhander past goaltender Clint Malarchuk to secure a 7–6 victory with 58 seconds to play—his fourth goal of the game. "I'm out of words," was the call by Penguins' play-by-play man Mike Lange as Lemieux once more had delivered a joyous memory at the most critical time.

All these moments of sheer brilliance from Lemieux, however, still couldn't get Pittsburgh in the playoffs, and they missed the post-season in five of his first six seasons. "There were some tough times," he said. "Not getting into the playoffs was taking its toll."

When the Penguins finally got there in 1989 for the first time in seven seasons, Lemieux surprised no one by scoring 12 goals in 11 games before being eliminated in the second round by the Flyers in the teams' first playoff encounter. This included an eight-point game with five goals in a pivotal Game 5 at home against Philadelphia, featuring a natural hat trick in the span of 4:40 of the first period—after a late Game 4 collision with Cunneyworth had left Lemieux with limited peripheral vision heading into the game. The Penguins won the game, 10–7, further solidifying their reputation as a team with defensive deficiencies that nevertheless often scored its way out of them.

The Penguins' captain absolutely terrorized the NHL in that 1988–89 season, piling up a career-high 199 points—only Gretzky has ever had more in one season—to win the scoring title for a second straight season. Despite being the most significant factor in the Penguins breaking their long playoff drought, Lemieux somehow lost the Hart Trophy as league MVP to Gretzky, who finished 31 points behind him during his first season in Los Angeles, where the Kings made the playoffs for the third time in four seasons.

Lemieux's regular season included an other-worldly eight-point performance at home against New Jersey on New Year's Eve, when he became the first NHL player to score a goal every way possible: even strength, shorthanded, on the power play, on a penalty shot and into an empty net.

The benefactor of playing on Lemieux's wing that season was right wing Rob Brown, who scored a career-high 49 goals. Unlike Young, Ruskowski or Cunneyworth, Brown was a naturally gifted finisher. He lacked speed but made up for it by understanding the way Lemieux played, and he wound up scoring 75 goals in his first 125 games with the team, a mark unmatched in team history, even by Lemieux.

"I saw the game on an offensive level. I couldn't do the things he did, but I could understand being in the right position for him and I could understand when he needed the puck," Brown said. "So I don't think I had to change. I'm playing with, at that point, the best player in the world and one of the greatest of all-time. My job was to make sure when I had opportunities, I finished.

"The biggest thing with Mario was just be ready no matter what. Other players, you could read the play and you'd know when the puck was going to be there or where it's going. But he was like the chess master who thinks four plays ahead of it, so you always had to be ready for a play no one else would see but he would see."

Like Cunneyworth, Brown marveled at the determination with which Lemieux played the game in an era when many stars were manhandled over the course of a season, although arguably none were subjected to the degree of illegal physical play that Lemieux endured during his career. He was a bigger target, and his frustration finally boiled over in January 1992, after a loss in Washington when he told reporters, "The advantage is to the marginal player now. They can hook and grab, and the good players can't do what they're supposed to do. Anybody can get away with it...that's the way this garage league is run." Lemieux had talked for years about the need for the league to give its stars the freedom allowed by the rule book so that they could sell the game.

"The abuse that Mario went though, the physical abuse, the clutching and grabbing, the holding, everything, and then to put up those numbers the way he did...because he was 6-4, he played through it. He never dove, never went down," said Brown. "To me, his ability to play though the absolute abuse that he went through and still be the best player in the world was probably his best attribute."

Lemieux's determination to overcome opponents was the attribute celebrated by his statue in front of PPG Paints Arena, which depicts him fighting off two Islanders' defenders in 1988 before scoring. Even the best of opponents struggled to defend Lemieux, and they all cited not only his skill level but also his size and reach as the largest challenges.

"It was impossible to defend the big boy," said Hall of Famer center Bryan Trottier, who joined the Penguins in 1990 after playing against Lemieux while with the New York Islanders. "He had such a reach, you just had to take his options away, and if you take his options away, then he starts shooting and attacking the net, so you're kind of caught between a rock and a hard place. It doesn't matter who he's playing with, he's going to generate some chances. What's the lesser of the two evils? I don't know. We started saying, 'OK, good luck (goaltender) Kelly Hrudey.'

"Mario was really a unique player. Nobody more graceful on the ice, he looked like he was barely moving and everybody else was in slow motion. He just made it all look so easy. You play too tight to him, he'll dance you. You play off him, he'll shoot or he'll pass. A really special player."

Bourque, a Hall of Famer who five times won the Norris Trophy as the NHL's best defenseman, was victimized by Lemieux on several occasions, including Game 4 of the 1992 Wales Conference Final. On the penalty kill, Lemieux used his reach to stop a pass from Joe Juneau, then burst up the ice one-on-one against Bourque, who didn't have time to turn himself to face Lemieux. Lemieux put the puck through Bourque's skates, picking it back up and then lifting a forehand shot past goaltender Andy Moog for an unassisted goal.

"He's deceiving because of his size," Bourque said. "When he really turns it on, he's got some great speed and strength and moves. And that reach on him...you could stop him and he could still have the puck on the other side of you and still score. That is tough."

Whether against a goaltender or a defenseman, when Lemieux put himself in a one-on-one situation, it was usually lights out for the defender. Lemieux took pride in this ability, which had been a hallmark of his game from his days as a youth. "Since I was real young, I was always able to go on the ice and beat anybody one-on-one if I wanted to," he said.

"Is 66 the best one-on-one player ever? I'd say No. 1 or No. 2," longtime NHL general manager and former Penguins' director of hockey operations Brian Burke told *The Sheet* podcast. "The only guy I'd put up there with him is (Jaromír) Jágr, both so big, such good feet and such good hands, they could make you look truly sick, make you look stupid, make you look foolish."

Said Murphy, a Hall of Famer who played against Lemieux for six and a half seasons before being traded to the Penguins, "It was quite apparent—because of his skill level and then add his reach onto that, that creates a whole 'nother problem—there just was no margin for error. You had to position yourself carefully and be aware. If there was some weakness, he would definitely expose it."

Many believe Lemieux did not receive enough accolades during his career for his defensive game, which often led to breathtaking shorthanded goals. He ranks fourth all-time in shorthanded goals with 49, including an NHL-record 13 in 1988–89. The only players who scored more—Gretzky, Mark Messier and Steve Yzerman—each played between 570 and 840 more games than Lemieux.

"Nobody killed penalties better than Mario," Johnston said. "People never mention that too much. He was in a class by himself, he could anticipate and read things...(as a coach) you had to use him if you wanted to stay in the game."

While Lemieux's defensive game was not always on full display in the regular season, it was certainly part of his playoff demeanor. Pierre McGuire, a member of the Penguins' scouting and coaching staffs for their championships in 1991 and 1992, witnessed first-hand Lemieux's play without the puck and could see the effect it had on opponents.

"He would envelop players. He was so good because his brain dissected the game so much quicker than anybody else and compound that with his wingspan and length of his stick and his desire to make plays happen, he was an intimidating force defensively," McGuire said. "I don't think he ever got enough credit for how good he was, especially in (penalty killing) situations. When he was plugged in, he was very, very good defensively. The way he closed gaps on opposition players, took away their space, it had to be unbelievably intimidating. Here's this big giant of a man, who has unbelievable athleticism and phenomenal offensive abilities, and he's closing the gap on you, and if you turn the puck over, he's probably going to score."

So Lemieux provided Pittsburgh hockey fans with not only a steady diet of perseverance but play that brought out the game's beauty and a nightly anticipation they might witness something special if they weren't watching him. They responded at the box office, as average attendance over his first six seasons with the Penguins jumped 135 percent to 16,018. In 17 seasons before Lemieux, the Penguins had sold out a total of 44 regular-season games; they sold out 137 over his first six seasons.

"He put the sport on the map here. What we hoped was that Mario would convert a lot of Pittsburgh sports fans to hockey fans, and that's exactly what happened," said Steigerwald, who noted that kids especially loved Lemieux. "He was a larger-than-life figure."

Fittingly, one of the early promotions the Penguins did with their star was a Mario Lemieux Growth Chart, a life-sized poster that was then slapped up on the bedroom walls of kids throughout Western Pennsylvania. As they charted their growth through the years, something else happened: those kids started playing hockey.

In the six seasons between 1990 and 1996, which included two Stanley Cup championships for the Penguins, USA Hockey player registration across the country grew 69.7 percent. In USA Hockey's Mid-American Region, which includes Indiana, Kentucky, West Virginia, Ohio and Western Pennsylvania, registration growth was double that, at 140.4 percent—with a majority of registrations coming from the Pittsburgh area.

In the two years before Lemieux arrived in Pittsburgh, the area had lost two ice rinks as the Sewickley Arena converted to soccer and the Monroeville Mall rink closed. Between 1993 and 1997, eight new ice skating facilities were built in the Pittsburgh area, several of them with multiple rinks, and the new facilities included the Penguins' first dedicated practice rink in Canonsburg, just south of Pittsburgh. None of this was coincidence.

"Things just exploded after that 1991 Cup," said Darcy Purvis, who served as executive director of the Pittsburgh Amateur Hockey League for 10 years and also served USA Hockey in several capacities. "People were so excited, Learn to Play programs were packed. Every rink was full. All the rinks were sold with the hockey hours, and in fact in a lot of places figure skating got pushed out because hockey got so big. There just was not enough ice."

More than a dozen players who have skated 150 or more games in the NHL were born in or near Pittsburgh, including Brandon Saad, J.T. Miller, R.J. Umberger, Vince Trocheck, Ryan Malone, John Gibson, Logan Cooley, Mike Weber, Matt Bartkowski, Nate Guenin and Stephen Johns, and many of them were part of this explosion of hockey's popularity among young athletes in the area in the 1990s. Ryan Malone, whose father, Greg, played 495 games for the Penguins, became the first Pittsburgh native to play for the Penguins in 2003 and was a productive player for them, helping the team to the 2008 Cup Final.

"When I was seven, I started watching Mario Lemieux and the Penguins on television and I got hooked on hockey," Umberger told the *Pittsburgh Post-Gazette*.

When the NHL All-Star Game came to Pittsburgh for the first time in January 1990, that's where many of the televisions in the Pittsburgh area were tuned. On the scoresheet, Lemieux was humming along, second in the league in scoring as the Penguins tried to build on reaching the second round of the playoffs the previous spring. All eyes were on him, and it surprised no one when he recorded a hat trick in the opening 18 minutes of the game and finished with four goals to win Most Valuable Player honors for the third time in his career.

But all was not right. Though his numbers never hinted at it, Lemieux had been experiencing back pain for months and finally talked about it in early February, telling the *Post-Gazette*, "It's bad every day but it's getting worse and worse." It was bad enough that his back pain came during a time when the Penguins were chasing the New York Islanders for first place in the Patrick Division, but even worse it threatened his chance to break a significant NHL record—Gretzky's 51-game points streak.

Pushing forward despite the pain, Lemieux recorded a point in 46 consecutive regular-season games until he was finally blanked by the Rangers at Madison Square Garden on Feb. 14, 1990. He left the bench during that game and didn't return until the final game of the season, when he scored one goal and set up another only to see the Penguins lose at home in overtime to Buffalo, knocking them out of a playoff spot. "At that point," Lemieux said of his streak ending, "I couldn't go anymore. I couldn't even skate. Knowing that I was very close to a record that's probably never going to be broken, that was the hardest part."

On the night his points streak ended, Lemieux had played in 93 percent of the Penguins' regular-season games since joining the team. Over the next seven-plus years, he played in just over 56 percent of their games. Opponents had been unable to stop him, but a series of medical setbacks would now present him with a different kind of challenge through much of the rest of his career.

In early July 1990, Lemieux underwent surgery to repair a herniated disk in his back, and he was skating again by late August. But by late September, he was again experiencing back pain, this time from a disk infection unrelated to his surgery. "I couldn't walk for a couple weeks. I had some doubts that I would ever play the game again," he said.

He didn't return to the lineup until late January, then led Pittsburgh to back-to-back Stanley Cups in 1991 and 1992, winning the Conn Smythe Trophy as playoff MVP in both seasons by averaging more than two points per game with a combined 32 goals and 78 points in 38 games as Pittsburgh became a hockey-mad city. The 18-year-old from Montreal had indeed saved the franchise.

"That was my only goal when I came into the league, to lift that Cup once," Lemieux said later. "I was fortunate enough to do it twice. For a kid growing up in Montreal, that was the dream that I had. As a player that took a last-place team and was able to build a championship team and win two Stanley Cups. That's how I want to be remembered: as a winner."

The Penguins appeared almost certain to make it three consecutive championships in 1992–93, when they won the Presidents' Trophy as the NHL's best team in the regular season with a franchise-record 119 points in the standings. But that season came with a shocking second-round loss to the Islanders and another significant medical issue for Lemieux, who was still occasionally being knocked out of the lineup with back pain. In early January 1993, the 27-year-old was diagnosed with Hodgkin's disease, a cancer that attacks the lymph nodes.

"I've faced a lot of battles in my life and always came out on top. I certainly intend to do the same with this disease," he said during a press conference that was televised live in Western Pennsylvania and in Canada. "It is scary every time you hear the word 'cancer.' I went back home after I saw (the doctors) and they gave me the news, and on the way down to my house I could hardly drive because of the tears...and (I was) crying the whole day. It was a tough day in my life. But once I learned about the disease, once I talked to my family and friends...the more I found out about the disease, the better I felt."

Doctors removed a small lymph node, prescribed a month-long series of radiation treatments and said Lemieux had an excellent prognosis for recovery. When he returned to the lineup March 2 in Philadelphia—having taken his last radiation treatment that morning—he scored one goal and set up another in a loss to the Flyers before which the Philadelphia fans gave him a standing ovation.

Just prior to the diagnosis, Lemieux was on pace to record 221 points that season—which would stand today as the NHL single-season record, better than the 215 points Gretzky put up in 1981–82. He was averaging an incredible 2.6 points per game at that point. After missing 23 games and completing his radiation treatments, Lemieux's 31-point lead over the New York Islanders' Pat LaFontaine in the scoring race turned into a 12-point deficit.

But Lemieux's points-per-game average after his radiation treatments improved to 2.8 over the final 20 games of the season, and he not only passed LaFontaine but beat him by 12 points to win his fourth scoring title and power Pittsburgh to an NHL-record 17-game winning streak. It was a remarkable return for Lemieux, who scored five goals in a 10–4 win at Madison Square Garden over the Rangers in early April, drawing another standing ovation from opposing fans. He was awarded the Bill Masterton Trophy for perseverance and dedication to hockey after the season.

Lemieux, however, had another back surgery for a herniated muscle in July 1993, and missed the start of the 1993–94 season, by which time the Penguins were averaging a team-record 16,714 fans per home game. He played only four games before the Penguins in mid-November announced he would be out indefinitely because of back pain. He wound up playing just 22 games that season as the Penguins lost in the first round of the playoffs to Washington, and four months later announced he would sit out the 1994–95 season to strengthen his back and deal with fatigue issues, per the recommendations of doctors.

Between the end of his 46-game points streak in February 1990 and the spring of 1994, Lemieux had discarded years of playoff frustration and captained the Penguins to two Stanley

Cups, but he had also been frustrated, scared and exhausted by repeated health challenges that could have finished his career.

Yet in June 1995, Lemieux announced he would return to play, an outcome he couldn't have predicted the previous summer. "At this time last year, I thought my career was over and I had no plans of coming back," he said. "But these last six months, I started to feel a lot better, a lot stronger, not as fatigued anymore...and my back is much better."

He roared back in the 1995–96 season, accumulating 161 points, his third-highest career total despite missing 12 games, and winning the scoring title. The Penguins averaged 4.41 goals per game, still the most in team history, and turned around their first-round playoff series against Washington with a four-overtime road victory in Game 4. But they fell one game short of reaching the Cup Final. Lemieux did not commit to returning for the 1996–97 season until early September but added that "this is probably going to be my last year. It's getting tougher and tougher year after year to get back in shape and to play at the level that I want to play. That's really the main reason. I've come to accept that I'm never going to be able to play the way I did five or six years ago, but I can still help the team."

Lemieux won his sixth and final scoring title in 1996–97, often playing on a line with Jágr and Ron Francis, a season highlighted by his four-goal third period at Montreal on Jan. 26, tying an NHL record for goals in one period. Lemieux's family was among the Molson Centre crowd, which understood it was likely their last chance to see him play and gave him a standing ovation after the game. "The ovation at the end was something very special, something I'll remember for a long time," he said.

Montreal fans always compared Lemieux not to his idol Lafleur but to their beloved Jean Béliveau, the 6-3 center who helped the Canadiens to 10 Stanley Cups. "If you had to make a comparison," said Johnston, a Montreal native, "that's pretty good."

In early April, Lemieux announced he would indeed retire at the end of the season. The acceptance of his physical situation he spoke about months earlier had wavered. "I've been playing at a high level for so many years, and all of a sudden not to be able to go on the ice and challenge a player one-on-one...the last few years, that hasn't been there," he said just before the end of the regular season. "That's something that I can't accept."

When the Penguins faced elimination in Game 4 of the first round against Philadelphia at home, every Pittsburgh fan saw the game as their last chance to see Lemieux play. On cue, he scored on a breakaway against goaltender Garth Snow with 1:04 left in a 4–1 victory, the Penguins' last home game of the season. In the modern era, Lemieux at that point was second in NHL history in points per game at 2.01 (Gretzky had 2.03) and first in NHL history with 0.82 goals per game.

The Hockey Hall of Fame waived its three-year waiting period and inducted Lemieux in November 1997, making him the ninth player accorded that honor. The others had been Béliveau, Dit Clapper, Gordie Howe, Red Kelly, Ted Lindsay, Orr, Maurice Richard and Terry Sawchuk.

Lemieux continued to live in Pittsburgh, and he had more time for his love of golf and more time for the Mario Lemieux Foundation, which he formed in 1993 to benefit local cancer research initiatives after his diagnosis with Hodgkin's disease. His decision to become a philanthropist has had an important impact on local families, as by 2025 the Foundation had gifted more than $40 million to cancer research and patient care initiatives in and beyond the Pittsburgh region. After his son

Austin was born prematurely in 1996, Lemieux and his wife, Nathalie, noticed families visiting their young patients lacked a way to engage their other children in the hospital and expanded the Foundation scope to create Austin's Playrooms. Today, more than 40 playrooms have been established throughout western and central Pennsylvania as well as on U.S. military installations.

Lemieux's time out of the hockey spotlight, however, was short. Boston businessman Roger Marino had joined Howard Baldwin as co-owner of the Penguins in May 1997, but was clearly calling the shots when the team began missing deferred payments due Lemieux from his last contract, an NHL-record seven-year, $42 million deal signed at the start of the 1992–93 season and restructured several times. The Penguins were struggling under the burden of multiple deferred contracts and an expensive arena lease but owed Lemieux $32.5 million in deferred payments, and he sued for them in June 1998. Four months later, the Penguins filed for Chapter 11 bankruptcy, and by early 1999, Lemieux, the largest creditor, was organizing a group to purchase the team.

If U.S. Bankruptcy Judge Bernard Markovitz was unable to accept a plan to keep the team in Pittsburgh, the NHL was prepared to consider moving it. But Markovitz on June 24 accepted Lemieux's plan, which called for him to convert $20 million owed him into equity while forgiving $7.5 million. His investment group, led by California billionaire Ron Burkle, contributed a total of $50 million. The group promised that all creditors would be paid the amounts which had been negotiated, and began navigating the long and winding political road that eventually led to the construction of Consol Energy Center in 2010—which replaced the NHL's oldest rink and cemented the Penguins' future in the city.

He had saved the franchise again, this time in a business suit and with the critical help of Burkle. Lemieux's ownership group held the franchise for more than 22 years—by far the longest of any owner in team history—before selling to Fenway Sports Group in December 2021. "The things he's done for the team off the ice really have no modern comparison," says hockey historian Eric Zweig. "It's a remarkable kind of second act."

While Lemieux's emergence as a hockey owner had been completely unforeseen at the time of his retirement, he still had one more major career surprise to deliver. Not long after the start of the 2000–01 season, he made a phone call to former teammate Jay Caufield, to whom he had remained close after playing with him from 1988 to 1993.

"I was coming back from Philly, got a call from him, and it was very subtle like, 'Hey, what are you up to in the next little while?' We talked kind of casual," Caufield said, "and he mentioned about trying to skate, and he said, 'Can you work me out?' All I said to him was, "What is your timeframe?'"

Lemieux was about to do what Lemieux always did—make a comeback.

With the exception of one game when he returned on the final night of the season to try and get the Penguins into the 1990 playoffs, Lemieux had missed 14 months because of back pain, then back surgery and a subsequent back infection in 1990. He had missed almost two months before returning to the ice just hours after completing a month of cancer radiation therapy in 1993. He had missed 18 months after back pain and fatigue caused him to sit out the entire 1994–95 season. Now, at the age of 35, he was about to attempt his most audacious comeback—three years and eight months after retiring.

Very few people knew Lemieux's plan, and his sharp sense of humor was on display when he convened a meeting of team executives. "Mario called us into his office, four or five department heads," recalls Tom Rooney, then the team's chief operating officer, "and he said, 'There's going to be some changes around here.' And he said it really cryptically, like everybody was going to get fired, and then he said, 'I'm coming back to play.' Our jaws dropped."

"I missed the game and missed the challenge of competing," Lemieux said. "I feel that being 35 isn't too late and I have a lot of great hockey left in me. This comeback, I feel, will be the easiest because I've been resting and I'm healthy and I have a fresh start mentally and physically. I play this game to win championships, and I feel this team is very, very close to competing for a Stanley Cup."

Another factor in Lemieux's decision was giving his four children, especially Austin, a chance to see him play. "He's a young kid who gets up early in the morning with a hockey stick in his hands and he loves the game of hockey, and he'll get to see Daddy play before it's too late," he said.

His secret workouts on an outdoor rink at suburban Neville Island with Caufield hadn't caused Lemieux any second thoughts, although Caufield has one particular memory.

"Only one time did I feel like it was a moment, like a make-or-break moment," he said. "Just one day. I told him a story about when I was playing football at North Dakota and they let me walk on to the hockey team. The first day I went to skate with them, there were no pucks. It was two hours of skating, and I hadn't been on the ice for almost a year and a half. Five minutes into the practice, I get down to the other end of the rink and I remember thinking to myself, what the hell am I doing out here?

"My legs...(future NHLer) Jim Archibald came up to me and said to just hang in. I did. I hung in. We're doing laps, four each way, I never stopped but guys were passing me on the third lap, my legs were so fried. Gino (coach Gasparini) said, 'You know what? You're on the team the rest of the way.'

"I told (Lemieux) that story just to break it up," said Caufield, who played one game for UND that season but signed a contract with the New York Rangers the following fall to start a nine-year professional hockey career. "It was a hump day. It was two weeks in, and he didn't feel right this one day. That was the only day he didn't feel right. He laughed at the story, we hopped back on the ice, and never once did he look back."

Lemieux hit the NHL ice like he had never left it. Cameras, of course, caught the gaze of Austin Lemieux as he watched his father's retired number descend from the re-named Mellon Arena rafters—an almost surreal scene—on the night of Dec. 27, 2000, as the Penguins hosted Toronto. In that magical atmosphere, Lemieux assisted on a Jágr goal 33 seconds into the game and added his own goal and another assist 3:50 apart in the second period on the way to a 5–0 victory. Playing as an owner, a situation without parallel in modern North American sport, Lemieux scored 35 goals in 43 games that season—including nine goals and 19 points in his first eight games—as Pittsburgh finished with the league's ninth-best record. As his boyhood idol Guy Lafleur had done with the Rangers and Nordiques, Lemieux had now also played as an active Hall of Famer.

Lemieux had two game-winning goals in the opening round of the playoffs against Washington and a critical tying goal with 1:18 to play in Game 6 against Buffalo in a second-round series which saw Pittsburgh win the final two games on overtime goals by Martin Straka and Darius Kasparaitis. The Penguins then fell to New Jersey after reaching the Eastern Conference

Final for the first time in five seasons. It was Lemieux's last playoff appearance, and he finished his career second overall in playoff points per game (1.61) to Gretzky (1.84).

Arthroscopic surgery to remove hip cartilage and a subsequent diagnosis of tendinitis in his hip limited Lemieux to just 24 games in 2001–02, although he played through that pain to help Canada win gold at the 2002 Winter Olympics in Salt Lake City. He racked up 29 points in an 11-game stretch early in a remarkable 2002–03 season—at the age of 37, with the next-to-worst team in the NHL—and finished with 91 points despite missing 15 games, 10 with a groin injury. At the pace he was scoring, Lemieux would have won the scoring title that season if he had missed only three games, despite the fact the only Pittsburgh winger with more than nine goals, Alexei Kovalev, was traded in early February. But the tendinitis in his hip ended his 2003–04 season after just 10 games, and he had surgery to address it in January 2004.

After the NHL's labor dispute washed out the 2004–05 season, the now 40-year-old Lemieux opened the 2005–06 season with the Penguins and new star Sidney Crosby; this time it had been one year and 11 months since his last NHL game. But he played only 25 games before an irregular heartbeat after practice in early December sent him to the hospital. He played one more game on Dec. 16 at home against Buffalo, joining Crosby in picking up an assist on a goal by Ziggy Pálffy. He announced his retirement for good on Jan. 24, 2006. "This is it," he said. "And it hurts."

The inimitable, majestic centerman had won two Stanley Cups, six scoring titles, two Conn Smythe Trophies as playoff MVP, three Hart Trophies as regular-season MVP, four Ted Lindsay Awards as the NHL players' MVP, the Calder Trophy, the Bill Masterton Memorial Trophy, the Lester Patrick Trophy for service to the hockey in the United States and an Olympic gold medal.

Lemieux's reputation hasn't changed in the 20 years since he left the ice.

In 2010, he was awarded the Order of Canada to recognize a lifetime of outstanding achievement, dedication to community and service to the nation. When he made a surprise appearance just before the puck dropped at the Four Nations Faceoff game between Canada and Sweden in February 2025 at the Bell Centre in Montreal, TV analyst and former NHL player Ray Ferraro was between the benches for TNT. "The ovation literally made the hair stand up on my arms," he said on *The Ray & Dregs Hockey Podcast.* "It was just amazing. It was like the King coming back. Here in this city, they revere, as they should, one of the greats in the history of the sport, Jean Béliveau, for his class and his style and his play. Mario would be our generation's Béliveau." When the NHL polled its top prospects before the 2025 Entry Draft, it asked them which NHL player they would go back in time to play with if they could. Lemieux was named on more ballots than any other player.

Today, Lemieux ranks second all-time in points per game at 1.88 (Gretzky averaged 1.92) and second all-time in goals per game at 0.75 (the Islanders' Mike Bossy averaged 0.76), the latter figure having been especially suppressed by his health issues over his last four seasons. When he turned 60 in October 2025, he was eighth all-time in points (1,723) despite playing just 915 regular-season games—fewest among the NHL's top 62 all-time scorers. Excluding his three-year, eight-month retirement after the 1996–97 season, he missed 446 games over his career due to injuries or illness, the equivalent of five and a half seasons. And he began and finished his career on numerous Pittsburgh teams that were not good enough to even qualify for the playoffs.

As remarkable as those figures are, they don't reflect how many games he played and produced during his career when he was considerably less than 100 percent healthy. "You wonder," said Brown, "if he would have played by today's rules and stayed healthy, the numbers he would have put up."

Hall of Famer Paul Coffey played seven seasons with Gretzky and five with Lemieux. "No disrespect to Wayne, who's the greatest player that ever played because you just cannot accumulate 2,800 some points," he said, "but the most talented, hands down, was 66. Now if he had stayed healthy... who knows? But he was the most talented guy I've ever played with."

5

Sid the Kid

When the Penguins sank to the bottom of the NHL standings for the third time in their history in April 2004, their struggles on and off the ice had not been surprising. None of the players acquired in the 2001 trade of Jaromír Jágr had helped the team. Mario Lemieux had largely missed two of his first three full comeback seasons with injuries. Attendance over the past three seasons had dropped more than 27 percent. The team also suffered from the absence of playoff gates and other revenue streams prevented by playing in the league's oldest building.

Only a third-period goal by Ryan Malone at St. Louis in mid-February, on the way to an overtime loss, kept the Penguins from losing 18 consecutive games in regulation—which would have been an NHL record. But there was an incredibly talented prospect up for grabs in the 2004 Entry Draft in Russian winger Alexander Ovechkin, who would go on to become the greatest goal-scorer in NHL history. Unlike the 1984 draft in which they positioned themselves to select

Lemieux, however, the Penguins now had another hurdle to clear before selecting Ovechkin—the NHL Draft Lottery. Debuting in 1995 as a way to discourage teams from free-falling to the bottom of the standings, the lottery had certainly delivered on its goal; in each of the previous four years, the league's worst team failed to land the first pick.

Despite having the NHL's third-worst record behind Chicago and Pittsburgh, the rival Washington Capitals won the 2004 lottery and drafted Ovechkin, the Penguins' poor luck offset by the availability of yet another exceptional talent in Russian center Evgeni Malkin, whom they drafted with the second overall pick. What no one in the hockey world knew on draft day, however, was that the Penguins' lottery loss was about to play a significant role in making them the biggest winners in arguably the most-hyped draft lottery in league history set to happen one year later.

When the league and the NHL Players Association could not agree on a new bargaining agreement after the 2003–04 season, the NHL for the first and only time in its history canceled an entire season. This was a devastating blow to players, owners and fans, but the league emerged in 2005 with an agreement that introduced a salary cap and revenue sharing with players that has since taken the game's financial and competitive health to robust levels. But the NHL in 2005 nevertheless was left with a sticky logistical problem—how to determine a drafting order for teams, all of whom wanted a fair shot at landing an even bigger prospect than Ovechkin—super-skilled Canadian center Sidney Crosby.

A native of Cole Harbour, Nova Scotia, just east of Halifax, Crosby at the age of 14 was already a well-known talent in Canada despite being four years away from eligibility for the NHL draft. Crosby caused the Halifax Mooseheads of the

Quebec Major Junior Hockey League (QMJHL) in 2002 to request the league adopt the Ontario Hockey League rule that allowed 15-year-olds to play junior hockey one year early as long as they play for their hometown team. This was denied, and by the time Crosby was drafted first overall by the QMJHL's Rimouski Oceanic in 2003, he had already been named MVP of the Air Canada Cup national midget AAA championship with the Dartmouth Subways and spent a season at Shattuck–St. Mary's, a private prep school in Faribault, Minn., with a long history of turning out NHL players, where he had 162 points in just 57 games.

The NHL opted to give each of its 30 teams a chance at the top pick in its unprecedented lottery held in New York on July 22. Each team was initially given three lottery balls, then lost one ball for each playoff appearance they made over the previous three seasons and lost one ball for each time they had chosen first overall in the past four drafts—with a maximum of two balls lost. These parameters left the Penguins, Sabres, Blue Jackets and Rangers as the only teams retaining three balls, giving them each a 6.25 percent chance of winning. Ten teams had two lottery balls (4.17 percent chance) and 16 teams had a single lottery ball (2.08 percent chance).

Had the Penguins won the 2004 draft lottery and picked first overall, they would have joined a group of 12 teams with two lottery balls and their odds of winning the lottery would have dropped 33.3 percent to 4.17 percent. But the Penguins' descent to the bottom of the NHL had again coincided with the availability of a talent with rare gifts, and their 2004 lottery loss was a significant boost to their chances of winning the 2005 lottery.

Penguins' general manager Craig Patrick pulled out all the stops, coming to the drawing carrying a four-leaf clover after a visit to St. Patrick's Cathedral. NHL Commissioner Gary Bettman called out each of the picks beginning with No. 30, and the other three teams with three balls in the lottery had all been eliminated by the No. 6 pick. Next went Crosby's boyhood favorite Montreal, which had drafted his father, Troy, in 1984. Eventually only Pittsburgh and Anaheim remained for the final two spots, and after the Penguins were announced as the winners, Patrick told the *Pittsburgh Post-Gazette*, "It's a very, very lucky day. It's about time."

The player the Penguins were getting, by contrast, had left nothing in his career to chance. He was as humble and hard-working as he was skilled and competitive, mature beyond his years and focused every day on trying to become a better player—regardless of past success. Having just led the QMJHL in scoring and having helped Canada to the 2005 World Junior Championship gold medal, "Sid the Kid" told reporters after the lottery that his first NHL goal was "making the team." This was already a given for the Pittsburgh management, but not for the kid who was turning 18 in two weeks.

A superb and powerful skater with incredible hockey sense and vision, high levels of motivation and determination and burgeoning leadership ability, Crosby surprised no one by immediately becoming one of the league's dominant scorers. He became just the seventh rookie in NHL history to record 100 points, finishing with 102 to eclipse Lemieux's team record. His 63 assists were the most ever by a rookie on a non-playoff team, as the Penguins finished next-to-last in the overall standings, having replaced coach Ed Olczyk with Michel Therrien in mid-December. Crosby's rookie production thus came during a season in which he was under a media microscope, making adjustments to the best league in the world and playing for a team that had changed coaches and was the least competitive of any team for which he had played.

No problem.

Lemieux had been forced to retire by an irregular heartbeat in January, but he joined Crosby in the Pittsburgh lineup for 26 games before doing so, effectively passing the torch as Montreal's Jean Béliveau had done in 1971 to Guy Lafleur and Los Angeles' Marcel Dionne had done to Luc Robitaille in 1987. And Crosby, who was living with Lemieux at the start of his career, seemed to also immediately share his landlord's penchant for delivering against the rival Flyers.

Crosby had a goal and an assist in his first game in Philadelphia, a 6–5 overtime loss, but his second appearance there on Nov. 16 was an early glimpse of the intangibles that drove him. In a matter of minutes late in the second period of a scoreless game, Flyers' defenseman Derian Hatcher twice got his stick up on Crosby, damaging multiple teeth and splitting his lip with the first one. Neither was penalized, though Crosby was given an unsportsmanlike conduct penalty for complaining about the non-calls. After the second intermission, Crosby set up a Malone goal and scored one of his own 56 seconds apart to give the Penguins a 2–0 lead, and after the Flyers tied it, Crosby delivered his first NHL overtime goal on a breakaway against Antero Niittymäki for a 3–2 victory. Over the first 20 years of his NHL career, Crosby scored more goals against the Flyers than any other team.

"Such a great competitor and fun to watch, I'll tell you that," remembered Mark Recchi, who joined Ziggy Pálffy as Crosby's linemates to start his rookie season. "When you see a young kid like that come in, it really helps to give you energy and get excited about the game. He was ready for the challenge and all the pressure he had on him. He was ready for it. He just let his play take over for him."

Right winger Colby Armstrong was recalled from the Penguins' AHL affiliate in Wilkes-Barre/Scranton in mid-season to make his NHL debut, and soon he was playing on Crosby's wing, where his play along the boards worked in tandem with Crosby's speed.

"I knew if I could get the puck and bring a guy to me and he's close by, I could get it to him and...total destruction. It was awesome and fun," said Armstrong, who finished 13th in rookie scoring in 2005–06 despite playing only 47 games. "He was so fast, just like a rocket ship. I would pull guys to me, and he would come under low with speed, 10 feet off me, and I could bring guys in enough that I could just lay a five-foot area pass in to him and he's going to have a clear shot up the ice. There's so many times I had an assist and I'm not even in the camera shot. I'm standing at our blue line and he's scoring a goal. That's what it was like. It just worked."

It was Ovechkin, not Crosby, who won the Calder Trophy as Rookie of the Year after recording 106 points, but the 2005–06 season was just the start of both young stars being measured against each other and playing an integral role in NHL efforts to market the game after it had been wiped from the world's sporting landscape the previous winter. Average attendance in Pittsburgh increased 33 percent in Crosby's rookie season to 15,804, and during his third season the Penguins sold out every home game for the first time in their history—the start of an astonishing streak of 14 consecutive seasons of doing so.

In late May 2006, Ray Shero was named to replace Patrick, and one of the first things he wanted to do was meet with Crosby. Their lunch in downtown Pittsburgh was Shero's introduction to Crosby as a unique member of the team.

"It was four hours," Shero remembered. "I had questions for him and gave him some homework, actually. He had been with the team for a year already and I hadn't. I asked him what three things we do well as an organization, what three things we could do better. It wasn't about the power play or this or that, it could be how we travel or whatever. He's a thoughtful kid. He asked if he could give it back to me later, because he wanted to work on it, give some thought to it.

"And after that, I'd meet with him once a year. There would be no set thing we were going to talk about. It was just that there was so much on his mind all the time. I would do a lot of listening. He would ask questions. He's a historian of the game, passionate about it and knowledgeable. He was incredible to work with."

By the start of the 2006–07 season, Crosby was surrounded by a young nucleus of players upon which Shero would help build a champion. Goaltender Marc-André Fleury had already played parts of two seasons with Pittsburgh, and now Malkin and 2006 second overall pick Jordan Staal, another center, joined the lineup on a full-time basis while defenseman Kris Letang made a brief NHL debut. Fleury was the oldest of this group at just 22, and the Penguins also had a supporting cast that included Malone, Armstrong, Ryan Whitney and checking forward Max Talbot—the latter three all 24 or younger.

When Crosby recorded 10 points over two games against the Flyers and Islanders in mid-December, he joined Wayne Gretzky (1980) as the only teenagers to hold the NHL's outright scoring lead in modern NHL history. Later that season Crosby became the only teenager in league history to win a scoring title, taking the NHL's Art Ross Trophy with a career-high 120 points, along the way continuing to drive the Penguins' production as it was obvious in his second season he was still challenging opponents to discover ways to stop him.

His powerful strides took him past forwards in the neutral zone and defensemen at the blue line, and he was always at home winning board battles for pucks or peeling away from defenders behind the net. He was the antithesis of a perimeter player, scoring most frequently around the net in areas that were more difficult to reach, and he could sense where a play was going and then execute his role in it—even if that sometimes meant bouncing pucks off goaltenders, something Lemieux would often do.

"He was such a relentless guy, that's the word that comes to mind," said Matt Cullen, who played against Crosby for 11 seasons before signing with the Penguins and winning consecutive Stanley Cups with him in 2016 and 2017. "He just keeps coming at you and coming at you and coming at you. He played at such a high pace and just outworked everybody on the rink, had a unique skillset...you could stop him once, but he just kept coming and you couldn't contend with it for the whole game."

Seven weeks after the Penguins were eliminated in the first round of the 2007 playoffs by Ottawa, Crosby at 19 became the youngest captain in NHL history. "You have to keep reminding yourself that he is 19 years old," Shero said. The captaincy made formal what those who had played with him could plainly see: leading the way, with both skill and his approach to working on his game and bringing together his teammates, came naturally to Crosby.

"You never see Sid without a 'C' on his jersey for a reason," said Talbot. "He's a calm leader, he doesn't speak often, it's not about what he says but what he does. It's about the character. You know every decision in his life is about the next game, to get better or to improve on something, whether it's the team or himself.

"I remember myself being a third- or fourth-liner, playing 12 to 14 minutes a night and to have an optional skate on Sunday after a big game where Sid played 22 minutes and it was so hard playing, and the next morning Sid would be the first one on the ice. I'd be so pissed off. As a fourth-liner you had some drinks the night before, and you wanted to relax on a day off, and you feel like you're tired almost, and then you look at your captain, he played twice as much as you and twice as hard and he's skating trying to get better and improve, so you had no choice but to follow. He leads by example: 'OK, if this guy's looking to get better every day, why am I not?'"

Chris Kunitz, who would become one of Crosby's longest-running linemates after being traded to Pittsburgh in 2009, came to the team as a Cup champion, having won with Anaheim in 2007. He had already been around great leadership, and yet he remembered how Crosby pushed the Penguins in the same way and helped them get off to an 11–5–0 start, best in the Eastern Conference, after a long lockout delayed the start of the 2012–13 season.

"We were all in Pittsburgh skating and doing drills. It was why we had a good start," Kunitz said. "A lot of teams were hanging out and being on the golf course. We had five to 15 guys September to January. It was just his ability to work and get better, even though he's the best. It literally doesn't matter the day or the year, he was always focused on getting better at some avenue of the game. He kept working and it would drag the rest of us to do it. That pushed everybody else in that locker room. Even though he's not saying it, he's not telling you do to it, you're just following him. You want to be with people who are trying to be the best all the time."

Cullen, a Cup champion in 2006 with Carolina, was 39 years old when he joined the Penguins. He had seen a lot in his long career, but Crosby showed him something new.

"He's an intelligent, thoughtful guy and he knows the game better than anybody," Cullen said. "He's got one of the best brains for hockey we've ever seen. And he's the hardest worker on the team, puts in more time than anybody. I've always been a big believer that if your best player is your hardest worker, you're setting the team up for success. I've never been around a guy who puts more into the game and cares more about the game. That sets up the tone of how the whole team is going to be operated. When your leader works that hard, everybody's got to work.

"And he has such a good awareness of what's going on within the group. It starts with a different level of care than most people have for their teammates. He cares about every guy. He gets to know everybody, he calls every single player that comes into the organization. Talk about selfless leadership. He cares about his teammates more than anybody, and guys love him for it. Just a different level of care coming out of him, and it means more when it's one of the best players to ever play the game. He leads by example better than anyone."

Crosby missed almost a third of the regular season in 2007–08 with a high ankle sprain but had still delivered a 19-game scoring streak early in the season and a memorable shootout-winning goal in the NHL's first Winter Classic game in Buffalo on Jan. 1. The Penguins reached the Stanley Cup Final before losing in six games to Detroit, a remarkable place for a young, still inexperienced team to be two seasons after narrowly avoiding finishing with the NHL's worst record.

Crosby had his third coach in four NHL seasons when Michel Therrien was fired late in the 2008–09 season and replaced by Dan Bylsma, but the Penguins shook off a prolonged mid-season slump to return to the Cup Final against Detroit again. Crosby led the playoffs with 15 goals and the Penguins won their first Stanley Cup in 17 years, making him the youngest player to captain a Cup champion. There was also a bit of mathematical symmetry to the Game 7 victory that the superstitious Crosby could appreciate—it was the 87th game of the 2009 Stanley Cup playoffs, won by the player who wears number 87 as a nod to his birthdate of Aug. 7, 1987.

"It's the stuff you dream of as a kid," he told reporters afterward. "It's reality now. We worked so hard. It's amazing to see how far we've come, and couldn't feel any better." Crosby celebrated his 22nd birthday with a Stanley Cup parade attended by an estimated 25,000 people in his native Cole Harbour.

The 2009–10 season, the Penguins' last in Mellon Arena, saw Crosby deliver a career-high 51 goals, winning the NHL's Maurice "Rocket" Richard Trophy as the league's leading goal-scorer, and despite a second-round defeat against Montreal, the Penguins seemed poised to be in the Stanley Cup conversation annually.

That season also saw Crosby push his international presence to a new level. He'd already won a gold medal with the Canadian team in the 2005 World Junior Championships, but now he was a critical member of Team Canada in the 2010 Olympic Games held in Vancouver. Given hockey's status as Canada's national game, any team representing Canada in an Olympic tournament plays under intense pressure, pressure that only increases when Canada is hosting the Games.

Team Canada finished second in its group, losing the top spot in its game against the rival United States, but marched forward to meet the Americans in the gold medal game on Feb. 28. The U.S. tied the game with just 25 seconds to play, and the gold medal would come down to one overtime shot. Crosby, held without a point in both the quarterfinals and semifinals, beat goaltender Ryan Miller at 7:40 of overtime to win the game, and his Golden Goal moment at General Motors Place served another Canadian generation as its "where were you when" moment, much the same way Paul Henderson's 1972 Summit Series winner in Moscow had done.

"Being in Canada, that's the opportunity of a lifetime," he said after the game. "You dream of that a thousand times growing up. For it to come true is amazing." Said Gretzky a few years later, "It seems like the more important the game, the more impact that he makes on a game."

In early November of the 2010–11 season, the Penguins' captain began a 25-game points streak, the second-longest in Pittsburgh history, that included 26 goals and 50 points. He was on pace to record 140 points, a level only nine players in NHL history had reached. He had multiple points in 16 of those games and at the age of 23 was clearly playing the most productive hockey of his career while the Penguins won 19 times to forge the best record in the league. The streak was broken in late December on Long Island, and everyone expected Crosby to kick back into gear three days later in another Winter Classic game, this time at Pittsburgh's Heinz Field against Ovechkin and the rival Capitals.

Instead, this game started Crosby on a career detour that lasted 14 months.

In the final minute of the second period, Capitals' forward David Steckel caught Crosby in the head with his right shoulder as Crosby was turning to go up the ice. Crosby stayed down momentarily and skated off the ice slowly, but returned to play the third period. However, in the Penguins' next game four days later, Crosby took a big hit behind the Tampa Bay net from defenseman Victor Hedman late in the second period, drawing a boarding minor. He saw limited ice time in the third period of what was a blowout Pittsburgh victory, but he missed the game the following night in Montreal with a concussion.

Crosby had figured in on an amazing 50 percent of all goals scored by the Penguins before missing the final 41 games of that regular season and all seven games of the Penguins' first-round loss to Tampa Bay in the 2011 playoffs. He had tried to stay part of his team, and he recalled during a press conference with his doctors later in the year that a February video session with his teammates "was something that felt like it was really stressing my system."

When he pushed himself during his annual intensive summer workouts, Crosby began experiencing headaches. He had seen specialists in Michigan and Georgia, but by the start of training camp in September 2011, Crosby was eight months into a gradual recovery with no timetable for his return, although he was skating with the team in early drills.

That return finally came on Nov. 21, 10 and a half months after his last game, in a 5–0 home victory over the Islanders in which Crosby scored on his third shift of the game and wound up with two goals and four points. But after playing eight games and racking up 12 points, Crosby's headaches returned and knocked him out of the lineup indefinitely. "I don't think 'frustrating' even describes it," he told the *Pittsburgh Post-Gazette*. But doctors almost two months later said they believed a soft-tissue injury in his neck, not a concussion, was the cause of his most recent problems, and after another three months out of the lineup, Crosby returned in mid-March—including the playoffs, he'd missed 108 of the team's last 116 games.

There were, of course, lingering doubts about how long Crosby might be able to stay in the lineup this time, but he soon dispelled them. He played in all 14 remaining regular-season games, averaging nearly two points per game, and then didn't hesitate to get involved in after-the-whistle encounters in a wild first-round playoff loss to the Flyers. He got involved with Philadelphia captain Claude Giroux in one Game 3 instance, and later with gloves littering the ice, he used his stick to push away Jakub Voráček's glove as Voráček reached down to retrieve it.

Asked after the game why he did it, Crosby put his competitive nature in a rare verbal spotlight. "I don't like him. I don't like any guy on their team," he said. "Guys are emotional and there's a lot of stuff going on out there. There's no reason to explain or sit here and say why I pushed a glove away. They're doing a lot of things out there, too. And you know what? We don't like each other."

Talbot, now playing for the Flyers, had been close to Crosby and really enjoyed his time in Pittsburgh before signing as a free agent with Philadelphia, although he admitted "in a way it was tough for me to do that move." When Talbot got home after Game 3 and saw the video clip of Crosby's comments about hating all the Flyers, he paused. "I'm like, crap," he said. "I sent a little text to Sid that night. I'm playing against him...'Even me, Sid?' His answer was, 'No, except you. We're good.'"

This was a period in Crosby's career marked by unexpected playoff frustration. The Penguins had lost their second-round series to Montreal in 2010, lost a 3–1 series lead while falling to Tampa Bay in 2011 without both Crosby and Malkin, who had undergone major knee surgery, and then suffered a meltdown of discipline while losing their 2012 series to the Flyers. Pittsburgh did reach the Eastern Conference Final in 2012–13—a season that also saw Crosby miss 12 games with a broken jaw—but scored only two goals while being swept by Boston, then blew a 3–1 series lead and lost in the second round to the Rangers in 2014 before going out in five games of the opening round to the Rangers in 2015.

During much of this period, Crosby played on a line with Kunitz and Pascal Dupuis, who had been obtained from Atlanta late in the 2007–08 season in the deal that brought Marián Hossa to the Penguins. The line, first tried by coach Dan Bylsma in late December 2009, didn't become a staple for Pittsburgh until the 2010–11 season, but that trio was a bedrock of consistent production for Pittsburgh when all three players were healthy.

Kunitz was a forechecking menace and brought a physical presence to the team, and Crosby was able to use Dupuis' superior speed to create opportunities.

"Myself and Duper were unselfish in the sense we knew what we were, we were not trying to become something else," said Kunitz, who had a career-high 35 goals and 68 points in 2013–14, most of the first half of which was spent on that line before Dupuis was hurt. "Duper's ability to play with speed and transport pucks...he did a lot of things. His mentality was being good defensively. Sid's creativity and ability to make all that space in behind and give us good passes, that put us in spots on the ice where we could have more success with the puck. It worked out really well."

Kunitz believes Crosby's efficient play along the wall, and his superior ability to make and finish plays on the backhand, were especially useful for the line.

"Just his ability to play on both sides of his stick. When he's along the wall," Kunitz said, "his body awareness, his ability to be on both sides of his body and be comfortable there, opened up everything. (Behind the net) he could make those passing lanes, instead of only being a foot wide, he could make them six feet wide."

Crosby in 2013–14 won both his second scoring title and second Hart Trophy as league MVP, later in the season also captaining Team Canada to its second consecutive gold medal at the Olympic Games in Russia. Crosby and Kunitz both had goals in the 3–0 win over Sweden in the gold medal game that brought Canada consecutive Olympic golds for the first time in 62 years and made it the first Canadian team in 86 years to win every game it played in an Olympic competition.

In the spring of 2015, the Penguins' early playoff exit meant Crosby could play in the World Championships in the Czech Republic, and he promptly helped Team Canada to its first gold medal in eight years of that competition as it won all 10 games it played. That made Crosby just the ninth Canadian to join the International Ice Hockey Federation's Triple Gold Club by winning the Stanley Cup, the World Championships and an Olympic gold—and the first ever to captain his team in all three. The following year he captained Team Canada to the World Cup of Hockey title.

The Oilers' Taylor Hall told the *Edmonton Journal* that Crosby joining Team Canada for the World Championships after the Penguins' playoff elimination "really set the tone for our team. When he came in, our whole mood changed. It was a win-or-nothing mentality. It was a learning experience trying to keep up with him...great player, great leader. You can see how he brings people into the fire."

What Crosby was most burning for, however, was another Stanley Cup, especially since the young and talented Penguins of 2009 had not come closer than eight victories away from a second Cup now in six seasons. They didn't qualify for the playoffs until the final night of the 2014–15 season, the first for coach Mike Johnston, and then found themselves out of a playoff spot in mid-December the following season when Johnston was replaced by Mike Sullivan.

The Penguins' offensive production took a dramatic fall under Johnston, from fifth in the NHL in Bylsma's last season to 19th in Johnston's first season (which saw Crosby start games with 13 different sets of wingers) and then to 27th by the time of his firing in 2015–16. Crosby had averaged fewer points per game under Johnston than he had under any other Penguins' coach.

With Sullivan pushing the team's pace of play, a huge benefit for Crosby's powerful skating, the Penguins' captain two weeks later began filling the net, scoring 18 goals in a span of 19 games, including five game-winners. In that same span, Malkin, Kunitz, Letang and Patric Hörnqvist all scored at least six goals and Pittsburgh was off and running toward the first of two consecutive Stanley Cups, with Crosby winning the Conn Smythe Trophy on both occasions.

Mid-season coaching changes are normally a death knell for teams with Cup aspirations; through the 2025 playoffs, only seven NHL teams had won the Stanley Cup after changing coaches in mid-season. The Penguins were the only team to do it twice, when Bylsma replaced Therrien in 2008–09 and when Sullivan replaced Johnston in 2015–16, and Crosby never forgot the emotions that came with those changes.

"Everyone feels like they have to prove themselves all over again. And as a team you feel really responsible," Crosby said. "It's one thing to lose, but coaches are losing their jobs, or jobs are on the line when you lose...it's not a good feeling. There's an urgency and desperation that comes with those changes, and for us, because of the groups we had, we had a lot of pride and wanted to right things as quickly as possible. The coaches who came in deserve a lot of credit in those situations, too, because they were able to get us on the same page quickly and get us in the right direction."

Shero remembered Crosby's reaction to the firing of Therrien, a coach with whom the Penguins had simply run their course amid reports of underlying tensions in the dressing room between the coach and his players.

"Always a team player, a team person. When we had to let Therrien go," Shero said, "Sid was the most pissed off of anybody. He really liked Michel, but he knows everybody is looking at him and saying it's him. No one (in management) asked Sidney Crosby what he thought. He never asked for that. It took Sid maybe three, four games to get over it. He was really in the dumps.

"It was hard to go through, and good to see he had his coach's back. People were saying Crosby had something to do with it. He had nothing to do with it. He was a young player at the time. We weren't playing well at the time, either. He's just a kid that cares."

Crosby's natural desire to support those around him goes beyond the rink and his team. Back home in Cole Harbour after the 2016 Cup victory, Crosby noticed a sign in the front lawn of a home in nearby Enfield asking him to sign a jersey. He later showed up unannounced at the home and did just that, chatting and taking pictures with the family before leaving. There are a myriad of Crosby stories similar to that one.

Through his play and the team's achievements, Crosby grew the game in Pittsburgh for a generation of fans, just as Lemieux had done. He did his part even more directly in 2008 by investing money and time to start Sidney Crosby's Little Penguins Learn to Play Hockey program, which presents players aged 5–9 with a complete set of hockey equipment and a chance to learn fundamental skills over eight to 10 weeks at more than 25 rinks around Western Pennsylvania, Ohio and West Virginia. By 2025, the program, also supported by USA Hockey and corporate donations, had given more than 17,000 children an introduction to the game. The program was so successful that in 2013 the NHL and NHL Players Association adopted the program into a league-wide initiative.

One of the program participants was Logan Cooley, a youngster from West Mifflin, Pa., just outside of Pittsburgh. Cooley attended the program at Rostraver Ice Garden, a rink 25 miles southeast of Pittsburgh which in the 1970s served the Penguins as a practice facility. He was a year and a half old when Crosby made his NHL debut, and 17 years later in 2022, he became the highest-drafted Pittsburgh-area native after being selected third overall by Arizona. By December 2023 at the renamed PPG Paints Arena in Pittsburgh, he and Crosby were in the faceoff circle together. "It's when I first stepped foot on the ice, and I knew from then hockey was what I wanted to do for the rest of my life," Cooley said of the program. "I kind of never looked back."

One thing that never stopped, whether winning Cups or missing the playoffs, was Crosby's focus on investing in himself through his legendary summer workouts, many with close friend and Halifax native Nathan MacKinnon of the Colorado Avalanche. Over his first eight seasons after turning 30, only 10 players averaged more points per game than Crosby did, despite the fact most of them began that period in their early 20s.

"He's deadly serious about preparation...having that mindset and ability to mentally prepare for a season at his level," said Armstrong. "That's one thing where I'm like, 'How is he still doing this?' Because it breaks a lot of people, the grind, it takes a little bit of the joy out of it for a lot of players.

Yeah, they play, but maybe they don't love it as much. He's just built different."

Sid was no longer a kid, but his continued excellence on the other side of 30—despite the team struggling in the playoffs or missing them entirely—would come to define much of this part of his career. The Penguins had matched their team record by winning a ninth consecutive playoff round in the first round of the 2018 playoffs, but they were beaten in the second round by eventual champion Washington to start a streak of five consecutive playoff series losses through 2022. They failed to qualify in the next three seasons.

But the Penguins' captain continued to deliver precision backhand goals, no-look passes, goals batted out of mid-air or scored off unique deflections, turbo-charged rushes through the neutral zone and catch-me-if-you-can skating drills for opponents behind the net. Among his many memorable goals was a particularly spectacular power-play rush in Buffalo in March 2017. Taking a drop pass from Justin Schultz, Crosby left his own zone and rolled through the neutral zone, skating around Ryan O'Reilly at the blue line and then headed between the circles straight to the Sabres' net. Using his left hand to fend off defenseman Zach Bogosian and controlling the puck only with his right hand before reaching defenseman Josh Gorges could knock it away, Crosby lifted the puck over the glove of goaltender Robin Lehner—essentially a one-handed backhander.

And he continued to play at an $8.7 million salary cap hit that was below what he could have demanded—in 10 of the 11 seasons between 2014 and 2025, his cap hit was not even the largest on his own team. Crosby improved his team's salary cap flexibility by playing for a contract well under market value, arguably, longer than any player in NHL history.

Crosby was 37 in March 2025 when he passed Gretzky by becoming the first NHL player to average a point-per-game through each of his first 20 seasons, a remarkable achievement under any circumstances. He made it 21 consecutive seasons in 2025–26 and by that time had also risen to seventh all-time in NHL scoring despite missing 224 games with injury or sickness in his career—the equivalent of more than 2.5 seasons—and despite his team having had 73 games taken away by the 2012–13 labor stoppage and COVID-forced scheduling reductions over two seasons.

Crosby signed a two-year contract extension in 2024 that wouldn't expire until just before his 40th birthday, and he did the once-unthinkable and passed Lemieux as the Penguins' all-time leading scorer on Dec. 21, 2025, against Montreal. Instead of slowing down on the international stage, he played in the 2025 World Championships in Scandinavia and captained Team Canada again when NHL players returned to the Olympics in 2026 in Italy, although he missed the final two games of the Winter Games with a knee injury as Canada took home silver.

"I think I've got to stay a little bit more active than I used to," he said not long before leaving for the 2025 World Championships. "I used to take a lot more time off the ice and get away from it. I really enjoyed that. I thought it was important to get away. I don't think I have that luxury anymore at my age just to put it away for that long, put the skates away. It's better to keep going at this point and stay on the ice a little more."

But he was playing and working with a purpose, which was not to prepare himself to move further up the NHL's all-time scoring charts but to help his team keep winning games. He talked about that in April 2025 when his NHL peers voted him the league's most complete player—for the sixth consecutive season.

"You're always trying to get better, find different areas of your game you can improve, no matter how long you've played," he said. "Ultimately those things hopefully translate to wins, so that's the motivation behind it, not necessarily individual things. They're things you believe in that are going to help translate into wins, so that's why you do it."

6

Geno

MAGNITOGORSK, RUSSIA. HELSINKI, FINLAND. EL SEGUNDO, California. Pittsburgh. As travel itineraries go, it's an interesting way to get from one steel town to another. As paths to the NHL go, it's a route as unique as it is long and will always belong to Evgeni Malkin.

In August 2006, the 20-year-old native of Magnitogorsk and the Penguins' No. 2 overall pick in the 2004 NHL Draft was making headlines across Russia and North America as he attempted to reach his dream destination—the NHL. Malkin was navigating his own emotional journey, pressured by his hometown Metallurg Magnitogorsk team to stay while trying to follow his own desire to test himself in the world's best league.

On Aug. 7, under extreme pressure at the conclusion of a meeting with his parents and team officials that lasted into the middle of the night, Malkin abandoned a longer existing contract with Metallurg and signed a new deal that would keep him at home for one more season—even though he said the team had reneged on a previous promise to allow him to leave for the NHL by this time. Metallurg had also pressured the Russian Hockey Federation to abstain from signing the International Ice Hockey Federation's transfer agreement, which legislated a standard $200,000 payout to Metallurg had Malkin left; the team was reportedly seeking millions in that circumstance.

But the transfer agreement was largely background noise, because Malkin could extract himself from even his new contract by submitting a two-week notice of his intent to leave, an old loophole in Russian law that sources told the *National Post* was not often employed because it left players who used it to be branded as traitors. More significant was the fact, reported later by several media outlets, that Metallurg general manager Gennady Velichkin had been withholding Malkin's passport.

When Malkin signed his new contract with Metallurg and left with the team for training in Helsinki, he got his passport back. And when he got to Helsinki's airport on Aug. 12, he vanished with the help of agent J.P. Barry and others. By Aug. 17, he was seen skating with NHL players at the Los Angeles Kings' practice facility in El Segundo, his two-week notice having been filed. He arrived in Pittsburgh on Sept. 4 and signed his first NHL contract the next day. It had been a whirlwind four weeks and an odyssey unlike any other taken by Pittsburgh players born outside North America—and highlighted Malkin's drive through the emotional weight of his situation to make his own way in the hockey world.

"I wouldn't like to speak about all that I've been through right now," Malkin told the *Pittsburgh Post-Gazette* through an interpreter upon arriving at Pittsburgh International Airport.

"The only thing I can tell you is that I'm really so happy to be here finally."

The 6-3, 195-pound center who spoke no English moved in immediately with Penguins' Russian defenseman Sergei Gonchar and his family. "He had a lot of pressure on him, and once he left (Russia), a lot of people were upset," said Gonchar. "I knew how tough it was for him, and I talked to my wife and we decided to help him."

One place Malkin didn't need any help was on the ice, as he had demonstrated again in his last season outside the NHL in 2005–06. He helped Magnitogorsk to a first-place finish but also excelled while playing in hockey's three biggest international events over a span of four months. He had 10 points in six games at the 2006 World Junior Championships, finishing second in tournament scoring to future teammate Phil Kessel while the Russians took the silver medal in January, and the following month he was the youngest player on the Russian team in the 2006 Turin Olympics, where he had six points in seven games. In May at the World Championships, Malkin had 10 points in nine games to tie for the team lead in scoring.

Gonchar had played with Malkin at Magnitogorsk during the NHL lockout of 2004–05 and said he knew then "it was just a matter of time till we were going to see something very, very special at the NHL level."

Malkin quickly began fulfilling that promise in his rookie season, becoming the first NHL player in 89 years to score a goal in each of his first six games, a streak he capped off in Los Angeles with two goals, including the overtime winner off an assist from Gonchar. The kid teammates nicknamed "Geno"—from Eugene, the English equivalent of Evgeni—won the Calder Trophy as NHL Rookie of the Year, after which the

Russian Hockey Federation had no problem including him on its team for the World Championships.

Malkin's size, vision and strength were immediately impressive, and by his second season he amassed 106 points—the quickest any player born outside North America had reached the 100-point plateau with the Penguins—and was named a First Team All-Star by the NHL. He put together a career-high 15-game points streak in his second season, and he was nearly unstoppable in the 2008–09 season, putting up a career-high 113 points in the regular season and then dominating the post-season, joining Mario Lemieux as the only Penguins player to win the scoring title and the Conn Smythe Trophy as playoff MVP in the same season as Pittsburgh won its first Stanley Cup in 17 seasons.

"He had the whole package, could read the game very well, put himself in good position all the time," remembers Gonchar, who played with or against Malkin for more than a decade. "One thing people didn't realize was how strong he is. It's so hard to knock him down in front of the net. He has the ability to make a play and find a guy. You feel like you're covering everybody and you lose a guy for a half second, and he takes advantage of it and finds his teammate. This is Geno."

The all-time NHL leader in assists among Russian-born players, Malkin not only proved adept at distributing the puck at the NHL level but also embraced opportunities to use his skill and size to beat defenders by himself—even multiple defenders. His confidence sometimes hurt him in instances where his chances of success were quite low, but like many European-trained players he usually preferred trying to make a play to dumping the puck and waiting for a chance on his next shift.

What was also obvious about Malkin, who grew to 6-5 and 210 pounds, was that he played at a high emotional level. This led him to sometimes take unnecessary penalties (he became the Penguins' all-time leader in penalty minutes in 2022–23), and his frustration at the way things were unfolding on the ice could sometimes be palpable. But that same emotion also helped drive him to become a difference-maker over his career, especially in the playoffs, and his heart-on-his-sleeve approach was an important part of his makeup.

"That's one of his great attributes: he plays with emotion," said former Penguins' general manager Ray Shero. "He's kind of a scary guy, he gets galloping around that ice and he's hard to stop. And he's got a fuse on him, and if you're an opposing player, you've got to deal with a lot of stuff going on there. A beast."

Remembered teammate Mark Recchi, "He had all the talent in the world. He had a great fire in his belly, too, you could tell."

An example of that came in Game 1 of the 2008 Eastern Conference Final against the rival Flyers. Malkin missed a shorthanded chance against goaltender Martin Biron early in the second period, then was crushed by Philadelphia's Mike Richards behind the net. Malkin was slow to get up as the play went the other way, but a Flyers' turnover led Gonchar to feed the puck ahead to Malkin, by now the only player near the Philadelphia blue line. Instead of making a move or picking a spot against Biron, Malkin simply skated between the circles and blasted a 20-foot slap shot past him—not an area and shot selection that go together for shooters on breakaway opportunities.

Winger Bryan Rust, who spent time on and off over the years on Malkin's line, said most players play with emotion but that with Malkin it "comes with the territory of being who he is, kind of being in the spotlight a little more. When you see him get kind of…when you see him turn it up a little, then you see him start to take over games."

Rust said Malkin's ability to use his elite skills to make unexpected plays meant reading off him "might be a little harder, but the more you do what you're supposed to do, he reads off that and he can do his own thing. He kind of thrives with guys who, he knows where they're going to be," Rust said. "He's always been a special player with the puck and with space, and anytime I was out there with him I was trying to use my skating to create that space for him. He does some special things with the puck, so your ability to play defense and get him the puck helps, and then go on offense and just kind of let him do his thing."

During the 2010–11 season, Malkin suffered the first of multiple significant injuries, leaving the lineup in mid-January with a right knee injury that forced him the following month to have surgery to repair both his medial collateral ligament and anterior cruciate ligament. But he responded with a magnificent season, scoring a career-high 50 goals and recording 109 points in 2011–12, winning his second scoring title and taking MVP honors as voted upon by the media (Hart Trophy) and the players (Ted Lindsay Award).

If future NHL fans want a glimpse of what Malkin looked like in his prime, his 2011–12 season would serve—and perhaps specifically three games against Tampa Bay during a six-week stretch from mid-January through late February in which he seemed simply unstoppable with Sidney Crosby out. At Tampa Bay, he recorded a natural hat trick inside 12 minutes of the third period to break a 3–3 tie and push the Penguins to victory with a five-point game; back home four weeks later, his two goals started and finished a rally from a 2–0 deficit for another victory; and two weeks later at home he delivered another hat trick, including a solo rush from his own zone in which he used his speed to leave behind defenders and then turned Lightning defenseman Brett Clark inside out before scoring, a goal which brought back memories of Mario Lemieux.

With Crosby playing only 22 games in 2011–12 due to a concussion, Malkin developed a tight chemistry with winger James Neal, and Neal delivered career highs in both goals (40) and points (81) as both players fed off each other with consistency. Only in Pittsburgh would Malkin be a No. 2 center, and when Crosby left the lineup, Malkin routinely elevated his game. Through his first 20 seasons in the NHL, he averaged 1.08 points per game with Crosby in the lineup and 1.33 points per game without him, an increase in production of more than 23 percent.

Malkin returned to play in his hometown of Magnitogorsk during the NHL lockout of 2012–13, again joining Gonchar as well as several other NHL players. It was his first time back in the Metallurg sweater of the Kontinental Hockey League since he left the team six years earlier, and he led the team in assists under coach Paul Maurice.

By this point, Malkin was an established danger on the power play, and he trailed only Joe Thornton and Alexander Ovechkin in power-play points through his first six seasons in the league. His ability to score from areas outside the crease gave defenders more to think about, and when rotations took him to the point he used his passing ability to create opportunities, often creating and finishing chances with Crosby. The pair, dubbed "The Two-Headed Monster" by Penguins' fans, often played together early in their careers and had combined on 389 regular-season goals through 2025–26.

Malkin's power-play effectiveness helped him play a major role as the Penguins became the first team in the salary cap era to win consecutive Stanley Cups in 2016 and 2017, and for the second time in his three Cup runs with the team he led all playoff scorers with 28 points in 2017.

General manager Jim Rutherford, who had watched Malkin almost single-handedly destroy Rutherford's Carolina team in the 2009 playoffs, saw Malkin's excellence as an outgrowth of his internal drive. "Everybody knows what they see, what a great player he is, but what I learned was how competitive he was," Rutherford said. "Anytime there was a little competition in practice of any kind, his compete was so good. It wasn't like he just wanted to get through the drills and get practice over. He loved to compete, whether in a big moment in a game or smaller moments in practice. He competed as good as anybody in the game."

Midway through the 2016–17 season Malkin became an unexpected part of the NHL's celebration of its 100th year. The league asked 58 individuals representing more than 1,800 years of experience in the game to select the league's 100 greatest players. While some notable players had been left off, including three of the NHL's top 20 all-time scorers in former Penguin Mark Recchi (No. 12 at the time), Doug Gilmour and Dale Hawerchuk, most observers considered Malkin the most surprising omission.

Malkin at that point was one of only six players in NHL history to win the Stanley Cup, the Hart Trophy, the Ted Lindsay Award, the Conn Smythe Trophy and multiple scoring titles, joining Crosby, Mario Lemieux, Bobby Orr, Wayne Gretzky and Guy Lafleur—three of whom, like Malkin, had had their careers significantly impacted by injuries or illness. Malkin downplayed the snub, later telling the *Pittsburgh Post-Gazette*, "I don't think about that. I just want to win."

One person surprised by Malkin's omission was Kevin Allen, who covered the NHL for *USA Today* for 34 years, was inducted into the media wing of the Hockey Hall of Fame and became one of the few media members to be awarded the Lester Patrick Trophy for service to hockey in the United States. Allen was among those voting for the 100 greatest players.

"I was really stunned. In this era I covered, you're not going far down that list before you get to Malkin. I really just couldn't believe it," Allen said. "He clearly has been one of the most dominant performers in the league. I don't think there was any doubt he was in the top 100."

His omission underscored the simple fact Malkin likely would have received even wider recognition throughout his career had his playing circumstances differed. He had entered the league just one year behind Ovechkin, a countryman who was drafted ahead of him and also was destined for greatness, and Crosby, who slotted ahead of him as the Penguins' top center and became one of the greatest legends the game has known. The careers of Crosby and Ovechkin were closely intertwined initially in league marketing and then subsequently by media coverage through their many regular-season and playoff matchups as division rivals, and Malkin in some respects often played in their shadows—much the same way Ron Francis, a Hall of Fame No. 1 center, did while playing behind Lemieux in Pittsburgh.

"He's actually an underrated superstar," Allen said. "The year he won the scoring championship (2009), Ovechkin was right behind him and Sid was third: one, two, three. We were at a place where we had three 'best players' in the league. Malkin was that. He never really got the attention he probably should have gotten based on his ability. If he were alone and not with other superstars, people would have viewed him at the time as the best player in the league. He was capable of carrying a team on his back.

"To get three generational players over a two-year period and have them all ascend together made it difficult for Malkin to find his own spotlight. Sid and Ovie found their spotlights alone, and it seemed like Malkin always had to share his," Allen added, although he noted Malkin didn't seem comfortable with the language and wasn't a player out-of-town reporters were likely to find after games.

Added Gonchar, "I think media hasn't given him the attention he deserves. At the same time, he recognized the situation. You look at all the teams that were winning, they always had a No. 1 and a No. 2...who maybe is not getting as much attention. I give him credit, he recognized the situation." Kyle Dubas, hired as the Penguins' general manager in 2023, told the *Cam and Strick Podcast* in 2025 that Malkin was "probably the most underrated player maybe to ever play."

Unfortunately for Malkin, various injuries continued to take him out of the lineup in the middle of his career, as he missed 20 or more games in five of the 10 seasons that followed his second scoring title in 2012. These included a series of upper- and lower-body injuries but most significantly another surgical repair of the anterior cruciate ligament in his right knee in early June 2021 after taking a hit against Boston in mid-March. Malkin rehabilitated his knee for six weeks after the hit and returned to play in early May, but his sore knee kept him out of two playoff games as the Penguins were eliminated by the Islanders.

After his second surgery, it was more than seven months before Malkin played again, wearing a brace for the 2021–22 season and, not surprisingly, showing signs at 35 and after two surgeries on the same knee that his mobility was not the same. His longtime teammates Crosby and Kris Letang had also missed significant amounts of time with injuries or illness over their careers, but through the 2024–25 season neither of them had missed as many games as Malkin (272, or the equivalent of almost three and a half seasons).

The summer of 2022 proved another emotional time for Malkin, as his $9.5 million contract was expiring and his agents were negotiating with Penguins' general manager Ron Hextall for an extension. Unable to reach a deal the day before he was set to become an unrestricted free agent for the first time in his career, Malkin told the team he would explore his options in free agency the next day at noon. Just hours before that deadline, however, he signed a four-year contract with an annual salary cap hit of $6.1 million.

Between 2023 and 2025 Malkin was largely injury-free but averaged fewer than one point per game in consecutive seasons for the first time in his career, although it didn't help that the rebuilding Penguins lacked the forward depth to consistently provide him with linemates that could take full advantage of his skillset. But he had a special moment in October 2024, joining Mario Lemieux and Crosby to become one of 20 players in NHL history to score 500 goals with one team in a 6–5 overtime victory over Buffalo, with Crosby picking up the lone assist—as Malkin had done on Crosby's 500th goal in February 2022.

"This is a great story. I don't know how it works, but I'm only assist to him 500 and he's only assist to me. It's like crazy. We probably deserve to do it, share this night together," Malkin said after the game in which he also became just the second Russian player to score 500 NHL goals. "I play with Sid, same team, but I try to do my best. I push to him, he push to me. We try to help each other. We try to push everybody."

That set the stage for a 2025–26 season that was the last of his contract and seemed at times destined to be his last in the NHL—he would turn 40 just months after its conclusion. But Malkin opened training camp by saying he would like "a chance to play one more year here," then soared near the top of the scoring race in the early weeks of the season, a place few people expected to find him. He wound up among the league's top 25 scorers of all-time after recording his 1,400th point late that season, after which he got that "one more year" in an extension offered by Penguins' general manager Kyle Dubas.

"It's his ability to raise his game. I think he's one of the best to ever do it," Crosby said. "His ability just to find another level. I could give you a thousand examples, times when we've had injuries or in the playoffs, just times when you really need somebody to step up. He's a gamer and has come through time and time again."

In late 2025 Malkin told Research Ground (formerly RG.org), "I don't see myself in another jersey—not in Florida, not in Colorado, anywhere. I've played my whole life in Pittsburgh. I love the fans, I love the city. I want to finish here. But there are always details. And, of course, I want to fight for another Cup."

7
Jags

ALMOST 40 YEARS LATER, THE START OF THE 1990 NATIONAL Hockey League Entry Draft's first round remains a bit of a curiosity, an exercise in which short-term certainty outweighed the potential for future greatness by a large enough margin to make the Penguins the event's biggest winners—although they were not picking until fifth.

Long before the NHL's general managers assembled in Vancouver for the draft, Czechoslovakian winger Jaromír Jágr was considered by many of them the best player available. The others rated highly were very, very good prospects and turned out to be very good NHL players—Owen Nolan, Petr Nedvěd, Keith Primeau and Mike Ricci joined Jágr in the group of five players nearly all observers expected to fill the first five picks in some order.

"No question, he's the most talented kid in the draft," Winnipeg GM Mike Smith said of Jágr. Quebec GM Pierre Pagé, holding the No. 1 pick, said "Jágr's probably the best of all, talent-wise." Well-known Edmonton scout Barry Fraser agreed, as did Vancouver GM Brian Burke, who had the No. 2 pick and added Jágr "would have been the best player in last year's draft, too." Bobby Clarke, who was sitting on the No. 4 pick before he was fired as Philadelphia's GM two months before the draft, had also declared Jágr the most talented player up for grabs.

But Detroit GM Jimmy Devellano, who had the No. 3 pick, was blunt. "We'll go the more traditional route," he said. "I don't feel we can take a boy and teach him a new language and go through all the other adjustments that are required." Those "adjustments" included possibly waiting for a year or longer for Czechoslovakian hockey authorities to clear a path for Jágr to leave. He had one year to go on his contract with his Kladno team, although he had signed as a youth, leaving the contract on shaky legal ground; he hadn't yet graduated from high school; and he also lived in the shadow of potential military service.

Through a translator the day before the draft, however, Jágr told reporters he believed he would join the NHL in January 1991 after the conclusion of the World Junior Championships, and that his military service might be able to be postponed for another 10 years. He was the first non-defecting Czech prospect to attend the draft, and that fact, along with Czechoslovakia holding its first free elections in four decades just weeks earlier, signaled that many things in that country were changing. So, too, did the fact Czechs Dominik Hašek, Robert Reichel and Bobby Holík were just four months away from starting their NHL careers.

In his book, *Jágr: An Autobiography*, written in 1997 with Jan Šmíd, Jágr said he "was already thinking about how I would rather play in America than Canada and especially in either

Philadelphia or Pittsburgh." The idea of enduring an uncertain wait for the player most scouts were fawning over, however, was still a non-starter for the teams ahead of Pittsburgh. Thus the 1990 draft for the Penguins—who could have slipped to the sixth pick if they hadn't been kept from a playoff spot by Uwe Krupp's overtime goal on the last night of the 1989–90 season against Buffalo—thus became one of the most important events in their history.

Remembers Pierre McGuire, then a scout for the Penguins, "For Philly, Ricci was a lot like (Bobby) Clarke. Detroit wanted Primeau; they had (Petr) Klíma and didn't want any more Czechs. Nedvěd had played (junior) in Seattle, right down the road from Vancouver, and was already a legend. Quebec wanted Nolan, they thought they'd play with him and (Mats) Sundin and shred everybody with offense. So we got the best player for the next 25 years in the NHL."

Jágr had more points over the next 25 years than any other NHL player, and it wasn't even close. His NHL career, which included a three-year sabbatical to play in Russia in his late 30s, spanned 24 seasons by the time he left the league at the age of 45. Today, he's still the second-leading scorer of all-time, surpassed only by Wayne Gretzky, and through 2025–26 his five scoring titles had been surpassed only by Gretzky, Mario Lemieux, Gordie Howe and Connor McDavid. He won four consecutive Art Ross Trophies from 1998 to 2001, a streak surpassed only by Gretzky, and won two Stanley Cups—all of that hardware coming while wearing a Pittsburgh sweater.

"How the hell did he go fifth?" former teammate and Hall of Famer Paul Coffey still asks. How, indeed. Jágr was in the Pittsburgh opening night lineup less than four months after the draft, and 24 months after the draft, Jágr became the youngest player in NHL history to win two Stanley Cups.

"The NHL by nature is a conservative league," said longtime *USA Today* hockey writer Kevin Allen. "There was a lot of concern about how long it was going to take Jágr to get here. A lot of GMs around the league would be saying, 'OK, we're going to take the safe pick, the one we can more easily project, where we know what's going to happen with him.' Who was the team who was willing to take a chance on a guy who was incredibly skilled?

"That's who the Penguins were. They weren't looking at passports. They were looking at who is the most skilled guy: 'We know how we want to play.' It made perfect sense for the Penguins to take him. Nobody viewed the game offensively the way the Penguins did. They wanted the guy who could light it up. That was part of their identity."

The Penguins placed Jágr with a local Czech family to live, enrolled him in classes to complete his high school education and enrolled him in English classes. Quipped coach "Badger" Bob Johnson, "I hope they start with hockey terminology."

Jágr, of course, was not a finished product at 18. The 6-2, 210-pound left shot could play either wing, had an incredibly strong lower body that helped him protect pucks and an undisputable ability to win one-on-one encounters. He had led his Kladno team in scoring the previous season, but the Penguins believed his wrist shot needed improvement and Johnson asked assistant coach Rick Kehoe to work with Jágr on that.

"He didn't have to use it (in Czechoslovakia), so we started right from the basics like we would when you're a young kid learning to shoot," Kehoe remembers. "He picked it up pretty quick, his hockey IQ was pretty high. Maybe back home when he was playing he could beat guys one-on-one, but here in the NHL when you're 18 years old, it's a little different.

"He adapted to the league. It took him a little while, but he worked hard at it, and it wasn't like he just took a few shots after practice. He stayed out there. There were times Badger would yell at me, 'Get him off the ice. We have a game tonight.' His release...there's times when you have to release it quick, and over time he learned all that. Plus, he had some pretty good guys to watch."

Lemieux was at the head of that class, and it was obvious to everyone on the team that once Lemieux returned from his back surgery in January 1991, Jágr couldn't take his eyes off him.

"There was a guy that wanted to be better," Coffey remembered. "There was a guy that wanted to be like Mario Lemieux. He watched Mario like a hawk, watched him in practice, watched how he controlled the puck. And his work ethic was as good as anybody I've ever seen."

Another Hall of Famer on that team, center Bryan Trottier, had similar memories of Jágr, with whom he spent a lot of time that season as a linemate along with Troy Loney.

"He knew the game on the big ice surface, but he had to learn North American hockey and the NHL," said Trottier. "He wanted to learn the give-and-go, he wanted to learn soft picks, he wanted to learn everything there was about NHL hockey. He was a great, great student of the game.

"I had the English-to-Czech book and I bought him a Czech-to-English book. His first two words to me were 'Big Bryan,' which was hilarious because he was much taller than me. He still calls me that. The time he spent in the gym trying to get stronger with (conditioning coach) John Welday was time well spent. And he wanted to be like Mario. He told me, 'Mario Lemieux is the greatest player in the world. I want to be like him. I want to play like him.' And sure enough, he became the best in the league."

Jágr had watched Lemieux play at the 1985 World Championships in Prague on television and was immediately taken by him, and practicing and playing with him had a profound effect on his adjustment to the NHL. "You learn a lot of things," Jágr said. "For me, he was like a teacher in the school. You go to school, you have a great teacher, you can learn a lot of things. That's what he was for me."

Jágr had 27 goals as a rookie, a season in which he worried about his ice time and was dissatisfied with his production while trying to find his way in a new culture with ongoing language challenges and without a driver's license. The Penguins' director of amateur hockey, George Kirk, drove Jágr where he needed to go. (When Jágr finally did get his driver's license, speeding tickets ensued.) He seemed down in the dumps by late November.

"He was in the throes of homesickness," Penguins' GM Craig Patrick said. "Realistically, the reason he was in this depression was because he didn't have a grasp of the language. He really didn't know what we were saying to him."

The Penguins' trade for Czech center Jiří Hrdina from Calgary in December 1990 proved to be a turning point for Jágr's assimilation. Limited to one point in his last 14 games until Hrdina joined the lineup, Jágr had 17 points in his next 15 games, some of them playing on Hrdina's line.

"He needed someone to talk to, even if it was just about the weather. He's smiling now in the airports, he's laughing. He's part of the team," Johnson said, "and he's played a lot more relaxed. He's trying things on the ice he had only tried in practice."

He scored 32 goals in a sophomore season that was forever marked by his dramatic contributions to the Penguins' Stanley Cup drive of 1992. Jágr had gone from a promising rookie to a difference-maker in the span of two seasons, then became simply a dominant NHL player. Over the last nine seasons of his Pittsburgh career, he led the NHL in goals, assists and points and won more scoring titles than any player born outside North America had ever won. Along the way he continued to work, continued to push himself to the highest standards and continued to display a love for the game that never left him—he was still playing occasionally as a minority owner of Kladno, his former team in the Czech Extraliga, at the age of 53. The Hockey Hall of Fame's requirement for inductees to be retired for three years was the only thing keeping him from membership.

"He had a drive to be the best. He took a piece from everybody he watched, especially the elite players," said Jay Caufield, his Pittsburgh teammate. "Where you can get blown apart in the NHL is in one-on-one battles. If you're young, you're not winning many one-on-one battles against grown men that were...nastier then. To be able to handle that and hold on to the puck against the best in the world only gave him more confidence in every other area of the rink."

"Jags," as his teammates came to call him, pronouncing the "J" with a "Y" sound, did it in his own unique way. He wore his hair in a mullet, pouring out from the back of his helmet. He liked heavy metal music and soon attracted girls everywhere he went, becoming the NHL version of a rock star. And he wore his distinctive No. 68, a memorial to the Prague Spring movement of 1968 when Czechoslovakia's reforms under Alexander Dubček brought occupation by Soviet troops but didn't quell acts of defiance from Czechs.

Jágr's disdain for communism had begun early, as both his grandfathers had been jailed for staying out of their native country's Standard Farming Cooperative, and caused him to paste a picture of American president Ronald Reagan in his gradebook as a symbol of the freedom he hoped might be his someday in the United States. After that story broke in North America, Jágr spoke by phone with the former president in November 1992, just hours before scoring in a home win over St. Louis—as he had promised Reagan. "It was my best day," Jágr said.

While Jágr did sometimes play with Lemieux after his rookie season, he more frequently played on a different line to allow the Penguins to deploy their two biggest offensive threats at different times, and a lot of his best days came playing beside centerman Ron Francis. Francis, a Hall of Famer who still ranks second only to Gretzky in career assists, was a consummate pro who had the smarts to position himself in the best places all over the rink and the vision and skills to distribute pucks to the right teammates. They were a dynamic team and made the Penguins an absolute nightmare to defend.

Jágr's skating ability allowed him to attack defenders wide, and his size and reach, while allowing him to keep defenders from the puck, also meant he was almost impossible to win battles against along the boards or down low in his offensive zone. After his rookie season, his points-per-game numbers rose for five consecutive seasons, and while his production was certainly helped by being surrounded by elite players, he was simply going places no European-born player had gone.

So when Lemieux was limited to 22 games in 1993–94 by back pain, Jágr responded by finishing ninth in league scoring with 99 points. When Lemieux was forced to sit out the entire 1994–95 season to rest and rehabilitate his back, Jágr became the first European-trained player to win the NHL scoring title. "I never thought anything like that could happen to me," said Jágr, who did a lot of his damage at even strength. "If you want to win a scoring title, you have to be on a good team and have a lot of help from your teammates. I have all of that."

The time Jágr spent on conditioning and strength development also paid off for him, as he missed only seven games with injury in his first six NHL seasons. His longest absence came when he was suspended 10 games in his second season for bumping referee Ron Hoggarth, a ruling the Penguins vehemently protested as Jágr, Lemieux and teammate Kevin Stevens were all ejected from a January 1992 game in Washington—eliciting Lemieux's famous "garage league" quote about NHL justice.

The 1995–96 season turned out to be the only one in which both Jágr and Lemieux dressed for at least 65 games in Pittsburgh, and the results were somewhat predictable. That was the highest-scoring team in Penguins' history, averaging 4.41 goals per game, and Jágr set career highs for goals (62), points (149) and points-per-game (1.81). Lemieux had 69 goals and 161 points, and the Penguins came within one victory of reaching the Cup Final in a playoff defeat to Florida, an outcome largely shaped by the absence of Francis, who had a broken bone in his foot.

Francis and Lemieux played on a line with Jágr for much of the 1996–97 season, after which Lemieux retired. It was now Jágr's turn to be center stage, although it took him some time to adjust to new coach Kevin Constantine, who brought with him a defense-first approach that was novel to the Penguins.

"I do remember there was a battle of wills between Jágr and Constantine about the way our team played," said Rob Brown, who returned to Pittsburgh that season as a checking winger. "I remember the defensive structure, (Constantine) was down to the inch defensively. Like, 'You are standing here. If you're standing three inches over here, you're in the wrong spot.'

Jágr was more of a free wheeler, so there was a battle between Constantine's way of playing and the way Jágr and the team had played for a number of years. It was a constant battle that was...noticeable."

The new tactical approach produced the best defensive team in the Penguins' history, but it did not noticeably compromise Jágr's ability to create. He won the first of four consecutive scoring titles in 1997–98, the same season he helped the Czech Republic to Olympic gold. When Francis signed with Carolina as a free agent, Jágr was named Pittsburgh's captain in October 1998. It was an unusual role for him, as he spent most of his youth playing with and against older boys and even played under an assumed name as a 15-year-old during an international tournament in which he was too young to formally participate. Thus captaincy had been largely out of the question. Now, he was ready for it.

"I'm getting older," he said just before the start of 1998–99 season. "I still love to have fun; I don't want to change that. Now I realize where the fun has to end. I've found the edge between the fun and the work. I changed so much during the summer. I don't get mad at all. There's no reason to get mad."

Francis was replaced as Jágr's center by the indefatigable Martin Straka, a small Czech center with terrific speed and solid skills, a 1992 first-round pick of the Penguins who had been traded in 1995 but had returned to the team in 1997 just as Pittsburgh's lineup began to be dominated by European players and, specifically, players from the Czech Republic. By the 2000–01 season, the Penguins had Czech legend Ivan Hlinka as their coach—just the third European-born head coach in NHL history behind John Gottselig and Alpo Suhonen—and sometimes iced lineups in which 15 of their 18 skaters had been born in Europe, including 10 in the Czech Republic.

Together, good friends Jágr and Straka helped engineer the biggest upset in team history in the first round of the 1999 playoffs against New Jersey, the top seed in the Eastern Conference. The Penguins trailed the series, 3–2, when they came home to face elimination in Game 6 on May 2, a time when a bankruptcy court decision was hanging over the team, which many in Pittsburgh feared might be playing its final game in the city. Jágr had missed four consecutive games with a significant groin injury suffered in the series opener, but he was in the lineup for Game 6—an appearance driven not by Jágr's health but by the team's desperate circumstances, both in the series and long-term.

With the Penguins trailing, 2–1, late in the third period, Jágr jammed home a centering pass from German Titov with just 2:12 to play, forcing overtime. Straka, who had 11 points over the final six games of the series, then beat Devils' defenseman Scott Neidermayer at the blue line, skated to the bottom of the left circle and sent a perfect cross-ice pass to Jágr, who quickly sent the puck past goaltender Martin Brodeur from the bottom of the right circle for a 3–2 victory at 8:59 of overtime, capping his most significant performance in a Pittsburgh sweater.

"It might be the last game in Pittsburgh. That's why I wanted to play so bad," Jágr told reporters after the game, in which he played almost 30 minutes. He added two assists, and Straka had a goal and two assists, in a 4–2 Game 7 win in New Jersey two nights later to complete the upset.

Jágr established an NHL record early in the 1999–2000 season by having a hand in 15 consecutive goals scored by the Penguins (scoring seven himself), but playoff success remained elusive as the team went out in the second round for the second consecutive season. The promotion of Hlinka from associate coach on the staff with coach Herb Brooks in the 1999–2000 season to head coach of the now Czech-heavy Penguins in 2000–01 sometimes seemed to have a deleterious effect on Jágr, who didn't like Hlinka's left wing lock system and infamously refused to take the ice for a Penguins' power play in an early November 2000 game against Philadelphia.

He later chalked it up to frustration over his play, but Jágr, who could be moody, was just getting started on what for him was a tumultuous emotional season. In the midst of a four-game pointless streak in late November, he told the *Pittsburgh Post-Gazette*, "I feel like I'm dying alive...I just don't feel comfortable here right now. It's not the same for me right now." His cryptic remarks took on even more significance when the *Post-Gazette* reported two weeks later Jágr had twice asked Lemieux, now the team's owner and about to embark on a legendary comeback, to trade him. "I wasn't happy with the way I was playing, and I thought that maybe the change would help me," remembered Jágr, who was averaging better than a point per game but was 11 points off the lead in the NHL scoring race on Dec. 1—a race he would eventually win for the fifth time, helped by Lemieux's return.

Jágr had not only Lemieux back but a team that included Straka, who was putting up a career-high 95 points; fellow Czech Robert Lang, who was putting up career highs in goals and points; and the supremely talented Alexei Kovalev, who likewise was having the best offensive season of his career. But Jágr's demeanor never really improved that season, and there were reports poor-performing investments had hurt his personal finances. His mood certainly wasn't helped by Lemieux telling reporters during the team's second-round series against Buffalo that Jágr needed to play better, or by Jágr's failure to record a single point in a five-game loss to New Jersey in the third round.

By this point, the economics of Jágr's large contract also came into play, as he was owed more than $20 million over the final two seasons of his deal while the Penguins were faced in the summer of 2001 with a raft of talented players about to hit free agency, including Straka, Kovalev, Lang and defenseman Darius Kasparaitis, all of whom wound up signing new contracts, most after arbitration. But a trade, suggested again by Jágr to general manager Patrick just after the conclusion of the playoffs, had become inevitable. In early July, he was dealt to the Washington Capitals for young prospects Kris Beech, Michal Sivek and Ross Lupaschuk—none of whom had an impact in Pittsburgh—and future considerations reported to be almost $5 million in cash.

Jágr lasted only two and a half seasons in Washington before being traded to the New York Rangers, and he wound up playing for eight other teams after leaving Pittsburgh. He won the first of two World Championships with the Czech Republic in 2005, along with former Penguins' teammate Jiří Šlégr becoming the only Czechs at that point to join the International Ice Hockey Federation's Triple Gold Club. After leaving the NHL for Russia's KHL in 2008, Jágr returned to the NHL in 2011 with Philadelphia—21 years after the Flyers passed on him at the draft. Both he and the Penguins were interested in a reunion, but Ray Shero, Pittsburgh's general manager at the time, had only one conversation with Jágr.

"He was saying (to some) he'd play for the minimum," said Shero, who was offering more than the league minimum salary. "Certainly we would have had him back, but in dealing with (agent) Petr Svoboda, Petr was like the more money offered, the more a sign of respect. I was like, 'Well, this is the salary cap world. That's not exactly how this works anymore.' It was hard to follow the bouncing ball."

When Jágr's remarkable NHL career ended in January 2018 with Calgary, Pittsburgh media outlets and fans renewed talk of a jersey retirement for Jágr, who never seemed convinced it would go over well in his old town. Former teammate and later Penguins' radio and television color analyst Phil Bourque flew to the Czech Republic to make the case for Jágr to agree to the honor, and it finally happened in February 2024.

Sidney Crosby, Evgeni Malkin and the rest of the Penguins donned mullet wigs for the pre-game warmup against Los Angeles that night, and Jágr joined them on the ice as well. In the pre-game ceremony, Jágr told the sold out crowd at PPG Paints Arena that his Penguins' career was "probably the best years of my life. I'm proud and happy to say the Pittsburgh Penguins are my second home."

8

Flower

THE 2003 NHL ENTRY DRAFT IS CONSIDERED AMONG THE very best classes in league history, a deep draft that featured future Cup winners Patrice Bergeron, Ryan Getzlaf, Eric Staal, Corey Perry, Jeff Carter, Mike Richards, Nathan Horton, Dustin Brown, Corey Crawford and Brent Seabrook as well as stars Joe Pavelski, Shea Weber, Ryan Suter, Brent Burns, Dion Phaneuf and Zack Parise. None of them had more fun than the kid taken first overall that season by the Penguins, goaltender Marc-André Fleury.

Given his surname, the French Canadian known forever to his teammates as "Flower" would provide a lightning-quick glove save. And a chirp. A stretch-to-the-max toe save. And a smile. A surprising poke-check. And a laugh. It was a powerful combination of personality and skill applied daily in a league that for some can be primarily marked by expectation, tension and pressure.

"It was just his love for being in the game," remembers teammate Colby Armstrong. "How many times I heard him in guys' faces after a big glove save: 'Oh yeah, you like that?' He yells at guys on the ice. He has the most fun with it. He's not in the fire and competing with his eyebrows furrowed, he's got a smile on his face and he loves it. That kind of infectious energy helped our group."

Especially in practice.

"Flower is the absolute teammate, the guy that makes it fun to go the rink," said Max Talbot, who played with Fleury in the NHL and AHL. "He shows up to the rink every morning with a big smile. We'd do any type of drill, (Crosby) and him would go at it until Sid would score or Flower would freeze it. It would slow down the whole practice. But they were competing so hard, always having fun competing, and for us, it's the way you should play hockey. There's one puck on the ice and these guys are competing so hard. His energy was just so big."

When general manager Craig Patrick traded up from the No. 3 pick to get Florida's No. 1 choice in 2003 from Panthers' GM Rick Dudley, the only GM in NHL history to have three times traded away the No. 1 overall pick, it made perfect sense for the rebuilding Penguins. They had missed the playoffs in consecutive seasons for the first time in 15 years and Fleury was a quick, athletic goaltender with great lateral movement who had already backstopped Team Canada to the silver medal in the 2003 World Junior Championships, being named the tournament's best goaltender when it was over.

But the Penguins were getting more than a promising goaltender. They were drafting an extraordinary teammate, a highly competitive presence and the first piece of the puzzle that would take them back to the Stanley Cup. Three summers later, the Penguins' roster down the middle featured Fleury,

Crosby, Evgeni Malkin and Jordan Staal. Twenty-two years later, upon his retirement in 2025, Fleury ranked second all-time to Martin Brodeur in regular-season games played and wins and third all-time behind Brodeur and Patrick Roy in playoff games played and wins.

That didn't surprise Brodeur, who after facing Fleury for the first time in October 2003, said: "It's rare to see a young guy who's in control like he is. He's the future. He's real impressive."

Fleury, of course, had to work to find that control. As a younger goaltender, Fleury admitted he "was all over the place" before working with former NHL goaltender and goaltending coach Roland Melanson. "He helped me be better technically, more stable. I wasn't good technically...I was just diving around. He helped me to do that. He was very good with me, very patient. He said I have to be more patient, not to go down on the ice so much. It's very important to be in control mentally and physically."

Despite playing behind a poor defensive team as a rookie, Fleury had a spectacular start to his NHL career, stopping 46 shots, including a penalty shot, in his debut, a 3–0 home loss to the Kings. He went 3–2–2 in his first seven starts with a .942 save percentage and was named NHL Rookie of the Month for October. But he was loaned to Team Canada for the 2004 World Junior Championships and later returned to his junior team in Cape Breton after he had lost 12 of his last 13 NHL decisions.

The Penguins could certainly understand the microscope Fleury was under, having become just the third goaltender ever chosen with the first overall pick in the draft, following Michel Plasse in 1968 by Montreal and Rick DiPietro in 2000 by the New York Islanders. He had suffered a devastating end to the 2004 World Junior Championships when his late clearing attempt struck teammate Braydon Coburn and bounded into his own net for the goal that decided the gold medal for the rival United States. Pittsburgh had to consider the state of his confidence, because it wasn't easy for their young goaltender.

"It's tough every night you don't win, tough on the confidence, every guy gets mad, then it gets hard to get out of it," Fleury said during his early time with the Penguins. "Some nights when you have five or six goals against you in one night, you kind of think, 'Oh my.' The guy's coming down on you and you think, 'Is it going to go in again? Can I stop one tonight?' Some nights it kind of gets in your mind a little bit."

But there were also financial aspects to Fleury's return to junior hockey, as the financially struggling Penguins were facing millions in bonus payments written into Fleury's contract if he stayed in the NHL. Those bonuses were also a factor in Fleury spending time with Pittsburgh's AHL team in Wilkes-Barre/Scranton in early portions of Pittsburgh's poor 2005–06 season despite a terrific training camp and the fact he allowed three or fewer goals in each of his first nine starts. But Fleury was resigned to controlling what he could control. It was part of his very mature approach to the game.

"Obviously, we were all thrilled with his on-ice skills, but we also learned to become very pleased and impressed with his off-ice demeanor and how he handled things," Patrick said at the time. "There were a lot of distractions, not all of them positive. But he's a special, special person."

One part of Fleury's approach that endeared him to teammates and coaches was his sense of responsibility on the ice. He simply rejected any notion that facing too many shots or too many high-quality shots were excuses for him to allow goals.

"That's the type of goaltender he is—every goal is his fault," said Ed Olczyk, the Penguins' coach in Fleury's rookie season. "He's a battler, and he works extremely hard, and that is one of his greatest assets." Lorne Mulleken, Olczyk's assistant coach that season, was a minor-league goaltender in the late 1970s and into the 1980s, and he loved Fleury's mindset. "When the puck goes by him, he shoulders that responsibility," Molleken said. "He always says to me, 'My job is to stop the puck no matter what.' That's a great attitude. I've been in this coaching racket now for 18 or 19 years, and you hear that. But he's very sincere when he says that."

This kind of thinking from Fleury was an outgrowth of his competitive nature, commonly cited by teammates as an important driver of his NHL success.

"We couldn't get off the ice; coaches had to kick us off the ice," remembered Armstrong, "because every little thing we did was like a game. Flower would remember how many times you scored on him in practice individually, and it was a game to him individually with each guy. He's like, 'You're not getting five on me today.' He knew where you liked to shoot. You could ask Marc now, 'Pick a random teammate, where does he like to shoot?' He could tell you exactly where. I tested him a few years ago and he called it, years later. He was a student of the game and it ran through his compete level."

Crosby could see that, too, during his rookie season in 2005–06. "He doesn't quit," Crosby said. "That's one thing you can't teach with a goalie, to have that second effort. Sometimes it's frustrating the more you lose, and it definitely starts to get at you after a while. It's obvious he never likes to lose. That's the way you need to be. That's why he's so good. That's the way we all need to think. I think I'm not one who accepts losing, and you feel for him, especially a goalie who's got a little more pressure on his shoulders than anyone else."

Among the most tangible displays of Fleury's competitive streak were his performances in shootouts, introduced in the

2005–06 season. At the conclusion of his Pittsburgh career in 2016–17, among goaltenders with at least 50 shootouts played, Fleury led all goaltenders in shootout save percentage (.740) and was third in shootout wins (53) behind Henrik Lundqvist and Ryan Miller, who had played in more shootouts than Fleury. His quickness was an obvious factor, but so too was his penchant for poke-checking the puck off shooters' sticks at the last minute, not a widely used tactic among his peers. It demanded an accurate read and some courage.

From March 19, 2013, through February 7, 2014, Fleury stopped 17 consecutive shootout attempts, and he compiled streaks of 11, 14 and 16 earlier in his career. On the 42 occasions in his career when a shootout save would win the game for Pittsburgh, he stopped the shots 31 times. He was machine-like, and not surprisingly Pittsburgh won more shootouts (73) during Fleury's time there than any other team during a time when shootouts were much more common than today and therefore more important to a team's finish in the standings.

Fleury was also very durable, as he made 60 or more starts in seven of the eight full NHL seasons between 2006 and 2015, excluding the lockout-shortened 2012–13 season. His only injury of consequence in that span came in 2007–08 when he missed 35 games with a high ankle sprain, but he won nine of his first 10 starts upon returning and was the rock backstopping the young Penguins as they went from a first-round exit in 2007 to within two victories of the Cup.

During the Penguins' run to the Stanley Cup Finals in 2008 and 2009, he started every single playoff game, famously sealing the team's first Cup in 17 seasons with a last-second Game 7 save on Detroit defenseman Nicklas Lidström. From his phenomenal play in the 2003 World Junior Championships, his outstanding opening month in the NHL and winning the

Stanley Cup to his difficult loss in the 2004 World Junior Championships and his shuttling onto and off Pittsburgh's roster in his early NHL seasons, Fleury had already been through a lot at the age of 24.

While he was having the time of his life on the ice, Fleury's personality didn't change in the dressing room, where he was an avowed prankster and became an esteemed teammate everywhere he played through the way he interacted with those around him. Always happy, always laughing, always having a good time.

"The way he was, I don't know if I'd ever seen anything like that, where he was chatty and loose and hanging out with the boys...(goalies) were kind of separated on an island, and he was the one guy that wasn't," Armstrong said. "He was hanging out with us. Having a guy like that, a first overall pick, he was so athletic and then on top of it he's this personality...it was unique and cool and fun all at the same time."

Neither did it change when things didn't go as well as hoped on the ice. Fleury's performance in a 2012 first-round exit against Philadelphia was the worst of his playoff career to date and matched what was going on around him as Pittsburgh lost its composure and took enough penalties for the Flyers' power play to decide the outcome. But when Fleury lost two of his first four starts against the New York Islanders in the first round of the 2013 playoffs, he was replaced by Tomáš Vokoun and never made another start that spring, which saw the Penguins eliminate New York and Ottawa before being swept by the Bruins to end a season that had included a team-record 25-game stretch in which they won 22 times.

Fleury responded by starting all 18 of Pittsburgh's playoff games over the next two seasons, compiling save percentages of .915 and .927, respectively, and becoming the first goaltender in team history to record consecutive playoff shutouts when the Penguins beat the Rangers in Games 2 and 3 of the second round in 2014. The Penguins' all-time leader in regular-season and playoff shutouts, he also registered a shutout on the final night of the 2014–15 regular season at Buffalo to help push the Penguins' streak of qualifying for the playoffs to nine consecutive seasons.

The 2015–16 season brought Fleury both elation and frustration. He put together the best season of his career to date, matching his career-high save percentage (.921) and establishing his best goals-against average (2.29) as the Penguins' superb second half left them with the NHL's fourth-best record. But he suffered a concussion in late March, knocking him out of the lineup until the middle of the second round, by which time rookie Matt Murray, who had won each of his last seven regular-season decisions, had already started his playoff career with five straight wins. Fleury would get only one more playoff start and it was Murray who played a major factor in Pittsburgh's 2016 Stanley Cup victory, with Fleury "doing an awesome job of mentoring and helping him," remembered center Matt Cullen.

Fleury's final season with the Penguins in 2016–17 was a perfect summation of the attributes that led him to draw praise from all his teammates. Over the second half of the regular season, Murray got 29 starts for the Penguins and Fleury just 11, but when a groin injury sidelined Murray at the start of the playoffs, Fleury was brilliant against Columbus and Washington in the opening two rounds. He won seven of his first nine starts, allowing no more than two goals in six of those seven wins, and his eighth and ninth playoff victories were both shutouts before Murray stepped back into the lineup in the middle of the Eastern Conference Final against Ottawa. Murray recorded the final seven victories that brought the

Penguins back-to-back Stanley Cups, and when Fleury was handed his third Stanley Cup on the ice in Nashville, he made sure to hand it to Murray next.

But Fleury had done something else behind the scenes that season that had an immense effect on the team's playoff run and its future plans. With an expansion draft looming to stock the new Vegas Golden Knights team, all existing teams were required to make a goaltender available who was under contract for the following season or about to become a restricted free agent. Pittsburgh couldn't protect both Fleury and Murray, and Fleury's contract included a no-movement clause that prevented him from being exposed in the draft. Pittsburgh was intent on keeping Murray, who was 10 years younger and had already won the Stanley Cup as a rookie. "It was just making a hockey decision, not an emotional decision," remembered Bill Guerin, then Pittsburgh's assistant general manager.

So prior to the NHL trade deadline in March, GM Jim Rutherford approached Fleury about waiving his no-movement clause, and he agreed to do so. "I said to him, 'Where do you want to go?' He said, 'I'd like to go to Vegas,' so I made sure that that happened," said Rutherford, who sent the Golden Knights a second-round pick in exchange for Vegas' commitment to select Fleury. This kept the Penguins' goaltending duo intact for the playoffs—which, as it turned out, was absolutely critical to their successful title defense.

"I thought it was the right thing to help the team, to stay with the team and finish the season here and have a chance to play for the Cup again," Fleury told the *Pittsburgh Post-Gazette.* In his only interview with the Pittsburgh media, team owner Ron Burkle told the *Pittsburgh Post-Gazette* in 2017: "I wish we could have given the $15 million (Penguins' share of the expansion fee) back and kept him forever."

Fleury's status as the most celebrated teammate in Penguins' history had been well earned, from the day he first walked into the Pittsburgh dressing room until the day in June 2017 that he became a Golden Knight. He backstopped Vegas to within three victories of winning the Cup in its inaugural season, won the Vezina Trophy as the league's best goaltender with the Golden Knights in 2020–21 and then played for Chicago and Minnesota before retiring after the 2024–25 season, an intention he had signaled before the season. He concluded his career as the second-winningest goaltender in NHL history and is headed to the Hockey Hall of Fame.

In late March, less than two weeks before his final NHL start, Fleury left the bench after the Wild's home victory over Washington only to see his longtime rival, the Capitals' Alexander Ovechkin, hurrying down the locker room runway to bring back his teammates who had left the ice. Ovechkin then led them to center ice for a playoff-style handshake line with Fleury.

When Fleury and the Wild were eliminated from the playoffs after a first-round loss to Vegas, he was asked to join Team Canada for the 2025 World Championships in Scandinavia. This gave him an unexpected but welcome opportunity to not only represent his nation but share a dressing room with Crosby again. "This is kind of perfect," he told The Athletic after a practice session in Stockholm. "And you know what I miss the most about playing with Sid? Days like this, just staying on the rink for an hour after practice, just challenging each other. Days like this, I don't want to leave the rink."

The Penguins and their fans obviously wanted him to stay, too. In September 2025 the team signed him to a tryout contract so that he could play part of a preseason game against

Columbus as a final send-off. He didn't allow a goal while playing the final period with Crosby, Malkin and Letang all in the lineup with him, and nothing showed the fans' attachment to the popular goaltender more than this: the game was a sellout.

9

Tanger

For Kris Letang, there was a personal symmetry to the way the opportunity unfolded.

With the Penguins and Sharks tied, 1–1, in the second period of Game 6 of the 2016 Stanley Cup Final in San Jose, the puck came to the Penguins' 29-year-old defenseman just inside the left point. Using his offensive instincts, he faked a slap shot, drawing Joe Pavelski out of position, and using his skating ability he then spun 180 degrees to the left wing boards and, relying on his hands, stickhandled past Joe Thornton and put the puck on his backhand as he skated below the goal line.

With his head up, he could see teammates Patric Hörnqvist and Sidney Crosby in front of the San Jose goal, and before reaching the back of the net, he sent a backhand pass toward both of them that became entangled in a sea of skates before Crosby found it to the right of goaltender Martin Jones and carried it behind the net. Letang had continued his skating path past the net and was at the bottom of the right circle when he saw Crosby go behind the net with the puck, Jones now hugging his right post. Letang knew what was coming next. He stopped and prepared himself for the inevitable Crosby pass, and when it came he fired the puck past Jones for the goal that proved to be the Cup winner in a 3–1 victory that brought Pittsburgh its fourth championship and first in seven seasons.

Letang's game has always been based on his skating ability, puck skills and desire to create, and those attributes all contributed to that goal—through 2025 the last Cup Final goal Letang scored. He also scored the critical Game 3 overtime goal that began the Penguins' rally from a 2–0 series deficit in the second round of the 2009 playoffs against Washington, but he never scored a bigger goal than that one in San Jose, which squelched the momentum of the Sharks just 1:19 after they had tied the game.

It was also the denouement of arguably Letang's best season in the NHL. He scored 16 goals and 67 points during the regular season, both career highs at that point, and his 15 playoff points were the second-highest of his career. He finished fourth in voting for the Norris Trophy as the NHL's best defenseman that season, having finished third three years earlier.

Receiving attention in Norris balloting had already become the norm for Letang, who received Norris votes in nine of the 12 seasons between 2011 and 2022, eight times being voted among the top 10 defensemen in a league that was typically seeing approximately 300 defensemen play in any given season. Two seasons in that span in which he failed to receive votes, 2014 and 2017, were the result of injuries that limited him to playing just 37 and 41 games, respectively.

The Montreal native was a third-round draft pick of the Penguins in 2005 and almost immediately began demonstrating that teams had erred by passing on him. He played on Canada's 2006 World Junior Championship gold medal team in Vancouver, then briefly stayed with the Penguins out of training camp in 2006, playing seven games, before he was returned to junior. He then captained Canada's 2007 World Junior team to another gold in Sweden and made the tournament's all-star team before finishing his junior career at Val-d'Or in the Quebec Major Junior Hockey League.

Hall of Famer Paul Coffey remembered Letang standing out in one of his early NHL preseason games and pointed him out to former teammate Bob Errey. "I can remember sitting in the Igloo with Errey doing something between periods, and I said to Bob, pointing down, 'That guy's a player.' I could tell. He's tough, he can skate, he can shoot."

Letang lasted all of 10 games in the American Hockey League before joining the Penguins for good in mid-November 2007, finishing sixth in scoring among the league's rookie defensemen that season. As he became a full-time NHL defenseman, Letang was very conscious of his need to be reliable in the defensive zone and not just a young player who could put up points.

"The question about me last year (as a rookie) was about my defensive game, so it was very important for me to focus on that," he said in the fall of 2008. "The coach did a lot of drills with me to get better defensively. Now it's going to be to continue that and bring more. I'm going to concentrate on being a better player in my zone, but still I've got my offensive sense, and you can't say to an offensive guy to be only concentrating on defense. You can't say to Sidney Crosby, 'Don't play offense.' That's my strength, and I think I'm going to play to my strength."

But Letang never stopped thinking about how difficult he could make things for opponents in his own defensive zone.

"It's something I take pride in. I want to be hard to play against every single night," he said. "I always wanted to make sure the other teams and the other good forwards don't like to play against me."

Crosby chalked Letang's approach up to the timing of his arrival in the NHL. "As the game's evolved, I think there's been more emphasis on defensemen being more offensive, but that was something that was a little bit less negotiable when he was coming in," Crosby said, "especially as a smaller guy, and he would have been considered a smaller defenseman at the time. So the emphasis would have been on defending hard, being strong, being tough to play against. If you were going to be slotted in those first couple pairs, it wasn't like you can be offensive and your partner can be the defensive guy. If you're going to be in the top four, you've got to play both sides of the puck."

Letang nearly doubled his offensive production in his first full NHL season, 2008–09, taking twice as many shots and playing more to his instincts. It didn't hurt to have veteran offensive defenseman Sergei Gonchar to watch every night in his rookie season, as Gonchar was the team's No. 1 defenseman and was playing heavy minutes, something for which Letang would later become known. Letang got an early taste of that in 2008–09, his ice time increasing almost three minutes more per night as Gonchar missed the first four and a half months with a shoulder injury. "It was fun to pick his brain and watch him play," Letang said of Gonchar, although he said he also learned quite a bit from Brooks Orpik, Mark Eaton, Philippe Boucher and Alain Nasreddine.

After Gonchar signed with Ottawa in the summer of 2010, Letang took over as the Penguins' No. 1 defenseman. For the only time in his first 17 NHL seasons, he played every game for

Pittsburgh in 2010–11 and finished tied for seventh in scoring among NHL defensemen—despite the fact Crosby and Evgeni Malkin, the forwards with whom he made so many plays, both missed the second half of the season with injuries. Among the NHL's top 12 scoring defensemen from 2010–2022, he played the fewest games and yet had the fifth-highest point total, six times finishing among the NHL's top seven scoring defensemen.

During this 12-year period, which included the prime years of his career, Letang's production in many ways mirrored his health. He suffered two concussions in 2011–12 and missed 31 games, the first of those coming on Nov. 26 from a hit by Montreal's Max Pacioretty that also broke Letang's nose; Letang returned to the game, however, and scored the overtime winner. He missed only three games the following season and tied P.K. Subban for the NHL's scoring lead among defensemen, averaging over a point per game and becoming a Norris Trophy finalist.

Along the way his puck skills led him to become a regular choice in shootouts, and through 2025–26 he led all NHL defensemen in all-time shootout appearances, goals and game-deciding goals. Over a one-month period in his rookie season, Letang converted the first four shootout attempts of his career, all on the road and the first two winning games for the Penguins.

His superb skating was always a critical part of Letang's success, and his longtime defense partner Brooks Orpik pointed to Letang's ability to skate away from opponents in the corner or behind the net in his defensive zone as being an important asset.

"You could see early on he was super gifted," said Orpik, who started nearly 200 regular-season games beside Letang.

"Skating ability is one thing that jumps out, and then his dedication off the ice, he's always been very gifted and kind of a freak off the ice. But he works at it off the ice, takes really good care of himself. That and his skating ability. You could see all the ability early on. It was just a matter of time for him."

Letang's intensive off-season strength training, in which he had been engaging since he was 14 years old, also helped him shoulder the big minutes coaches asked him to play and respond to the physical demands of competing against often bigger forwards in his own zone. "I just think it was an advantage I could work on, and I was willing to do it," Letang said. "Growing up, I was never the most skilled player or best player on my team, and I had to gain some sort of advantage, and I thought conditioning and strength was one way."

When Brian Dumoulin reached the NHL in 2013 with the Penguins, he noticed what a difference Letang's approach made for him. Dumoulin wound up starting more than 300 regular-season games beside Letang, more than any other player, and believes that time was important in his own development.

"When I saw how hard he worked, I understood how he could play like that. He didn't cheat the game," Dumoulin said. "He was playing hard offensively and hard defensively. I've seen other people try to play those minutes and they have to sacrifice somewhere; they might not be finishing checks in the defensive zone. But he was so physical and so strong and so in shape and kept it up throughout the season. He was so demanding of himself, and he wanted those minutes and he could carry those minutes.

"I was very fortunate to have seen him when I was at a young age, see why he's so good. He's closing in on 40 years old and still playing 22 minutes a night and still an awesome player.

It was so good for me to be able to see: 'OK, I get now why, I see his work ethic and how he carries himself.'"

Letang played an average of 24 minutes or more in 14 consecutive seasons from 2010–2024, and through 2025 only the Los Angeles Kings' Drew Doughty had averaged 24 minutes or more in more seasons during that timeframe. Months from his 39th birthday in late 2025, Letang was still playing more than 21 minutes a night.

"It doesn't surprise me one bit," said former NHL defenseman Todd Reirden, who was an assistant coach working with the Penguins' defense for eight seasons. "He's just such a special person on and off the ice, and the way he's dedicated to his craft and to being a hockey player is like few I've seen in my 30 years of being involved in the NHL. It's not surprising when you couple that with the drive and competitiveness of a player who had to beat the odds even to get to the NHL.

"He's always wanted to be cutting edge on his training. When we first met one another he was the fifth defenseman on the team…then to move forward from there, we had to try to get his minutes up and he conditioned himself to be able to play upwards of 23, 25 minutes and then we had to get him to maximize the 23 minutes. He changed his training completely, and he went and trained one summer with MMA, and that was based on 45-second shifts and maximizing every time he was on the ice. I've done this with other players in the league, but none have figured it out as well as he has."

Through all those minutes and all those years, Letang always emphasized trying to feed the Penguins' creative forces up front. That meant he sometimes hung onto the puck a few seconds longer than normal, looking for openings and inviting hits, a habit coach Mike Sullivan tried to convince him to eliminate in the name of playing a simpler game. That also meant Letang would take gambles, either with pinches from the point or passes through the middle of the ice, that other defensemen would avoid.

"He has one turnover, it doesn't affect him. That's the best part about him," said Dumoulin. "You've got to give him that leash because the majority of the time he's going to make that play. And you need to make that play in order for us to create a chance, because Sid only needs one chance, (Malkin) only needs one chance and it's a goal. And now it's a 2–0 lead instead of a 1–0 lead, and that's such a big difference when you can give those guys just one opportunity.

"We were willing to take that chance, because the majority of the time he would hit Sid up the middle or create a three-on-two and we'd score on it. That was something I was comfortable with. A guy like Tanger will roam a little bit and make reads, so you have to be comfortable reading off him. I was able to do that and was fine doing that. I knew he could make the plays. I knew when he was going to jump down and pinch and I'd come over and support because I knew if I could be on top of that guy, that potential two-on-one—if (Letang) did get beat—was gone."

Orpik called Letang "a bit of a rover...a little bit of a wild card. That was one of the great things about him, he had the ability to jump up in the play and even if he made a mistake, his legs could get him out of trouble and get him back in position to cover up." Added general manager Jim Rutherford, "He's a game-changer...you see him play sometimes, you know, he can play a little bit casual at times because he's so talented, but nobody wants to win more than him."

Letang was for years the only defenseman on the point of the Pittsburgh power play, using his skating ability to get from one side of the ice to the other quickly and relying also on the chemistry he had developed with Crosby in particular. In October 2018, he passed Coffey to become the Penguins' highest-scoring defenseman, and early in the 2025–26 season he became just the 20th defenseman in league history to record 600 assists.

"He's played some major minutes over his career, had an important role on both sides of the puck that whole time, so to see that number and know how much he takes the defensive side serious, it's not always easy. That's a hard game to play," Crosby said when Letang hit that milestone. "He's created a lot of offense, and we've been on the receiving end of those passes and those plays. It's a great number and something that speaks to how hard he works and what he puts into the game."

Letang played in six NHL All-Star Games through 2025, reaching the 2012 game in Ottawa despite having missed 21 games early that season with his first concussion. He was named an injury replacement for Winnipeg's Dustin Byfuglien, in large part, because he had been on pace to record the highest point total of his career when he was hurt.

But Letang's health had a way of deserting him just as he was having his best moments, and that was certainly true in 2013–14, the season after he was a Norris Trophy finalist. Knee and elbow injuries knocked him out of the lineup first, and then he faced a scary and completely unexpected development.

On the morning of Jan. 29, 2014, Letang's wife found him on the floor of their home, conscious but "not able to function," he said. Days later, doctors told him he had suffered a stroke, and subsequent testing revealed he had a hole in his heart wall that was likely congenital. He was relieved to be told by doctors that he would be able to resume playing at some point, and he started practicing with the team six weeks later and returned to the lineup in early April.

His teammates had been shocked to learn that a 26-year-old known for his intense off-season strength conditioning and with the stamina to play 25 minutes a night for several seasons had been felled by a stroke. He suffered another stroke almost nine years later, in late November 2022, diagnosed at a local hospital after reporting a migraine. The day Letang's second stroke was announced, coach Mike Sullivan told reporters, "The biggest challenge for me today was to try to find a way to keep him off the ice. He wanted to skate today. That's just an indication of Tanger's passion to play and wanting to get back with his teammates."

Twelve days after he was diagnosed, Letang was back in the lineup. He had surgery to repair the hole in his heart wall in April 2025.

After his stellar 2015–16 season culminated in his Cup-winning goal, Letang's 2016–17 season was particularly difficult physically. In the first half of the season he missed one month with injuries, and upon recovering, he played five games and was sidelined for 10 days with a knee injury, then played three weeks before his season was ended by a herniated disc in his neck. He had put up 34 points in 41 games despite the injuries, but now he would be forced to watch the Penguins defend their Stanley Cup title. "That was tough. I knew we had a good team and could do great things," he said.

In 2023, Letang won the Masterton Trophy, awarded annually through a vote by the Professional Hockey Writers' Association, to the player "who best exemplifies the qualities of perseverance, sportsmanship and dedication to hockey." It was his second time as a finalist for the trophy, as he was also nominated in 2015, and that was hardly surprising to the Penguins. They had also seen Letang devastated by the death of his father in 2023 and, previously, the death of his Val-d'Or and Team Canada teammate and close friend Luc Bourdon in 2008. "He's definitely had a lot of obstacles and things away from hockey to deal with," Orpik said.

When he was presented the Masterton Trophy at the NHL Awards Ceremony, Letang said, "I'm the most proud because today I am a father, and my kids will see this in the house and they're going to know that their father never gave up in anything."

They may also get to see him in a Hall of Fame jacket. In addition to his Masterton Trophy, three Stanley Cups and two World Junior Championships gold medals, Letang had a real opportunity to finish his career among the top 15 defensemen all-time in assists and points. Paul Pidutti, who has contributed to TSN, The Athletic and Daily Faceoff, developed a system of measuring Hockey Hall of Fame worthiness and believes Letang's accomplishments merit his induction.

"I think because of all those partial seasons and missed time, it masks his true brilliance," Pidutti said. "I think he was playing in the Norris conversation levels for 10 or 12 years, and when you miss a quarter of a season or 10 games, your points totals, your Norris votes, they don't get there. Had he missed full seasons instead, and had gotten to play in a few 80-gamers at his peak, he would have been a Norris finalist a handful of times at minimum. He played at a really high level for 12 years."

The Pidutti Point Share System scores players on six factors: production, efficiency, seven best seasons, playoffs, international competitions and award shares. It doesn't try to measure character or intangibles, but Pidutti said Letang's Masterton Trophy was "a real sign of respect. A lot of times it's related to one season where somebody came back (from injury), but I think in his case it was a career achievement award, like we just can't keep this guy off the ice. His story is great, it's inspiring. He's a warrior."

Letang's current contract carries him through the 2027–28 season, and Reirden in 2025 said Letang had changed through the years to make that longevity possible. "He can skate forever. But now you'll see," Reirden said, "he's more under control than ever right now. It's because of the desire to continue to have his career go on. When you play that hard every shift, to be able to have 20-plus seasons is a very difficult thing.

"Early on, he was a high-risk player...now it's supporting the rush and seeing things that originally he didn't see, and we watched tons of video together to help build that skill. For him now it's really understanding what he's seeing on the ice, and he knows he doesn't have to just rely on raw skill. The thing about him is the adversity he's gone through really tells the tale, really makes it a special situation."

PART 3

HALL CALLS

10
Stars, Inc.

By the end of the 1983–84 season, the Penguins had come by their status as the worst-performing surviving member of the NHL's 1967 expansion class honestly. They had won one seven-game playoff series. They often failed to use the NHL draft as a building block but instead as a source of assets to be used in pursuing a quicker path to success, a strategy that failed them. Their lack of ownership stability and financial strength for their first 12 seasons undermined their broader efforts to attract free agents, find any meaningful playoff success and build a larger and more dependable fan base—which forced them in some ways to start all over again in the 1980s.

They had their moments and some stars over that era that brought the team recognition, including the brief stardom of Michel Brière; Greg Polis (1973) and Syl Apps (1975) winning NHL All-Star Game MVP honors; the high-scoring 1974–75 team opening the playoffs with five straight wins and featuring talented rookie Pierre Larouche; the consistent excellence of

Jean Pronovost and Rick Kehoe; Lowell MacDonald winning the Masterton Trophy in 1973 and Kehoe (Lady Byng) and Randy Carlyle (Norris) both winning trophies in 1981.

But by the start of summer in 1984, the Penguins were largely a non-descript franchise. They finally had some financial stability under owner Edward DeBartolo Jr. but still no guarantees about a long-term future in Pittsburgh, given his season ticket demands of the team in the mid-1980s, when the team admitted it was in "a crisis situation." The team remained something of a niche interest among most of the city's sports fans, second-page news behind the Steelers, Pirates and often the University of Pittsburgh's teams. They had missed the playoffs in eight of their 17 seasons, had averaged fewer than 10,000 fans per home game in seven of them, and they had just become the third team in 20 years to finish last overall in consecutive seasons. One of the other two, the Colorado Rockies, had already moved.

But the Penguins' nadir as a franchise came at precisely the right moment in NHL history, and with some roster management made it possible to draft Mario Lemieux, who more than four decades later is still considered by many the most talented player the game has ever seen. But the mid-1980s optimist who believed it was not necessarily a crazy leap of faith to envision the Penguins eventually building a winner around Lemieux could not have dreamed what an incredible contrast the next 40 seasons would be.

Since Lemieux's blades first hit the NHL ice in Boston in October 1984 through the conclusion of the 2024–25 season 40 seasons later, the Penguins won five Stanley Cups, more than any other franchise, and had one or more future Hall of Famers on their roster in every one of those years. They won the most playoff games (193) and the most playoff series (37, tied with

Detroit), scored the most goals and also won more regular-season games than all but Boston, Washington and Detroit.

After GM Eddie Johnston drafted Lemieux, Penguins' general managers in the 36 years between 1987 and 2023 brought to Pittsburgh 18 more players who have either joined Lemieux in the Hockey Hall of Fame or have a chance to do so in the future. Johnston also traded for Paul Coffey, and GM Tony Esposito drafted Mark Recchi and traded for Tom Barrasso. GM Craig Patrick, who acquired the majority of these Hall of Famers during his long tenure in the job, acquired Bryan Trottier and Sergei Gonchar as free agents; traded for Joe Mullen, Larry Murphy, Ron Francis, Luc Robitaille and Sergei Zubov; and drafted Jaromír Jágr, Marc-André Fleury, Evgeni Malkin, Sidney Crosby and Kris Letang. GM Ray Shero traded for Marián Hossa and Jarome Iginla; GM Kyle Dubas traded for Erik Karlsson.

Outside of the goaltenders, both of whom won multiple Cups in Pittsburgh and are among the top 25 all-time in wins, these Penguins' general managers were not acquiring players known for their physical play or primarily as defensive stalwarts. This group includes some of the most gifted scorers in the history of the game. The six defensemen were all among the top 26 scoring backliners in NHL history in 2026, and seven of the 10 forwards were among the top 25 scoring forwards of all-time.

The arrival of Lemieux kicked off an era in which the Penguins were known not only for their championship success but for building teams heavy with stars and based primarily on their creative scoring skills. The Penguins and goals went hand-in-hand. They would often allow four or five goals in a game and simply outscore opponents on the way to victory. From Lemieux's arrival through the 2025–26 season, Pittsburgh ranked No. 1 in the NHL in goals scored, power-play goals scored, playoff goals scored and, excluding recent expansion teams, power-play efficiency. The Penguins in this period 21 times were among the league's top-five scoring teams and 16 times boasted a top-five power-play unit—both numbers unsurpassed by any other team.

Matt Cullen's long NHL career saw him play his first 19 seasons against the Penguins before joining them to win two Stanley Cups, and he always looked forward to seeing them come up on his team's schedule.

"They were such a high-powered offensive team, I loved playing Pittsburgh because I loved that style of hockey," he said. "It was puck possession hockey, and at that time it wasn't the case throughout the league. It was heavy, it was slower, the old-school hooking and holding, and they were a unique team in that they played with a lot of skill, kept the puck, tried to make plays. The style was puck possession hockey, up-tempo, a lot of offense. I always felt it was one of those teams that played hockey the right way. It was a transition period from the old-school game to the newer game, and I always appreciated that."

Fifteen times a Pittsburgh player has won the Art Ross Trophy as the NHL's leading scorer, most by any team since the trophy was first presented in 1948. Lemieux won six of those, Jágr five, Crosby two and Malkin two. In the 14 seasons from 1988 to 2001, Lemieux and Jágr won the trophy 11 times between them.

"One of the traditions we have in sports is teams kind of known for defensive excellence, and it's almost tribal, handed down through the years. The Bruins are a pretty good example of that. They played good defense and they're hard hitting," said longtime hockey writer and Hockey Hall of Fame media member Kevin Allen. "It's much harder to carry on a tradition of having offense. When I think of the Penguins, I do think of superstars, getting the best players, not only getting the players they have in the draft, but also bringing in guys."

Not surprisingly, this approach worked at the box office. Beginning with Lemieux's second season, the Penguins set team records for average attendance in each of the next five seasons despite only one playoff appearance. Pittsburgh sold out the vast majority of its games for seven straight seasons beginning in 1986–87, and attendance went to yet another level after the drafting of Crosby in 2005. From February 2007 through October 2021—a span of 14 full seasons and parts of 16 seasons—the Penguins sold out 633 consecutive regular-season and playoff games.

While Pittsburgh fans had regular exposure to future Hall of Famers, the Penguins' pursuit of skilled players hardly stopped there. Patrick acquired Rick Tocchet (a career-high 48 goals and 109 points in 1992–93), Petr Nedvěd (a career-high 45 goals and 99 points in 1995–96), Alexei Kovalev (a career-high 44 goals and 95 points in 2000–01) and Ziggy Pálffy. Shero traded for Bill Guerin and James Neal (a career-high 40 goals in 2011–12). GM Jim Rutherford traded for Phil Kessel (a career-high 92 points in 2017–18).

"They're always thinking about big-time players, guys who play at a high level, an elite level: 'If they get four goals, we want to get five.' That's been their identity, having star power and being able to outscore the opposition," Allen said. "They've been important to the league because of that identity as well. People want to see them play because of the way they do play. They've always been able to light it up; they've had top players and they can put the puck in the net."

Kovalev, for example, never won a Cup or a scoring title with Pittsburgh, but was a supremely gifted player with the puck. Rob Brown, who scored a career-high 49 goals and 115 points with the Penguins in 1988–89, remembered Kovalev not only for his notable game contributions but what he could do in practice when they were teammates with the Penguins from 1997 to 2000.

"The best was after practice, we'd have these games three-on-three or four-on-four, the Russians had a team, the Czechs, the Swedes, the Canadians," he told the *Spittin' Chiclets* podcast in 2024. "Kovalev would come down, he would beat all four of us and go in on a breakaway, and instead of (taking a shot) he would go behind the net, come out to center again just so he could go through us all again. It was embarrassing."

While the Penguins made plenty of trades to acquire skill, their ascendency to becoming an elite NHL franchise was, ironically, based on the draft. Their roster management in 1983–84 speaks for itself, and of course they benefited from hockey serendipity; their two plunges to last-place overall finishes in 1983 and 1984 and then again in 2004 placed them squarely in position to draft Lemieux and Crosby, players that make everyone's short list of the league's greatest players.

"You're down at the bottom of the heap and you get those players, it shows how fortunate the Penguins have been through the history of the team," said the legendary Scotty Bowman, who won nine Stanley Cups as a coach, including in 1992 with Pittsburgh. "That's not a formula I think we're going to see too often in the NHL, that teams would get more than generation-type players, not back-to-back, but pretty close."

Pittsburgh twice enjoyed a run of high draft positions that saw them get top-five picks in five consecutive drafts. The Penguins selected Lemieux, Craig Simpson, Zarley Zalapski, Chris Joseph and Darrin Shannon from 1984–88, then selected Ryan Whitney, Fleury, Malkin, Crosby and Jordan Staal from

2002–06. Five of those 10 players went on to win the Stanley Cup in Pittsburgh, while the other five were all traded in deals that brought Coffey, Francis, Barrasso, Chris Kunitz and Brian Dumoulin to the Penguins, where those players won a combined 10 Cups.

Yet the Penguins' success story is more than simply the outgrowth of being terrible at precisely the right time in NHL history. Drafting those five Cup winners was one thing; ensuring the right return for the five high draft choices who were traded was another. Drafting, signing or acquiring players who had lower initial visibility in the hockey world but who wound up playing major roles in Pittsburgh was also critical, including the drafting of Mark Recchi in the fourth round after he'd been passed over twice; the trade for Kevin Stevens just months after he was drafted in the sixth round by the Kings; and the drafting of Letang, Matt Murray and Jake Guentzel in the third round, just to name a few.

Pittsburgh was not the only team to experience this kind of opportunity since the start of the modern draft. Washington, Quebec/Colorado and Ottawa join the Penguins as teams to have top-five picks in five or more consecutive drafts in the modern era, and the Edmonton Oilers had a top-seven pick in six consecutive drafts from 2010–15, only once picking lower than third and four times selecting first overall. Only the Penguins and Avalanche turned those windows into Stanley Cups.

The Capitals had top-five picks in seven consecutive drafts from 1976–1982, taking Rick Green, Robert Picard, Ryan Walter, Mike Gartner, Darren Veitch, Bobby Carpenter and Scott Stevens. Quebec/Colorado had top-five picks in five consecutive drafts from 1988 to 1992, including two such picks in 1988, selecting Curtis Leschyshyn, Daniel Dore,

Mats Sundin, Owen Nolan, Eric Lindros and Todd Warriner. Ottawa had top-five picks from 1992–96, taking Alexei Yashin, Alexandre Daigle, Radek Bonk, Bryan Berard and Chris Phillips. Edmonton's top-five picks brought them Taylor Hall, Ryan Nugent-Hopkins, Nail Yakupov, Darnell Nurse, Leon Draisaitl and Connor McDavid.

Of all these players, only Leschyshyn won the Cup playing for the franchise by whom he was drafted. None of the Ottawa draftees won the Cup, and among the Oilers' picks only Hall (with Carolina in 2026) did so. While it's true there are Hall of Fame players among these lists for the Capitals, Nordiques/Avalanche, Senators and Oilers that don't quite reach the levels of Lemieux and Crosby, it's also true Pittsburgh made solid picks through these years to get players that either won the Cup with them or were good enough to bring back players in trades that would become key Cup contributors for the Penguins—something only the Nordiques did in the trading of Nolan, Sundin and Lindros.

Longtime hockey writer Ken Campbell, for *The Hockey News* in 2024, ranked all 32 NHL franchises' Mt. Rushmore of best players as he saw them and placed the Penguins' group of Lemieux, Jágr, Crosby and Malkin second only to Edmonton's Wayne Gretzky, Mark Messier, Jarri Kurri and McDavid. "I really, really struggled with who I should put No. 1," he said. Gretzky, Messier and Kurri were all gone from Edmonton by the summer of 1991, and McDavid did not play his first game for the team until 24 years later. The Penguins, however, had one of those four players on their roster for 41 consecutive years and counting when the 2025–26 NHL season began.

While the Oilers, Red Wings, Lightning, Devils, Avalanche and Blackhawks all won three or more Cups with Hall of Fame players in the four decades following Lemieux's arrival in

Pittsburgh, the Penguins came to represent stardom for longer than any other franchise in this time period, giving Pittsburgh hockey fans an incredible gift for more than four decades.

In 2025–26 the Penguins were also celebrating a milestone of that legacy stardom as they marked the 20th consecutive season Crosby, Malkin and Letang had all played together—the longest such run for three teammates in any North American professional sports league, having passed the Yankees' trio of Jorge Posada, Derek Jeter and Mariano Rivera two years earlier.

"It means a lot. It's so rare," Crosby said. "The fact we came in at such a young age and grew up in the league together, experienced so many things, good and bad, a lot of ups and downs, but sticking together through all that and achieving the memories we have and growing up through it, is pretty special. It's one thing to be able to play in the league this long, that's not common, and to be able to share it with that group, that's really unique and something I'll always be grateful for."

Those three came by their longevity the hard way, each of them having persevered through difficult injuries or physical conditions—Crosby a scary concussion, Malkin two major surgeries on the same knee and Letang two strokes. Each of them had been prevented from playing an entire post-season due to injury, Crosby and Malkin in 2011 and Letang in both 2015 and 2017. Together, and with Fleury before he departed the team, those three created an environment for success.

"It's the culture that they set, the expectation they have for each other, how hard they push each other every year," said Brian Dumoulin, who played with them for 10 seasons. "Those three, they're almost like brothers, but it's not like it's always good times, they're the best of friends and there's never any hardship. They are so hard on each other, they demand so much from each other every game. They demand perfection every game. It's that demand...I couldn't imagine having that pressure and that demand on each other for 20 years each and every game. It's created like a brotherhood almost, they love each other, they hate each other, they get over it, like an old married couple a little bit. It's great to see. I get why they played so long together."

Their run together was nearly cut short in the summer of 2022 by management. Rutherford's shocking resignation the year before set the stage for the hiring of Ron Hextall as GM and Brian Burke as president of hockey operations, and The Athletic later reported both had been hired at least in part because they were willing to move on from Malkin or Letang or both—a condition The Athletic said had been set by team president David Morehouse. But Fenway Sports Group, which had purchased the team in late 2021, did not share that vision; Letang signed a six-year extension that summer and Malkin a four-year extension, although he came within hours of reaching free agency before that deal was done.

Like Crosby, both Malkin and Letang signed contracts for less than their market value. Burke told Jeff Marek on *The Sheet* podcast in 2025 that Pittsburgh had been told by one NHL general manager he was prepared to sign Letang for five years at a $9 million cap hit; Letang signed with the Penguins for six years at $6.1 million. "So (Letang) came in at the low end of the expectations of what we were told teams were going to pay for him," Burke said.

Staying together was important to them. "I always say, it's a dream to play with same guys together, forever, you know?" Malkin told *Pittsburghpenguins.com*, and he signed a one-year contract extension in May 2026.

Injuries to all three meant that by the late portions of the 2025–26 season, they had actually dressed together for just over 60 percent of the games for which they were all on the Penguins' roster together. But they were a force when healthy, not only winning three Stanley Cups but combining for more than 1,000 goals, surpassing 1,000 games played and approaching 3,000 points when dressed together in the regular season and playoffs. It was an amazing run by three of the biggest stars ever to play for a team that began its existence as nothing special and became, as Allen put it, "the Showtime of the NHL."

11
Beantown Connections

THE PENGUINS HAVE STRONG HISTORIC TIES TO THE STATE of Massachusetts and the city of Boston. More than 20 percent of all American-born players to skate for the team were born in Massachusetts, and all but three of those were born within 30 miles of Boston. Nearly one of every four former college hockey players to skate for the Penguins played somewhere in Massachusetts, two-thirds of those at either Boston College or Boston University. Pittsburgh's longest-tenured coach, Mike Sullivan, was born 35 minutes southeast of Boston in Marshfield, Mass., and played at Boston University.

Thus it is no surprise that three of the biggest stars in Penguins' history have direct ties to Boston: Joe Mullen, Tom Barrasso and Kevin Stevens.

Mullen was born in Hell's Kitchen, New York, and first learned the game on roller skates, but it was at Boston College from 1975–79 that he put himself of the radar of NHL teams. A phenomenal offensive force, Mullen remains arguably the greatest goal-scorer in Boston College's modern history with 110 goals in 111 games. One of the few Boston College players to have his jersey retired, Mullen was undrafted but earned a contract from the St. Louis Blues, and by his second and third full NHL seasons, the right winger was a 40-goal scorer.

Mullen was traded in 1986 to Calgary, where he scored a career-high 51 goals to help the Flames to the 1989 Stanley Cup, a season which saw him score 16 goals in 21 playoff games and win his second Lady Byng Trophy for the combination of gentlemanly play and a high standard of playing ability. But in the summer of 1990 he was traded to the Penguins for a second-round draft choice.

"I wasn't looking to go. It was kind of a surprise to me," Mullen said, "but I was pretty happy, because I was moving to a good team, a team that had a shot at it."

Mullen three times scored 30 or more goals in Pittsburgh, and remarkably did so at the ages of 35, 36 and 37, including memorable back-to-back four-goal games in December 1991. At just 5-10 and without great skating speed even in his younger days, Mullen simply had a feel for the game, an uncanny knack of finding open space on the ice and a finishing ability that ranks among the best in league history. Among 500-goal scorers, only Mike Bossy, Jari Kurri, Mario Lemieux and Bryan Trottier have better career shooting percentages than Mullen's 18.0.

"He was the ultimate anticipation player. He knew where things were going before they happened, and he had to be that way. We had races from one end to other, he'd be last or second-to-last most of the time, looked like he still had the roller skates on," remembered teammate Bob Errey with a chuckle. "But he did everything right. If you want an example of a guy who got the most out of his skills, there's a great example. He never took a shift off. Just had a hockey mind."

Mullen had multiple goals in each of the last three rounds of the 1991 playoffs as the Penguins claimed their first Cup, and he scored three goals to help the Penguins rally past Washington in the first round of the 1992 playoffs before an injury—the second major injury of his career to his left knee—in the second round against the New York Rangers ended his season. Yet he knocked home 33 goals the following season.

"It was just the ability to push yourself a little bit," he said. "You need little bit more each year, because you're getting old."

The first American to reach 1,000 NHL points in 1995 and the first American to score 500 NHL goals in March 1997, Mullen was awarded the Lester Patrick Trophy for outstanding service to hockey in the U.S. in 1995 and was inducted into the United States Hockey Hall of Fame in 1998 and the Hockey Hall of Fame in 2000.

Born in Brockton, Mass., about 20 miles south of Boston, Stevens entered Boston College just four years after Mullen's graduation. He had been drafted in 1983 by the Los Angeles Kings, who traded him to Pittsburgh three months later, and the big left wing put up improved numbers every season he played for the Eagles, culminating with 35 goals in his senior season—the second-most in school history.

At 6-3 and 210 pounds with great hands around the net, Stevens was on a path to stardom as a power forward. Before he reached the NHL with the Penguins, he had already represented the U.S. in the 1987 World Championships and the 1988 Olympic Games. After a brief post-Olympic stint with the Penguins, he spent only 45 games in the International Hockey League the following season before becoming a full-time NHL player in March 1989—scoring 11 goals in 17 games after his recall.

In his early seasons with Pittsburgh, Stevens most often played with Dan Quinn, John Cullen and, after his acquisition from Hartford, Ron Francis. But Stevens quickly became a dominant scorer and a major force on the power play, sharing the team lead with 40 goals in 1990–91 and then following that up by leading the Penguins with 17 goals in the 1991 playoffs—a single-season team playoff record—as the team earned its first Stanley Cup.

"I liked playing in the playoffs," he said, "just enjoyed the play and the pressure."

Stevens' dominant playoff performance preceded a busy time for Penguins' general manager Craig Patrick, for whom Stevens was just one of a number of important players seeking new contracts. Patrick was nothing if not painfully patient, and Stevens essentially forced his hand by signing a five-year, $5.3 million offer sheet from the Boston Bruins that Pittsburgh then matched.

"I wanted to stay in Pittsburgh...I just felt to make it easy, I'll sign and hopefully they'll match it," he said. "Thank God they did."

A boisterous and magnetic personality in the Pittsburgh dressing room, Stevens started the 1991–92 season on Lemieux's left wing with Mark Recchi on the right, and the result was predictable. He scored 54 goals that season and followed that with 55 in 1992–93, and from 1990 through 1994, regular season and playoffs, only Brett Hull scored more NHL goals than Stevens. Stevens added 13 more goals in the 1992 playoffs as the Penguins defended their title, and through 2025 he remained one of only 13 players in team history to average a point per game over their playoff careers with the team.

"The first couple years they put me with Mario, I couldn't play with him. The first Cup I played with Ronnie and Joey," Stevens remembered, "but it took me a while to figure him out. He always wanted the puck, but Cully wanted the puck all the time, and Ronnie wanted the puck all the time, and I didn't want the puck, so it was perfect. I wanted the puck where I could shoot it. I didn't want to carry the puck. Mario would get the blue line, and I could just go to the net and take guys (with me). He just wants space, he'll get the line and buy some time, and if guys don't go with you to the net, he'll give it to you."

His 1992–93 season, however, was a turning point in Stevens' life. In New York after a game in March 1993, he told SportsNet, he had tried cocaine. Two months later, his violent Game 7 collision with Rich Pilon of the New York Islanders knocked him out before he could brace himself for his fall to the ice, and that fall shattered multiple bones around his face, necessitating reconstructive surgery. Stevens relied on pain pills to help him, and soon he was battling addiction. He returned from his playoff injury to score 41 goals for the Penguins in 1993–94, but his career would never be the same. He missed almost half the 1994–95 season with an ankle injury, and that summer he was traded to the Bruins, the first of four different teams for which he would play over the next six seasons.

Stevens was arrested for cocaine possession in St. Louis in 2000 while playing for the Rangers. He returned to the Penguins to finish his career and retired in 2002, and the Penguins hired him as a scout in 2005. But after several seasons Lemieux personally ensured Stevens got to a rehabilitation facility. Stevens broke his neck in a car accident in 2014 and the following year was arrested on federal drug charges that resulted in probation and a requirement from the judge to speak to the community and try and help those fighting addiction.

Stevens and his sister Kelli Wilson then formed Power Forward, a non-profit based in Marshfield, Mass., that fights addiction through education, empowerment and innovation, providing recipients complete funding for a six-week stay at safe, structured and vetted sober living homes following Substance Use Disorder treatment. Stevens has done more than 300 speaking engagements to tell his story and inspire others in their struggles, increasing the visibility of his organization to the point where the number of funded recipients in 2025 represented a 700 percent increase over just two years earlier. Power Forward also started a first-of-its-kind D.O.E.R. Program for Dog Ownership Enhancing Recovery, placing trained service dogs into sober homes to help residents.

Appearing on NBC's *The Today Show* in 2024, Stevens said, "My hockey legacy is great, but I think I'm here to help people." He was inducted into the United States Hockey Hall of Fame in 2024, where he joined 11 other former Penguins: Mullen, Bob Paradise, Gordie Roberts, Mike Ramsey, Mark Johnson, Kevin Hatcher, Ed Olczyk, Bill Guerin, Scott Young, Matt Cullen and Barrasso, the only former Pittsburgh goaltender through 2026 to reach Hall of Fame status. Barrasso was inducted into the U.S. Hockey Hall of Fame in 2009 and the Hockey Hall of Fame in 2023, and neither of those outcomes would have seemed crazy when he splashed onto the NHL scene in 1983.

A Boston native, Barrasso was a dominant presence at Acton-Boxboro High School northwest of Boston before being drafted fifth overall by Buffalo in 1983, and he promptly became the first goaltender in league history to jump directly from high school to the NHL, becoming the youngest goaltender in 40 years to play in the NHL. If that wasn't enough, he won the Vezina Trophy as the league's best goaltender that season as well as the Calder Trophy as NHL Rookie of the Year, adding to the legend of the Sabres' general manager who drafted him—Scotty Bowman, who would coach Barrasso to the Stanley Cup nine years later in Pittsburgh. At 6-3 and 210 pounds, Barrasso had not only size but confidence and what was then a more novel skill for an NHL goaltender—the ability to deftly play and move the puck. His 48 career assists remain the NHL record for a goaltender.

"I watched the Bruins when I was a kid, and Gerry Cheevers handled the puck quite a bit. I think everybody who skates wants to shoot pucks," Barrasso said. "I don't think I realized what an asset it was until probably high school, but it's certainly invaluable if your goalie can help out your team by getting the puck and moving it up the ice."

In November 1988, Pittsburgh general manager Tony Esposito, a Hall of Fame goaltender who, like Barrasso, caught with his right hand and had a Calder Trophy to his name, acquired Barrasso from the Sabres and thus provided the Penguins with a high-profile goaltender for the first time in their history. Barrasso had finished second in Vezina Trophy voting the previous season but was off to a poor start with the Sabres at the time of the trade; in his first playoff series with Pittsburgh five months later, Barrasso's .930 save percentage against the New York Rangers was an important part of the Penguins' first-round sweep.

Later that summer, his daughter Ashley was diagnosed with cancer, and late the following season Barrasso left the team to join her for the start of treatments that were successful in saving her life. In 1990–91, he won 27 games, his highest total in five seasons, and then backstopped the Penguins to their first Stanley Cup, punctuating that playoff run with an 8–0 road shutout of Minnesota in the deciding game.

Barrasso was the right goalie at the right time for a Pittsburgh team built around skill and scoring prowess. His ability to move the puck and feed the attack played to the Penguins' strengths, and while the volume of chances they allowed meant his numbers would rarely be outstanding, he proved adept at making saves at critical junctures in games, especially at the most important time of the season.

"Playoffs is timely goals and timely saves, and we'd get that," said defenseman Larry Murphy. Added Recchi, "We would win, 5–4, but he never left the fifth one in when it really counted. Look at (Grant) Fuhr, (Andy) Moog, same type of thing. He was always really calm in there. He believed in what he was doing, and you felt that confidence that he was going to be there for us."

Being there for his defense corps meant making their jobs a little easier. "The way he played the puck was a big help," Murphy said. "He was more than willing to go out and get the puck, especially if you'd have a couple of guys bearing down on you, where if you got to the puck, you wouldn't have many options. He'd get out there and throw it up the boards. He was always a picture of composure in the net."

Barrasso's play in the 1992 playoffs was even better, as he compiled a .927 save percentage during the team's 11-game winning streak to conclude their successful Cup defense. He limited Chicago to a single goal in Games 2 and 3 of the Stanley Cup Final, including a 27-save shutout in a 1–0 Game 3 victory in Chicago that realistically ended the Hawks' chances of winning the series.

"Going into every game, you know Tommy's going to come up with the saves," teammate Rick Tocchet said late in the 1992 playoffs. "He basically says, 'Worry about your own job and I'll worry about my job.' And that's what he does."

Barrasso was then often plagued by injuries, missing virtually all of the 1994–95 (wrist) and 1996–97 seasons (shoulder). But after Lemieux retired for the first time following the 1996–97 season and new coach Kevin Constantine brought a more defensive approach to the game, Barrasso responded in 1997–98 with career-best numbers for games played (63), shutouts (7), goals-against average (2.07) and save percentage (.922). Traded to Ottawa in 2000, Barrasso left the Penguins as their all-time leader in games played, wins and shutouts among goalies.

"There's a lot of pressure on a goalie, especially when you have a team that has a chance to win," Stevens said. "He was a phenomenal player. We don't win anything without him."

12

Championship Genes

In the eight seasons from 1979–80 to 1986–87, either Bryan Trottier or Paul Coffey won the Stanley Cup seven times. Trottier was the No. 1 center for the New York Islanders' dynasty that won the first four Cups of the 1980s, and Coffey was the No. 1 defenseman for the early years of the Edmonton Oilers' dynasty that unseated the Islanders to win four Cups between 1984 and 1988 and five Cups over seven seasons ending in the spring of 1990.

On their way to the Hockey Hall of Fame, Trottier and Coffey excelled not only at the most important times of the season but across the nine-month journeys that took their teams from training camp to championships. A high-scoring two-way centerman who thrived on competition and brought superb playmaking ability to an Islanders' attack led by he and longtime linemates Mike Bossy and Clark Gillies, Trottier also won the Calder Trophy, Conn Smythe Trophy, Art Ross Trophy, Hart Trophy and King Clancy Memorial Trophy. An amazing skater who with the puck single-handedly deflated armies of forecheckers and also had the skill and vision to initiate and finish plays at the other end of the rink, Coffey won three Cups with the Oilers and three Norris Trophies as the league's top defenseman.

But both players left the franchises with which they had earned so much recognition to come to Pittsburgh—Coffey in a November 1987 trade after a contract impasse with the Oilers, and Trottier as a free agent in 1990. And each came to the Penguins with a bit of a chip on his shoulder.

"When I had my contract holdout with the Oilers, there were other teams that were wanting my services, and for lack of a better term, they sent me here because I'd never win again. That's what they told me," said Coffey, who was 26 at the time of the trade. "The only thing they discounted was Mario. I couldn't get here fast enough. I liked the city and it gave me a chance to play with him. It was special."

When the Islanders failed to win a playoff round for the third straight season in 1990, they bought out the final two years of Trottier's contract, making their all-time leading scorer a free agent for the first time in his career. Trottier was promptly on the radar of Pittsburgh general manager Craig Patrick, whose new team had won one playoff round in 11 years.

"Craig was the first one to offer a contract," remembered Trottier. "On July 1, I made a few phone calls, Detroit, L.A., Toronto, even the Rangers. I thought, 'Hey, the first one to throw a contract at me, if it makes sense, I'm going to go.' I thought why not try and help the Penguins. Mario, (Tom) Barrasso, Coffey...I was looking at their lineup and saying I don't think they're that far away. To have the good fortune of going from the Islanders team and being unappreciated by the organization and coming here, and every little thing I did, the fans, or the media or the organization, just appreciated it. It's fun to be appreciated."

Both had plenty of hockey left in them, and both brought far more than their skillsets to a Pittsburgh franchise that had never won anything. Their leadership skills were just as important to the Penguins teams with which they would wind up winning more Cups.

"Both of them changed Penguins hockey forever," said winger Phil Bourque, who lifted the Cup with Trottier and Coffey. "Because they changed the culture. They did. Changed the mindset, changed the way we practiced, the way we worked out, the way we believed in each other, the way we treated each other. Everything changed in that locker room. Those two guys made us believe we were winners. Before that, we always hoped to be winners. We never really believed. We hoped we'd win a series or win two series, but those guys made us absolutely believe we could win a Stanley Cup."

General manager Eddie Johnston's trade to acquire Coffey was easily one of the most important in team history. The Penguins sent No. 2 overall 1985 pick Craig Simpson, No. 5 overall 1987 pick Chris Joseph, center Dave Hannan and defenseman Moe Mantha to the Oilers for Coffey, enforcer Wayne Van Dorp and forward Dave Hunter. Johnston had worked on the trade "for quite a while. They asked about Simpson, and I was a little hesitant, but at the time I had to make that trade for Coffey. He and Mario were like Orr and Esposito in Boston, one helped the other. They got along good, their communication was terrific and their leadership was perfect."

On cue, Coffey made a dramatic Penguins debut on Nov. 25 in Pittsburgh against Quebec on Thanksgiving Eve, a beloved traditional game for Penguins' fans. Pittsburgh was losing, 4–0, late in the second period before he assisted on three power-play goals to help turn the game into a 6–4 Penguins' win. Despite not having a training camp and missing the first 21 games, Coffey finished fifth in scoring among NHL defensemen that season, leading all of them in points per game.

The Penguins were still trying to build their forward depth around Lemieux at the time of the trade, but Coffey instantly drew defenders to himself on his countless rushes up the right side of the ice, and that meant space was being created in a new way for Lemieux. "It was a big change to be able to play with a great defenseman like Coffey," Lemieux said. "He opened things up for me with his skating and passing ability, and I had a great time playing with him."

Defenseman Randy Hillier, often paired with Coffey in Pittsburgh, had also played with Hall of Famer Ray Bourque in Boston before coming to the Penguins, and he remembered the difference in how those two skated.

"Ray was such a heavy, thick guy, he plowed through the ice, and he could skate and you could hear him. Coff skated on top of the ice, just glided," said Hillier, who later served six seasons as an assistant coach with the Penguins. "He never wanted the puck standing still. If you gave him the puck because you had traffic on you and he was standing still, he'd just fire it back at you. We'd play catch with it, bring the forwards in on a forecheck, and he'd do a little circle in the slot area. I'd go to the corner, draw someone over and then lay it over to him in full flight, and he's gone. As soon as he gets the puck and he's moving forward, he's got you by two or three steps. We all know what he's going to do, and yet you can't defend it. Everyone backs off because he's got such great speed...he was electric with the puck."

When the Penguins finally reached the playoffs for the first time in seven years the following season, Coffey's presence was a huge stabilizing factor for the team, especially in a first-round sweep of the New York Rangers as he had nine points, including two goals in a Game 1 victory.

"When you start bringing people into the locker room like that...just the way he went about his business, he was the same demeanor every day. He brought that winning way and what it takes," said Jay Caufield, who came to Pittsburgh in Coffey's first full season with the team. "They know when to say things. It mattered when they said something. There are some guys that talk all the time, and after a while, that falls on deaf ears. Guys that spoke when it mattered most, like when Mario said anything, immediately people would pay attention. Coffey was the same way."

Coffey was not shy about sharing his thoughts, either. When the Penguins dropped the opening game in their second-round playoff series against Washington in 1991, Coffey criticized coach Bob Johnson for not shortening his bench. "We didn't play to win, man. When you play to win, there's certain things you do," he said. "You've got to play your guys that are willing to work, that's all. You can't be fair to everybody."

Phil Bourque said those comments showed Coffey's heart was in the right place. "He said the things people were thinking and never in a selfish way, coming from a place of wanting to win more than anything else," he said. "Some people will say they want to win more than anything; players like Trots and Coff will do anything. It's one thing to say it, it's another thing to do it. It came from a place of desire to win."

When Coffey was traded in February 1992, after five seasons with the Penguins, he was their all-time leader among defensemen in every major offensive statistic. Now, 34 years later, his points-per-game average of 1.33 still remains the best in franchise history among defensemen. He was inducted into the Hall of Fame in 2004.

Trottier's success with Pittsburgh was due, in part, to the way he embraced his role as a bottom-six forward at that point in his career, a player who could still contribute on the ice but whose experience and leadership would likely have the most impact on those around him. "It's not easy for a Hall of Fame player at the end of your career and you're down to 12, maybe 14 minutes a game," said Scotty Bowman, who coached Trottier to the Cup in 1992. "He was still a competitor."

Remembered scout and assistant coach Pierre McGuire, "Trottier was really the guy that never got enough credit for what he would say behind the scenes or on the bench," and not surprisingly Trottier would later serve four seasons as a Pittsburgh assistant coach.

What Trottier did get a lot of credit for was easing Jaromír Jágr's professional assimilation into the NHL game, as Jágr spent a lot of time in his rookie season playing with Trottier. Even in Jágr's second season in 1991–92, Bowman would sometimes reunite them. "Trottier seems to be able to get a lot of hockey out of Jágr," Bowman said.

When Lemieux went out of the lineup in the second half of that season, Bowman simply inserted Trottier into Lemieux's position on the top line with Mark Recchi and Kevin Stevens, and Trottier responded with 11 points over five games—matching his previous output for the season. His ice time had increased, his role had changed and yet Trottier seemed to turn the clock back without a problem.

"He had a youthful enthusiasm about him, even at that age," remembered Hillier. "He loved being around the rink, loved being around the guys. His attitude was so infectious, he was great with young kids, guys like Jágr...he just wanted to be part of it, wanted to be a complementary piece, even after being a superstar and arguably on one of the greatest lines in hockey history. He was such a great player, a 200-foot game, could score, could shut you down, had a nastiness to him...he was perfect for this team and could play up and down your lineup."

Trottier was still an excellent faceoff man during his time with the Penguins, which helped him to play an important role as a penalty killer. In January 1992, he was named one of two Senior All-Stars added by the league to the NHL All-Star Game in Philadelphia, his eighth career appearance in the game. He was inducted into the Hall of Fame in 1997.

13
Immediate Impact

Ron Francis was so associated with the Hartford Whalers, where he spent his first 10 NHL seasons and later another six seasons in their second iteration as the Carolina Hurricanes, that he became aptly known as "Ronnie Franchise." He joined the Whalers for their third season in the NHL in 1981 and was still playing for the Hurricanes in 2004, along the way becoming the franchise's all-time leader in games, goals, assists and points.

But much like internal decisions had led Edmonton to trade Paul Coffey and the Islanders to hand Bryan Trottier free agent status two years early, the Whalers set the stage for Francis' departure when coach Rick Ley stripped Francis of his captaincy in December 1990. "The owner (Richard Gordon) and I probably didn't see eye-to-eye, is the best way to put it," said Francis. Still, it was a shocking move three months later when Francis, Ulf Samuelsson and Grant Jennings were traded to the new home of stars on the move—Pittsburgh.

"Before we got traded, Ulf and I had a conversation about our team in Hartford," remembered Francis. "He asked me if we were capable of winning the Cup, and I said I didn't think we were good enough to win it in Hartford. After a couple of games here, we went for something to eat one day and I said, 'Remember that question you asked me a week ago? Well, I think this team is.'"

Still second all-time in career assists to Wayne Gretzky, Francis fit the Penguins perfectly, giving them a No. 2 center who could not only distribute the puck to the team's talented wingers but give its top-six forwards a defensive presence not in the wheelhouse of John Cullen, the talented young center who was part of the package sent to the Whalers' general manager Eddie Johnston, who had been running the Penguins just three years earlier.

Only 28 at the time of the trade, Francis had 11 points in his first 14 games playing behind Mario Lemieux, an absolute matchup nightmare for opponents, and he added 17 points in the playoffs as the Penguins won their first Stanley Cup in 1991.

"Plus, he was that security blanket if Mario wasn't able to go," remembered Bob Errey. "Like a defensive conscience. His defensive mind, he was defense first...he was the ultimate turn, play defense and turn defense into offense guy. He was our No. 2, but he was No. 1 on most any other team. He was so smart, knew how to play the middle the of ice, a present day (Aleksander) Barkov.

"It wasn't just his on-ice play, I think it was his off-ice demeanor, too. He was calm, intelligent, poignant, a brilliant man, really, in terms of what was said and when he said it. All that was equally important. Just a calming force. We needed some of that voice of reason."

Francis will forever be remembered in Pittsburgh for his performance against the New York Rangers in the second round of the 1992 playoffs. He set up Kevin Stevens' game-winning goal in the second period of Game 1, later adding an insurance goal of his own, then had six goals and 10 points in the final four games of the series after Lemieux was sidelined with a broken hand. His goal to win Game 4 remains among the most dramatic overtime goals in team history.

"I remember it was just his body language, the tone in his voice, the chatter on the bench, the more demonstrative chatter in the room, it was a message to us," said Phil Bourque. "Without him saying it, it was like, 'I'm stepping up without Mario.' It was obvious what he was doing."

Inducted into the Hockey Hall of Fame in 2007, Francis had an impact well beyond his first two seasons in Pittsburgh, playing a major role for the Penguins when Lemieux missed a majority of the 1993–94 season and all of the 1994–95 season. Francis had points in every game as the Penguins began their 1994–95 season on a 12–0–1 run, and he finished fifth in NHL scoring that season—the highest finish of his career until he finished fourth the following season with a career-high 119 points as part of the highest-scoring team in Penguins' history.

"He was always in the right spot at the right time," Mark Recchi said.

Pittsburgh was absolutely the right spot for Recchi, who played junior hockey for his hometown Kamloops Blazers of the Western Hockey League under future Stanley Cup–winning coach Ken Hitchcock. He had been passed over in both the 1986 and 1987 NHL Drafts, the first while playing in New Westminster and the latter after his Kamloops season was ruined by a broken ankle. But just as they had done two years earlier when drafting the Blazers' Rob Brown in the same round, the Penguins heeded the urging of scout Bruce Haralson and selected Recchi in the fourth round in 1988, just months after he had helped Canada to the gold medal at the 1988 World Junior Championships.

"Everybody kept saying, 'You're too small,'" said the 5-10 Recchi, who then quickly made his presence known at the professional level.

He scored 50 goals in just 63 games with the Muskegon Lumberjacks of the International Hockey League in 1988–89 and then helped them to the Turner Cup title with 21 points in 14 playoff games after playing 15 games with the Penguins. In 1989–90, he scored seven goals in his first four games with Muskegon before departing the minor leagues for good, and he then became the lowest-drafted rookie ever to score 30 goals for the Penguins. In his first full NHL season, 1990–91, he scored 40 goals and finished fourth in NHL scoring with 113 points playing much of the early part of the season beside center John Cullen and left wing Kevin Stevens, the Penguins' memorable Option Line whose members were all bidding for new contracts.

"It was awesome. We were best friends off the ice, we fought on the bench, yelled at each other...we drove each other," Recchi said. "Three different players, but all competitive."

Recchi was solidly built and played a relentless game, battling for pucks all over the ice. Getting knocked down was just part of the game, and Recchi kept getting back up and making things happen in the offensive zone. Penguins' play-by-play man Mike Lange aptly nicknamed Recchi "The Wreckin' Ball."

"There's nothing wrong with a guy 185 pounds being an aggressive bulldog out there," said coach Bob Johnson. Added Cullen, "You don't see Mark going second into the corner, third into the corner. You don't see him bailing out. Small guys have to do it. You're not big, so you better not back down or you'll be out of the league."

Stevens was Recchi's roommate on the road for years and called him "a phenomenal player, a little guy with a heart of gold. The guy could score from anywhere, he could make plays, he was strong on the puck, Recchs had everything. For a guy in a big league back then, a small guy who got to those areas to score goals, he had a big heart—as big as anybody's."

Certainly Recchi's production had become the biggest part of his game. "I never thought I'd be able to get as many points as I did as quickly as I did," said Recchi, who was particularly effective on the rush as a left shot playing on his off wing, the precise situation in which he scored the late game-winning goal against Boston in Game 6 of the Prince of Wales Conference Final that put the Penguins into the Stanley Cup Final for the first time in 1991. Only Lemieux had more points than Recchi during the 1991 playoffs.

"He was that hop-on-his-skates type of skater, and he did bring us a ton of energy," remembered teammate Troy Loney.

Recchi was on pace for 45 goals in 1991–92 when he was surprisingly traded to Philadelphia in February, leaving Pittsburgh at the same time general manager Craig Patrick sent Paul Coffey to Los Angeles as Patrick added size and toughness he thought was missing in a bid to defend the Cup. "I didn't expect it, and it hit pretty hard. We heard things," remembered Recchi, "but the year before we went through some stuff, too, and we got through it and then took off, so we always felt we were going to be fine because of what we had been through. It was definitely a shock."

Recchi became a 50-goal scorer in his first full season with the Flyers and fashioned an incredible career, proving a consistent and durable player, skating in 1,652 NHL games, eighth-most in league history. He signed with the Penguins for the 2005–06 season and began it on rookie Sidney Crosby's right wing, picking up a goal in the opening game to give Crosby his first NHL point, but was traded later that season to Carolina and helped the Hurricanes to the Stanley Cup before returning to Pittsburgh and becoming one of the few players to have three stints with the Penguins.

His long career ended on top when Recchi helped Boston win the Cup in 2011. He was inducted into the Hockey Hall of Fame in 2017 just as he was beginning a three-season stay as an assistant coach with the Penguins.

Like Recchi, Larry Murphy had a reputation for durability and multiple Stanley Cups in his future when he came to the Penguins in December 1990 in an unusual trade that saw the Penguins and Minnesota North Stars swap four veteran defensemen—Murphy and Peter Taglianetti moving to Pittsburgh and Minnesota natives Jim Johnson and Chris Dahlquist heading to Minneapolis—who would face each other five months later in the Stanley Cup Final.

Murphy had burst onto the NHL scene with 60 assists, a record for a rookie defenseman, with Los Angeles in 1980–81, and he soon established himself as one of the most productive offensive defensemen in the game. Moving to Washington in 1983, he established career highs for goals and points in 1986–87, when he finished third in balloting for the Norris Trophy as the NHL's best defenseman.

A right shot to complement the left-shooting Coffey, Murphy soon established himself as an important presence on the Penguins' power play, proving himself quite adept at keeping pucks in the offensive zone with his stick and moving the puck smartly. "He had great hand-eye coordination, and he'd get the puck to the net for you," said Joe Mullen.

While not a big body-checker or a notably quick skater, Murphy had the size to move opposing forwards in front of the net and played a cerebral game that relied on his ability to read the play, use a poke-check and position himself where he could succeed consistently without the puck. "You didn't see him get burned very often," Loney said.

One of the best examples of Murphy's adaptation to the game was his frequent decision, when he could feel forechecking pressure coming, to simply loft the puck high toward the opponents' end of the rink—but not too far to create an icing call. He had learned what his teammates called the "Murphy Dump" while playing junior hockey for coach Gary Green in Peterborough.

"He used to have the defense line up on the goal line at the end of practice, and have us fire the puck, loft it in the air. He thought it was a good skillset to have," Murphy said. "I spent a whole year doing that. I had the confidence I could do it, and it was an effective tool, it got the puck out of the zone, could take the pressure off, and offensively it was a good tool, too, if you threw it high and if you could land it behind the other defense. It's tough for the other defense to find the puck if you had guys bearing down on you."

Murphy was at his best on the power play, and he set single-season team playoff records for power-play goals by a defenseman in 1991 (later matched by Kris Letang) and power-play points by a defenseman in 1992 (later surpassed by Sergei Gonchar). After the trade of Paul Coffey, the only defenseman in team history to record more points in a season than Murphy, Murphy ran the Penguins' power play at the right point, and the Penguins finished with the league's second-best power play in Murphy's first full season in that role in 1992–93.

Murphy later won back-to-back Stanley Cups under Scotty Bowman with the Detroit Red Wings in 1997 and 1998 and today ranks fourth all-time among defensemen in games played and fifth in scoring. He was inducted into the Hockey Hall of Fame in 2004.

PART 4

THE CUP SEASONS

14
Top of the Mountain, 1991

When the Penguins hosted the Buffalo Sabres for their final game of the 1989–90 season, they needed a win or tie to clinch consecutive playoff berths for the first time in eight years. The importance of the game for Pittsburgh was underscored by the presence in the lineup of Mario Lemieux, who had missed the past 21 games and was headed for back surgery but saw a chance to help push his team across the line. Playing at about 80 percent, he scored one goal and assisted on another, but Uwe Krupp's overtime goal sank the Penguins, 3–2.

Almost 20 minutes after the game, many of the Penguins were still in uniform, sitting in silence at their dressing room stalls. Tony Tanti was slumped against a wall. As coach and general manager Craig Patrick walked through the room, amid the near-silence, someone mentioned to him that the outcome had been typical for this franchise. "That's going to change," he said tersely.

The summer of 1990 laid the platform for that change with Patrick's hiring of "Badger" Bob Johnson as coach and the legendary Scotty Bowman as director of player development, giving the Penguins an other-worldly front office. Johnson, who won three national championships in a 15-year career as coach at the University of Wisconsin that gave him his nickname, was a positive thinker who had spent five seasons as coach of the Calgary Flames, taking them to the 1986 Cup Final. Bowman was the winningest coach in NHL history and winner of five Cups with the Montreal Canadiens, a master strategist behind the bench. Patrick, Johnson and Bowman are all in the Hockey Hall of Fame as builders, and Patrick, a Detroit native, and Johnson, a Minneapolis native, are also in the United States Hockey Hall of Fame.

Soon after those hirings, Patrick drafted Jaromír Jágr, made a trade with Calgary for right wing Joe Mullen and signed four-time Stanley Cup champion Bryan Trottier as a free agent center from the New York Islanders. It was quite a summer, and just days before the start of the season, he traded for defenseman Gordie Roberts from St. Louis on Roberts' 33rd birthday, adding to the veteran presence on the roster. Also new to the team were defenseman Paul Stanton, an eighth-round draft choice in 1985 who had spent four years at the University of Wisconsin; defenseman Jim Paek, a ninth-round 1985 draft pick who became the first native of South Korea to play in the NHL; and winger Jeff Daniels, a sixth-round draft pick in 1986. The first month of the season saw seven players make their debut in a Penguins' sweater.

The biggest unfolding story of the season, however, was not the roster turnover and its effect on the team, nor Pittsburgh's play under the new coach. Lemieux had undergone back surgery in the off-season, and there was no reliable timetable for a return, which would have more impact on the Penguins' fortunes than any other factor. But three young players whose futures with the team were in serious question wound up playing integral roles in helping the team through it.

Left wing Kevin Stevens, acquired from Los Angeles in a trade seven years earlier while starting his career at Boston College, right wing Mark Recchi, a fourth-round draft pick in 1988, and center John Cullen, a free agent signing in 1988, were all playing out their contract options. Johnson put them together, and of course they were dubbed "The Option Line" while dominating the NHL scoring charts. They combined for 15 points in a season-opening win at Washington, with Stevens recording six points, still an NHL record for an opening night. With the game tied, 4–4, and just under eight minutes to play, the trio delivered three goals, accounting for nine points in the span of 6:39, for a 7–4 win.

By Dec. 1, all three were among the top 10 scorers in the league, with the undrafted Cullen just two points behind Wayne Gretzky for the scoring lead, while the Penguins, a game under .500, were the third-highest scoring team in the NHL. *Without* Lemieux.

"We loved playing together, being on the same team. We lived together off the ice," said Stevens of his linemates, "and it was awesome. Cully was such a good center, and Recchs could do anything, score or pass. The line worked well together. Cully, I remember playing against him in college, he was an unbelievable player. It's funny he was never drafted. Cully's hands were as soft as any pair of hands in the league. He was just smaller in a league that was big, but he was tough and could make plays. He took a beating, too."

But the team's defensive cohesion was lacking, and by mid-December Pittsburgh had won just two of its last 12 games and sat nine points out of a playoff spot. In the span of 10 days, Patrick made three trades to acquire winger Scott Young from Hartford; Czech center Jiří Hrdina from Calgary, to help acclimate fellow countryman Jágr; and defensemen Larry Murphy and Peter Taglianetti from Minnesota. Pittsburgh won 16 of its next 21 games, the final two of those with Lemieux in the lineup, as he returned Jan. 26 at Quebec.

"I just liked the way they played the game, a real puck possession team, and that's the way I liked to play the game, so I knew it was going to be a real strong fit," said Murphy, an offensive-minded defenseman who was joining his fourth team. "I knew right away this was going to work out great for me."

The Penguins' power play, already one of the best in the NHL, surged an additional 6.5 points in the first month with Lemieux in the lineup. He averaged more than two points per game in that span, picking up right where he had left off when his 46-game scoring streak had ended almost a year earlier.

"Having Mario out there caused teams to approach their penalty kill a different way," Murphy said. "He drew a lot of attention, and overall it would make your job somewhat easier. They were so concerned about him…it definitely skewed their approach, and we had a great ability to realize when they overplayed him to work away from him. And if they didn't, of course, it was never a bad play to get him the puck."

But by March 1, when the Penguins concluded a five-game road trip without a victory while allowing 28 goals, they had won only four of their last 14 games. Injuries had cost them veterans Randy Hillier (foot), Mullen (neck), Trottier (groin) and Taglianetti (lung) through parts of the middle of the season, but it was obvious Pittsburgh was not a finished product even with Lemieux back. The Penguins were third in the Patrick Division, just three points behind second-place Philadelphia, but they were also just six points away from being out of a playoff spot.

During a three-day break in the schedule after the disastrous road trip and just one day before the trade deadline, Patrick on March 4 made the biggest trade in team history. He sent Cullen, defenseman Zarley Zalapski and depth forward Jeff Parker to Hartford for center Ron Francis and defensemen Ulf Samuelsson and Grant Jennings. Francis gave the Penguins a No. 2 centerman who would be a No. 1 on most teams, and Samuelsson played with a biting physical edge that made the Penguins a more difficult team to face; Samuelsson and Francis over the next 15 months would each score a Cup-winning goal. By late March, Pittsburgh was dressing a lineup featuring five defensemen who hadn't been with the team to start training camp.

The Penguins were unbeaten in their first seven games after the trade (6–0–1) and went on a 9–2–1 post-trade run that neatly coincided with the first- and second-place Rangers (1–8–1) and Flyers (2–8–0), respectively, falling apart. A 7–4 victory March 27 in Detroit gave Pittsburgh the first division title in team history.

Pittsburgh had home-ice advantage for its first-round playoff series against New Jersey, but the Devils scored twice in the span of 50 seconds early in the third period to break a 1–1 tie and produce a 3–1 victory in Game 1. Future Hall of Famer Peter Stastny had two goals, including the game-winner, and the 56 penalty minutes dished out over the final five minutes of the game put the series on an emotional plane right away.

Game 2 thus took on an urgency for the Penguins, but the Devils under coach Tommy McVie were making things difficult on the division champions. Regulation ended 4–4 after Alexei Kasatonov's goal early in the third period for New Jersey, but with his team being outshot in overtime, Barrasso came up with several big saves before Jágr scored his first playoff goal at 8:52 of overtime, holding off John MacLean as he carried the puck along the right wing boards and then pulling it around defenseman Ken Daneyko before outwaiting goaltender Chris Terreri and scoring on a wrist shot.

"That was about as intensely played a hockey game as I've ever seen," said Johnson, whose team got goals from three bottom-six forwards in Jágr, Phil Bourque and Troy Loney. But the Devils were nevertheless feeling good about the start of the series. Laurie Boschman was shadowing Lemieux with fair results and Claude Lemieux was irritating the Penguins. "If we play the way we played here both games, we're going to win this series," Stastny said. "There's no doubt about it."

Mullen's return to the lineup from February neck surgery in Game 3 at New Jersey figured to boost Pittsburgh, but Brendan Shanahan scored twice and Doug Brown tied the game for the Devils shorthanded with just 5:14 left. Pittsburgh's inability to protect a late lead looked ominous, but the Penguins then caught a break. Bourque lofted the puck high into the New Jersey zone to relieve pressure, a tactic he learned from Murphy, and Devils' defenseman Eric Weinrich knocked it out of the air and right onto the stick of Recchi. Recchi, who had opened the scoring in the game, then closed it with a goal at 19:10 to give the Penguins a 4–3 victory and their first series lead, 2–1.

The Devils dominated the opening period of Game 4, outshooting Pittsburgh, 15–3, and taking a 2–0 lead that led to a convincing 4–1 victory to even the series. Claude Lemieux scored twice, and defenseman Viacheslav Fetisov got his stick into Coffey's face early in the third period, knocking Coffey out of the game with a scratched cornea. Trottier took his second 10-minute misconduct penalty in three games as Claude Lemieux continued to get under his skin. "He probably doesn't like the way I play," Lemieux said. "That's too bad."

Back in Pittsburgh for Game 5, with Coffey and Trottier out, the Penguins rallied from a 2–0 deficit to tie the game before Claude Lemieux's power-play goal proved the difference in a 4–2 win that put the Penguins on the brink of elimination after allowing three power-play goals and going 0-for-7 on the power play themselves.

Few knew Barrasso had also suffered a separated shoulder in the third period of that game, so when the Penguins arrived in New Jersey for Game 6, it was backup Frank Pietrangelo making his Stanley Cup playoff debut as part of a lineup that was still missing Coffey. Coffey's absence was having a profound effect on Pittsburgh's slumping power play, and Mario Lemieux had just two even-strength points through six games as the Penguins limped into a rink in which they had lost six of their last seven games. They were in trouble.

"We have to steal one," Recchi said.

MacLean opened the scoring for New Jersey, but Stevens then scored twice in 2:28 to give Pittsburgh a lead for the first time since Game 3. Pietrangelo took a delay-of-game penalty late in the period, however, and the New Jersey power play that had scored six times in the past three games had a chance to tie it. Moments later, when Pietrangelo tried to cover a loose puck, MacLean poked it away from him and right onto the stick of Stastny, who looked up to see a yawning net. But Pietrangelo flung his catching glove back and snatched the resulting shot at 15:33, stunning everyone in the Brendan Byrne Arena.

"He had an open net. It's just instinct to reach back and put anything you can in there. He hit my glove," Pietrangelo said. It became known in Pittsburgh as "The Save," one of the markers of the team's first Stanley Cup championship. Jágr added the Penguins' second power-play goal of the period four minutes later and Pittsburgh had an unpredictable 3–1 lead after 20 minutes.

Francis scored early in the second period for a 4–1 lead, but Weinrich and Claude Lemieux scored 1:16 apart midway through the period to draw within a goal. The Devils appeared to tie it at 18:28 after Boschman redirected a Claude Lemieux pass behind Pietrangelo, but referee Bill McCreary waived the goal off, saying Boschman had kicked it in, and Pittsburgh held on for a memorable 4–3 victory. "It changed the momentum of the hockey game completely," Boschman said. "It hit my skate and then hit my stick. But what are you going to do?"

Asked afterward if the win was the biggest of his hockey career, Pietrangelo said, "It's the biggest until Monday night." Back home for Game 7, Pietrangelo made his first Civic Arena start in nearly four months, with Coffey back in the lineup and defenseman Ulf Samuelsson now out with a broken hand. Coffey and Mario Lemieux had goals, Hrdina scored twice and Pietrangelo stopped 27 shots for the first Penguins' playoff shutout in 15 years, a 4–0 win that gave the Penguins the first Game 7 win in team history. "They played their hearts out," said Johnson, whose team lost Mario Lemieux for the final two periods due to back spasms.

Next up for the Penguins were the Washington Capitals for what became the first of seven playoff meetings between the teams in the span of 11 years—the start of a boisterous rivalry that is still going strong today. The Capitals had eliminated the Rangers in the first round, and they surprised the Penguins by scoring three times in the third period to erase a 2–1 deficit and take a 4–2 victory in Game 1, getting goals from defensemen Calle Johansson, Kevin Hatcher and Al Iafrate. The Penguins took some solace in getting Samuelsson and Lemieux back in the lineup, but they had little jump. "Maybe we're emotionally drained," said Pietrangelo, who had established a team-record playoff shutout streak of 112:19 before Johansson scored early in the second period.

As they had done in the first round, the Penguins evened the series in overtime of Game 2, this goal coming from Stevens at 8:10 off a pretty two-on-one setup from Francis for a wild, 7–6 victory in which Recchi had two goals and four points to take over the league's playoff scoring lead, benefiting from his recent switch to a lighter stick. Stevens' second goal of the game enabled the Penguins to escape after blowing another third-period lead, as Dino Ciccarelli had scored twice and Johansson once in the opening 11 minutes of the third period to put Washington ahead, 6–5. The tying goal belonged to fourth-line winger Randy Gilhen, who took what for him was the highly unusual step of jumping off the bench to replace Pietrangelo during a delayed penalty to Washington. His backhander beat Mike Liut, who had replaced starter Don Beaupre, at 15:25 and set the stage for Stevens' heroics.

As the series shifted to Washington, the Pittsburgh defense corps was being devastated by injuries. Taglianetti had yet to play in the series because of severely bruised tendons on the top of the foot impacted by skate laces. Samuelsson had taken injections to play the last two games with a broken hand, but it was now too swollen to grip a stick. Coffey had played Game 2 with a full face shield after a Dmitri Khristich shot broke his jaw in Game 1, but a Dale Hunter elbow to that jaw in Game 2 forced surgery and put him out of the lineup indefinitely.

Randy Hillier and Paek jumped into the lineup, but it was the return of Barrasso that turned the series.

The Penguins won Games 3 and 4 in Washington by the same 3–1 score, and Barrasso made 64 saves in those two games. "The last two games he's played, he's been unbelievable," Lemieux said of Barrasso. Said Stevens, "People don't realize how good he really is, because we kind of left him back there on his own the last couple years. But he's as good as they come."

Back home with a chance to end the series in Game 5, Barrasso made another 33 saves in a 4–1 victory that pushed the Penguins to the third round of the playoffs for the first time in their history. Barrasso finished the series with a .970 save percentage, a dominant performance that left the Capitals frustrated. "When you win the first game of the series here and you play well in most of the games, losing four straight shouldn't happen," said Washington coach Terry Murray.

The Penguins faced the Boston Bruins in the Wales Conference Final without Coffey, but they got Samuelsson and Taglianetti back, as trainer Skip Thayer used a plastic bag filled with peanut butter inside Taglianetti's skate boot to make it possible for him to tie his skates. Samuelsson, the Penguins' most physical defenseman, would be a key figure against Bruins' power forward Cam Neely. Those two had played many games against each other as Adams Division rivals when Samuelsson skated for Hartford, and they were after each other from the start.

Pittsburgh, unfortunately, was sloppy in its own zone and dropped a 6–3 decision in Game 1 at Boston, with Bob Sweeney shadowing Lemieux, Neely scoring twice and the Bruins getting two power-play goals after too many men on the ice penalties by the Penguins. There would be no Game 2 rebound this time for Pittsburgh, however, as Craig Janney scored a late five-on-three goal to tie the game and Vladimír Růžička won it for the Bruins at 8:14 of overtime, 5–4.

Lemieux was brilliant in this game, turning a 3–2 deficit into a 4–3 lead in the span of 1:59 of the third period, stealing the puck from goaltender Andy Moog and setting up a Recchi goal and then stealing the puck from defenseman Don Sweeney and beating Moog on the backhand. But Janney's goal came after a tripping call to Taglianetti and a high-sticking call to Roberts just 17 seconds apart by referee Dan Marouelli, and the Penguins were incensed that Boston had been given a two-man advantage that late in a tight playoff game—an unusual occurrence.

The Penguins were again in trouble. They had never won a playoff series when trailing, 2–0, and this was a veteran Bruins team that had been to the Stanley Cup Final in two of the previous three seasons. Pittsburgh, in the Cup semifinals for the first time in their history, needed to win four of the next five games to advance. Stevens, born 25 miles south of Boston in Brockton, Mass., couldn't have cared less about the bleak outlook.

"We can beat this team," he said moments after the devastating Game 2 loss. "And we will beat this team. I'll say it right now, we'll beat them."

Many of Stevens' teammates said later they had similar feelings, but it's unlikely any of them would ever have dreamt of expressing them quite like that. But Stevens was a big personality in that dressing room and didn't let his emotions mute what he was feeling. Years later, Stevens said his statement was "anger. It was frustration, but I knew we were going to win. I didn't say it to put any pressure on us. I just felt that way. I didn't even really remember saying it, to tell you the truth, until it was written. I believed in our guys. I guess I was the only one dumb enough to say anything. But I think we all felt the same way, we felt we deserved Game 2, just felt our team was better than their team."

Pittsburgh played like the better team in Game 3 back at home, winning 4–1 behind 27 saves from Barrasso and one goal and one assist each from Lemieux, Francis and Stevens. The Penguins knocked Moog out of this game, which began and ended with some fireworks. Boston tough guy Chris Nilan fired a puck at Jay Caufield near the end of the pre-game warmup, and they engaged in a shoving match at the entrance to the Bruins' dressing room before being separated; Nilan dropped the gloves with Troy Loney midway through the first period. The game concluded with 13 penalties in the third period, which also saw Neely leave the game with a charley horse after taking a big check from Samuelsson.

On the off day, that Samuelsson check became the series' prime narrative. Boston coach Mike Milbury decried Samuelsson's hit and lit into Johnson. "For all Bob Johnson's seven-point plans, there must have been somewhere in that seven-point plan: 'Make sure you take as many cheap shots as you can against the other team's star players.' So the professor of hockey, as he so often projects himself, is also subtly a professor of goonism, and we can't take that any longer," Milbury said. "They've drawn a line in the sand, or somehow on the ice, and far be it for me not to accept the confrontation."

Neely told reporters he felt Samuelsson stuck out his leg in delivering the check, and added he had no respect for Samuelsson because he played with a face shield. One loss had the Bruins' emotions boiling over. Told of Milbury's remarks, Johnson said, "We're interested in playing a flow game, a speed game. I don't know what he's talking about. It's confusing, but it's interesting."

For Game 4, Milbury inserted four new players into the Boston lineup, including Lyndon Byers, who hadn't played a game in five months. All four players took penalties as the Penguins earned another 4–1 victory to even the series. Barrasso had 29 saves and Lemieux scored a critical third-period goal just 1:45 after the Bruins had cut the Pittsburgh lead to 2–1. In the victory, Recchi extended his points streak to 12 games while Lemieux reached 11 and Stevens nine. The Pittsburgh stars were feeling it, especially after Milbury's comments.

"I came to the rink...probably as fired up as I'd been all year. I was ready to play at 1:00," Johnson said. "The statements they made...it fired up our players, but it really fired me up as a coach."

The Penguins had won just two of their last 21 games at Boston Garden heading into Game 5, but they swamped the Bruins, 7–2, for their first lead in the series. It marked the first time a Pittsburgh team had ever scored seven goals in a game at Boston, regular season or playoff, and the first time the Penguins had ever scored seven goals in a road playoff game. Lemieux had four points to take over the NHL playoff scoring lead and Stevens piled on two more goals and four points.

Back home for Game 6, the Penguins watched the Bruins build a 2–0 lead in the second period on goals by Neely and Ken Hodge, but goals by Murphy and Bourque tied it before the end of the period, part of a four-point effort by Murphy. After defensemen Roberts and Sweeney traded goals in the third, Recchi scored with 4:20 to play and Lemieux added an empty-net goal for the 5–3 victory that sent Pittsburgh to its first Stanley Cup Final. Neely skated past Samuelsson without acknowledging him in the handshake line.

"This is just a stepping stone," Bourque said after the game. "This is great, this is nice. But to go this far and not get the Cup would be a crime. I want the Cup."

The Cup Final against the Minnesota North Stars was the first between two 1967 expansion teams and featured a Minnesota team that was 12 games under .500 in the regular season, the second-worst record of any team to ever play for the Cup. The North Stars had beaten Chicago in six games in the opening round, St. Louis in six games in the second round and then needed only five games to eliminate the defending Cup champion Oilers. Their power play was clicking at just under 27 percent, they were scoring more goals than even Pittsburgh and they were 7–1 at home.

But this was a Pittsburgh team playing with nine future Hall of Famers and a confidence unknown to any Penguins team before. "Everybody's got a lot of trust and respect for everybody else in the room," said Bob Errey. "We put a lot of faith in everybody, that they can do their own jobs. We have a lot of character players in this room, and that's the only reason we're here right now. We haven't had that in the past. Every player on the team can pick up anybody else, simply by saying something or doing something on the ice. We're not looking around, waiting for somebody else to pick us up."

For the fourth time in as many series, the Penguins dropped the opening game, 5–4. Neal Broten's second goal of the game late in the second period broke a 3–3 tie and the Penguins converted just one of eight power-play chances while Coffey missed his 10th game with a broken jaw. Recchi's points streak ended at 14 games, a remarkable run for a guy earning just $105,000.

Coffey returned for Game 2, playing only on the power play as the Penguins again went 1-for-8, but that one goal from

Stevens gave Pittsburgh a 2–0 lead late in the first period. Mike Modano answered for the North Stars in the opening minute of the second period, and Minnesota slowly began taking over the game. Losing the first two games of a series on the road, as they had done in Boston, was one thing; losing the first two games of the Final at home might have given the Penguins an insurmountable deficit. "If you could pick one time in a game we needed a lift from our best player," Bourque said, "it was right then and there."

And Lemieux provided it. Taking a pass from Bourque in his own zone, Lemieux whisked through the neutral zone and skated one-on-two against defensemen Shawn Chambers and Neil Wilkinson. He deked Chambers to the outside—Chambers had caught him on an outside move earlier in the game—and drew the puck back to the inside on his backhand between Chambers' skates. Chambers waved desperately with his stick and fell down, and Lemieux by this point was already beyond Wilkinson. Goaltender Jon Casey, seeing Lemieux now alone and on his forehand, was out aggressively at the top of his crease, but Lemieux went to the backhand while falling down to score what most consider his signature goal with the Penguins.

Said Stevens, "Mario is Mario...only he could do that." Stevens added another goal 1:28 later and the Penguins evened the series, 4–1.

Lemieux was still the story in Game 3—because he didn't play. He took the pre-game warmup but his shocking scratch from the lineup with back spasms suffered after bending over to tie and untie his skates put the game under a completely different lens. "It was like Christmas morning, practically," the North Stars' Stew Gavin told the *Minneapolis Star-Tribune*. Johnson put Trottier between Lemieux's regular linemates,

Errey and Recchi, but Pittsburgh managed only 15 shots through two periods and fell, 3–1.

Lemieux, who was in some pain in the first-round series against New Jersey, was still in pain. Patrick ordered Lemieux not to talk about his status, and while it seemed unlikely he would stay out of the lineup, neither was it business as usual for him preparing to play. Before Game 4, Lemieux summoned Tracy Luppe, part of the Penguins' game night locker room staff. "He's like, 'Red, come in the training room with me and grab my skates,'" remembered Luppe. "I said, 'What's going on?' He goes, 'You have to tie my skates or I can't play. I can't bend over to tie my skates.' I think it was Coff who goes, 'Yep, Red, everything is on your shoulders right now. We don't win, it's your fault.' I was nervous, the best player in the world, the team is in the Final..."

Everyone in Pittsburgh was nervous, but Lemieux returned in Game 4 with a goal and assist in a 5–3 victory that ended Minnesota's eight-game home winning streak, evened the series and quieted talk of Cup parades and White House visits that had been in the Minneapolis air. The Penguins scored three times in the opening 2:58, becoming the quickest team to reach three goals in a Cup Final game. Power-play goals by Brian Propp and Modano 5:15 apart late in the second period made it a 4–3 game, however, and Loney took a high-sticking major with 6:57 left that opened the door for Minnesota to tie it. "I thought, if they win, I won't be able to live in Pittsburgh. I'll have to move," Loney said. But Pittsburgh did not allow a single shot for 3:49, at which time Casey took an interference penalty to negate the power play, and Bourque added an empty-netter.

Pittsburgh chased Casey by scoring four times in the opening 14 minutes of Game 5, Recchi scoring twice and Lemieux once while adding two assists. But Barrasso left the game after the first period with a groin injury, and a seemingly comfortable 5–2 lead after two periods was endangered by Ulf Dahlén and Dave Gagner goals early in the third. The Penguins didn't finish off their 6–4 victory until Loney scored with 1:39 left. "We just couldn't contain them," Minnesota coach Bob Gainey said.

With the Stanley Cup at the Met Center in Minneapolis for Game 6 and Barrasso back in goal, the start followed a now-familiar script. Broten took a penalty nine seconds in, and the Penguins turned it into a power-play goal and scored three times in the opening 14 minutes to chase Casey again. Pittsburgh got three more goals in a span of 5:29 late in the second period, and Lemieux finished the playoffs with points in each of his last 18 games by providing a goal and three assists—his 44 playoff points were the second-most in one playoff year in NHL history. The resulting 8–0 victory was the largest margin of victory ever in a Cup-clinching game, and the Penguins had reached what Johnson called "the top of the mountain," fittingly doing so in the town where he was raised.

"We lost our best player early in the season, and in the playoffs we had injuries again and just kept playing," Coffey said. "We had 20 guys who played their hardest every night. That's what makes a great team, a Stanley Cup team. We deserved to win."

15

Back from the Brink, 1992

While Penguins' fans basked in the glory of the team's first Stanley Cup in the summer of 1991, general manager Craig Patrick faced a busy off-season. He had eight players hitting free agency and a dozen others entering their option years, and he was also serving as general manager of Team USA for the September Canada Cup tournament that would include games in Pittsburgh.

The Penguins lost Randy Gilhen to Minnesota in the expansion draft to fill the roster of the new San Jose Sharks, a draft in which the North Stars were able to participate under terms of a complex arrangement with the NHL that granted Minnesota owners George and Gordon Gund the expansion team while they sold the North Stars to a group headed by Norman Green. Scott Young also left to play in Europe, and the ever-patient Patrick signed no new deals for two and a half months, no doubt influenced by the impending $65 million sale of the team to Howard Baldwin and Morris Belzberg—an NHL record transaction that wasn't official until Nov. 18.

Left unprotected in the 1991 Expansion Draft, Bryan Trottier re-signed in mid-August, and Gordie Roberts, Gord Dineen and Jim Paek re-signed in early September. Mark Recchi did not sign until mid-September, and Kevin Stevens signed in late September. Ron Francis did not reach a new contract until Oct. 25 and missed the first nine games of the season, and there continued to be rumors the new owners were planning to trade players for cash.

So there was a lot of significant business going on around the Penguins, but it all seemed meaningless on the night of Aug. 29, when coach "Badger" Bob Johnson was rushed to Mercy Hospital and then underwent a two-hour operation the following morning to remove a brain tumor. "I'm devastated," Patrick said. Said backup goaltender Wendell Young, "It doesn't seem fair. It's a rough thing to try and sort out. You think the upcoming season is so important, contract this and contract that...it puts life in perspective."

Tim Taylor assumed Johnson's duties as coach of Team USA in the Canada Cup, and Scotty Bowman oversaw the Penguins' training camp and was expected to be formally named the team's coach at some point while Johnson remained hospitalized with brain cancer. Johnson, who doctors discovered also had a second tumor that hadn't yet been removed, could not speak but wrote down his thoughts on facing Sweden when Taylor and Patrick visited him in the hospital. He was always a coach.

Johnson attended the Penguins' Sept. 19 exhibition game against Calgary in Denver, and the entire Penguins team visited their coach in his off-season home of Colorado Springs, Colo., four days later. But the 60-year-old coaching legend, inducted into the U.S. Hockey Hall of Fame six weeks earlier, passed away on Nov. 26 at his home.

"You look back at what he's done for this city and this team in one year, and it's pretty incredible," Mario Lemieux said at the time of Johnson's death. "Everybody liked him, and I think that everybody who played for him had a lot of respect for him. The way he came in and was always positive in any situation, it brought a lot of confidence to everybody. It changed the whole outlook of what we were trying to achieve. We're really thankful he was a part of our lives."

Lemieux was thinking about Johnson even 16 years later, after announcing his retirement in the spring of 1997. "He really turned the franchise around in bringing a winning attitude to the franchise," he said. "He really helped my career the first day he stepped into Pittsburgh. I own him a lot. I owe him two Stanley Cups."

The Penguins added a patch to their sweaters, "Badger 1931–1991," and painted his famous mantra, "It's a great day for hockey," on the ice at the Civic Arena for the Penguins' next home game, where it remained for the entire season. That game, played against New Jersey the day after Johnson's death, included a candlelight pre-game ceremony featuring Karla Bonoff's touching "Goodbye My Friend," and many at the rink were in tears.

Getting back to hockey had been difficult for the Penguins. Bowman was not named interim coach until days before the season opener, and the Penguins won just five of their first 14 games and were learning the reality that every opponent now had a different level of application when playing the defending champions. Shortly after Francis' contract was finally signed, they began to look more like themselves, winning 17 of 24 games. "What we have to do, and I know what Bob would want us to do," said goaltender Tom Barrasso, "is to go on and try to win another Cup, to try and put together the type of dynasty here that he would want to be a part of."

Knee injuries to Trottier, Jiří Hrdina and Paul Stanton caused them each to miss a month, but Recchi and Stevens rebounded from sluggish starts and Jaromír Jágr was becoming a much bigger offensive presence with 30 points in his first 25 games. Mullen scored 16 goals over a 16-game stretch from late November through late December, including back-to-back four-goal games Dec. 23 and 26. But beginning with a New Year's Eve home loss to New Jersey, the Penguins won just four of 19 games as two familiar problems returned: Lemieux was missing time with back pain, and the Penguins were leaking in goals to the tune of 4.4 per game.

As he had done the previous season, Patrick made another bold move, in mid-February trading Paul Coffey to the Kings for defensemen Jeff Chychrun, Brian Benning and the Kings' first-round 1992 draft pick. He then sent Benning, the pick and Recchi to Patrick Division rival Philadelphia for right wing Rick Tocchet, defenseman Kjell Samuelsson and goaltender Ken Wregget. While moving on from two gifted players and a first-round pick, the Penguins got bigger and tougher while changing the makeup of their defense corps.

"We've definitely been known as a wheeling, skating offensive team, and today's deal definitely turned that around a little bit to give us more balance," Gordie Roberts said. Coffey had been the subject of trade rumors for much of the season, and the man who in mid-October had passed Denis Potvin as the leading all-time scorer among NHL defensemen admitted it had affected his play.

"I was out on the ice last night. I stayed till about 2 a.m.," Coffey said after the trade, "just doing stuff, packing my sticks and that. I went out on the ice by myself, just looked around. It was dark...seeing that little thing about Bob (Johnson), that was touching, taking a look up at the ceiling and seeing the Stanley Cup banner. That's the thing I'm going to remember."

Recchi was shocked by the trades, which multiple media outlets outside of Pittsburgh reported also included cash coming to the Penguins. His good friend Stevens held nothing back in reaction to Recchi's departure. "We definitely needed some help somewhere," said Stevens, who had been numbed by the trade of friend John Cullen the previous season, "but I don't know if this is the way we should have gone about it. Recchi turned down more money in Philadelphia at the beginning of the year, figuring he was giving something back to the Penguins, and this happened...it just goes to show you that you've got to look out for yourself." Added Trottier, "The Recchi trade was a tough pill to swallow. When he left, there was some frustration."

Samuelsson played a simple but effective game for the Penguins, and Tocchet was an injection of skill and toughness that made a huge difference for the team. Tocchet the following season put up career highs for goals and points, and during his Pittsburgh career he averaged almost three penalty minutes per game while putting up 1.19 points per game, the latter figure surpassed only by Lemieux, Jágr, Coffey and Sidney Crosby.

The Penguins didn't win any of their first four games after the trade, and by the end of February, Pittsburgh held a one-point lead over the New York Islanders for the fourth and final playoff spot in the division. The transition from the effervescent Johnson to the staid Bowman had not been easy for the Penguins, who didn't like the slow pace of Bowman's practices, and before long Bowman was rarely on the ice for practices and let assistants run them—an arrangement Patrick said was his idea—while Bowman used the time to visit his family in Buffalo, which had been a priority for him when joining the Penguins' organization the previous season and remained so. On game nights, said assistant coach Pierre McGuire, "Players knew Scotty would crush the other coaches with matchups."

But the Penguins pulled themselves together and began winning, including a notable March 15 game at Chicago Stadium in which Tocchet, his jaw broken when hit by a Lemieux shot, returned to the game and scored two goals 7:23 apart in the third period to erase a 3–1 deficit and spark the Penguins to a 4–3 victory. It was part of an 11–3–1 stretch by Pittsburgh that was renewing optimism for another long Cup run—at least until the afternoon of April 1, when the Penguins' stop-and-start season stopped again.

That day NHL players voted nearly unanimously to strike, their collective bargaining negotiations with the league stunted by disagreements over the length of a new deal, pension issues and NHL merchandise and trading card marketing and licensing, among other items. The strike came little more than four months into Baldwin's ownership of the team, and the Penguins' need to meet budgets with playoff revenue was probably more intense than that of most other teams. Trottier, president of the NHL Players Association, told the *Pittsburgh Press* he believed trading card royalties were the biggest issue and that players wanted a larger portion of what they were sharing with owners. The strike was settled after 10 days, saving the season, and Baldwin certainly played an important negotiating role in enabling the Penguins a chance to defend their championship.

Pittsburgh lost two of its last three regular-season games after the strike but finished third in the division, and there was some serious levity in their meaningless final game in

New York against the Rangers, a 7–1 loss. Barrasso was given the night off with the playoffs just days away, and Bowman wanted both Wregget and Young to get action in the game. So he told them beforehand he would be replacing them at regular intervals throughout the game, which he did nine times during breaks in play. But the goaltenders took it to another level early in the third period when they decided to change on the fly, a move most people had never seen in an NHL game.

The Penguins dropped the first game of a playoff series for the fifth consecutive time when Washington's Peter Bondra scored twice in a 3–1 Capitals' win in Game 1 of the first round. Pittsburgh seemed destined for a quick response when it scored two power-play goals in the opening eight minutes of Game 2, but instead the Penguins then surrendered six unanswered goals in an ugly 6–2 loss in which Bondra had three more points. Lemieux recorded a hat trick in a 6–4 Game 3 victory back home in Pittsburgh, although the game was tense late when Al Iafrate and Kevin Hatcher scored goals 3:51 apart before Lemieux's empty-netter.

Then the wheels nearly fell off, with Dino Ciccarelli scoring four goals in a 7–2 Washington rout in Game 4, as the Capitals chased Barrasso for a 3–1 series lead. Washington returned home with a chance to knock out the defending champs, and the Capitals built a 2–1 lead halfway through Game 5. The Penguins were on the road and on the brink, a mere 30 minutes from elimination. But the Capitals didn't score another goal that night as the Penguins fully meshed with a dramatic tactical switch they made before the game, deciding to play a neutral-zone trap they called a 1-4 delay.

"If we couldn't establish an instantaneous forecheck, we just backed off in the neutral zone. We would lock lanes," said McGuire. "We really frustrated their guys, especially their defense who liked to jump up and try to manufacture offense. We took those defensemen out of the game because they couldn't beat our guys up the ice. That's where the magic changed in that series."

Bowman called the Capitals' defense corps of Kevin Hatcher, Al Iafrate, Sylvain Côté and Calle Johansson "really special" and said the Penguins had to react. "We didn't want to change a team that was high scoring, but at the same time we were up against a team that had something that most teams didn't have," Bowman said. "If we wouldn't have tightened up...we talked a lot with Mario, Mario was always listening to everybody, so we said we're going to have to do a different style to beat this team, and he said he's willing to try it and willing to support it."

So Lemieux covered the strategy in a players-only meeting in the dressing room before the game, and Jay Caufield said the meeting "in my opinion turned the series around." The Penguins turned it into a 5–2 victory as Errey scored the first of four unanswered goals midway through the second period and former Capitals' defenseman Murphy scored the game-winner late in the period on the power play. Errey finished with two goals.

"All their defensemen were killing us joining the rushes. We weren't even competing with them," said Errey. "I had probably one of the best playoff games I ever played, given the importance of it. It was almost 'less is more.' I'm not in there trying to run people over behind their goal line unless I'm 100 percent going to get the puck, I'm just retreating and they're just coming into our trap. It was something that was pretty unfamiliar for Penguins hockey."

Remembered Hatcher, "Of all teams to go into a trap and be very successful at it, them...it really surprised us."

The Penguins' application of their new system was bumpy in Game 6 back in Pittsburgh, however. On the way to a four-point night, Stevens scored two early goals, but the Capitals responded with four unanswered goals, the first three in a span of 5:49 late in the first. But Mullen and Bourque tied it with goals midway through the second period, and Lemieux scored the final two goals of the game for five points on the night and a wild 6–4 victory that evened the series.

In Washington for Game 7, Lemieux beat goaltender Don Beaupre shorthanded late in the first period and Jágr's power-play goal midway through the second period was the series winner in a 3–1 victory as the Penguins became the 11th team in NHL history to overcome a 3–1 series deficit. Washington managed only 19 shots, and Lemieux finished the series with 10 assists and 17 points, both team records. The Penguins had ended the series in a more typical Pittsburgh way, converting five of their last six power-play chances.

"I think a lot of people doubted us, including you guys," Stevens told reporters, "yet we never lost faith in ourselves. That's why we're winners. We're not losers. We're winners, and we knew we were winners."

Next up were the New York Rangers, who had won the Presidents' Trophy with the NHL's best regular-season record and had outlasted New Jersey in a seven-game first-round series. Francis' first goal of the playoffs midway through the second period was the winner in a 4–2 Game 1 victory at Madison Square Garden, but everything about Game 2 was a disaster for the Penguins.

Just seconds into a power play at 5:05 of the opening period, with the Penguins already ahead, 1–0, the Rangers' Adam Graves slashed Lemieux, who left the game with a broken left hand that knocked him out of the series and ended his streak of recording a point in each of his last 25 playoff games. Thirteen minutes later, Kris King leveled Mullen, who suffered a season-ending knee injury. Bowman used only nine of his 10 forwards the rest of the way, but the Penguins nevertheless built a 2–1 lead after two periods only to allow three late goals in a 4–2 loss, King getting the game-winning goal. "A lot of things going on out there," said Troy Loney, "were totally absurd."

Graves, who said he had no intent to cause injury and was not known as a reckless player, became public enemy No. 1 in Pittsburgh as the series shifted there, and he was in the New York lineup while the NHL continued to weigh a possible suspension. On cue, he scored the opening goal of Game 3. Without Lemieux and Mullen, the Penguins' power play went 1-for-10 in a 6–5 loss with King again getting the decisive goal at 1:29 of overtime. The Rangers had played two games without injured captain Mark Messier and had won them both, had the series lead and the prospect of hosting two of the final three games of the series if need be.

Of all the times the Penguins seemed to be in trouble during their 1991 and 1992 Cup championship runs, Bourque said he felt this situation was the most serious of all. "That Rangers team was loaded," he said. "They had guys who could punish us. We were without Joey and Mario."

Incredibly, the Penguins didn't lose another game.

Graves was suspended for four games prior to Game 4, but Messier returned to the lineup to score twice and New York held a 4–2 lead with less than 10 minutes to play. Then Francis completed arguably the most impactful game of his Pittsburgh career. He beat goaltender Mike Richter from outside the blue line with 9:33 left, and Jágr used his strength on the puck to set up Loney's tying goal just 1:25 later. New York coach Roger Neilson yanked Richter, and at 2:47 of overtime, after Jágr had drawn a penalty, Francis deflected a Larry Murphy shot past John Vanbiesbrouck for the hat trick and a 5–4 victory.

When Francis went home after the game, he saw seven or eight hats hanging on a tree in his front yard. By the following morning, he said, "there were about 30 hats in the tree. For a second-round series, that was as emotional as it could get."

In New York for Game 5, the Jágr Show continued. He scored on an early penalty shot to give Pittsburgh a 2–0 lead, then scored the game-winning goal with just 5:33 left for a 3–2 victory. Two nights later, Jágr delivered another game-winning goal midway through the second period of a 5–1 victory in which Barrasso made 33 saves, eliminating the Rangers and pushing the Penguins back to the Wales Conference Final. Then, facing the Bruins again, Jágr delivered another dagger with a goal at 9:44 of overtime that gave Pittsburgh a 4–3 win in Game 1.

"Jágr went to a level that blew me away," Bourque said. "That's when he became a superstar. Before that, he was a good young player with potential, but in 1992, every shift he was on the ice, you're like, 'This guy is taking over the game.' It was next level."

Expected to miss four to six weeks with his broken hand, Lemieux missed only two weeks and returned to score two goals and set up another in a 5–2 Game 2 win over the Bruins. The Penguins then went to Boston and completed a sweep, giving them eight straight playoff wins over Boston dating to their 1991 series. Lemieux had eight points in just three games of the series, while Jágr also finished with eight points.

Game 3 saw Stevens, the Boston-area boy whom the Bruins had signed to an offer sheet before the season, score four goals. The first of those was a thing of beauty, as Lemieux picked up a rebound in the Pittsburgh slot, quickly turned and took off with

Jágr on his left and Stevens on his right. Lemieux sped through the neutral zone and skated between the Boston defensemen, then went around Jim Wiemer just inside the Bruins' blue line, dropping the puck to Jágr on the edge of the left circle. Jágr quickly fed it to Stevens, who was streaking toward the net from the right circle, and he sent it past Moog. The speed, size and skill of those three, on a rush like that at this point in their careers, made them practically indefensible.

Game 4 featured another incredible Lemieux goal, this one shorthanded to make it 2–0 in the first period. Again creating offense from defense, Lemieux deflected a Joé Juneau pass from the far right circle, gathered it at the top of the circle and pushed it toward Ray Bourque, who was skating with his back to Lemieux and had no time to turn around. Lemieux pushed the puck between Bourque's skates, picked up the puck in front of Bourque, fended off a hook and then, right on top of Moog, quickly pinged the puck to the top corner of the net. Asked legendary Canadian play-by-play man Bob Cole, "Have you ever seen such finesse?"

The Penguins had won seven consecutive playoff games, but they had nothing on the Chicago Black Hawks, who had won a league-record 11 straight after sweeping Detroit and Edmonton in the second and third rounds, respectively. The teams meeting in the Stanley Cup Final had each finished the regular season with 87 points, but Pittsburgh began the series at home by virtue of having more victories, including that dramatic 4–3 win in Chicago in March that now loomed even larger. "If we lose that game, we don't open the Stanley Cup Final in Pittsburgh, we open in Chicago," McGuire said.

Playing in their first Cup Final in 19 years, the Hawks jumped out to a 3–0 lead in the opening 14 minutes of Game 1 and were still holding a 4–1 lead late in the second period before Tocchet and Lemieux scored 59 seconds apart to make it a one-goal game. Jágr then delivered arguably the most aesthetically beautiful goal of his Pittsburgh career to tie the game with just 4:55 left. He intercepted a Brent Sutter pass just above the left circle in the Chicago zone, then stickhandled around Dirk Graham on his way to the left wing boards, pausing to scan the situation in front of him. When Sutter then charged at him, Jágr put the puck between Sutter's skates, then regained possession of it right before František Kučera could reach it, getting around Kučera on the backhand and then skating toward the edge of the right circle before beating Ed Belfour with a backhander. It was a stunning display of skill.

"Probably the greatest goal I've ever seen," Lemieux said later. "He can beat a guy one-on-one at will." Added Tocchet, "There aren't enough adjectives in the vocabulary to keep describing Jaromír's goals."

Pittsburgh had to kill off a penalty to Larry Murphy two minutes later, and Lemieux then drew a penalty on defenseman Steve Smith with 18 seconds remaining. Francis won a draw that bounded back to Murphy at the right point, and Belfour stopped his wrist shot from the top of the circle. But Chicago's Steve Larmer had drifted out toward the blue line, and Lemieux left his post at the left point and headed for the net, depositing the rebound of Murphy's shot into the net with 13 seconds to play, a goal etched indelibly on the minds of Pittsburgh fans for a 5–4 victory that turned the series inexorably toward the Penguins.

"When you've got fellas like Jaromír and Mario, there's always time left," said Bowman, whose team became the second in NHL history and first in 48 years to rally from a 4–1 deficit and win a Stanley Cup Final game. Decades later, he said he could "still see the goals going in in my mind."

The Game 1 victory sucked the air right out of the Black Hawks. Errey scored a shorthanded goal midway through the first period of Game 2, and Lemieux scored twice inside three minutes late in the second for a 3–1 Pittsburgh victory, and Barrasso stopped 27 shots for a 1–0 win when the series returned to Chicago for Game 3. Graham recorded a hat trick in less than 10 minutes of the opening period of Game 4, but the Penguins had answered with three of their own goals to chase Belfour. Murphy and Francis scored goals 3:08 apart early in third period and Pittsburgh won, 6–5, to earn its second consecutive Stanley Cup title and match the Hawks' record 11-game playoff winning streak.

"I don't think any team—with the parity today, because of the (salary) cap—will ever win 11 straight to win the Stanley Cup again," said McGuire. The Penguins' streak continued the following playoff season and eventually reached 14, still the NHL record.

"Last year was great, but this year is even sweeter," Loney said amidst a loud dressing room celebration. Tense contract situations, Johnson's death, a change in ownership, inconsistent play, the transition to a new coach, the trade of the well-liked Recchi, a players' strike, the loss of three of their first four playoff games as defending champs...it had been a trying season. Despite it all, the Penguins became the eighth team in NHL history to win consecutive titles.

"You can't win championships with just great players," Stevens said. "You win championships with great teams. We've got a team. We've got great players, sure, but we've got a team of 25 guys who pull together every single night they put their skates on. That's the only way we can win."

The Penguins seemed poised to make it three consecutive titles the following season, winning the Presidents' Trophy as the league's best regular-season team with a franchise-record 119 points. This included an NHL-record 17-game winning streak, highlighted by a memorable 10–4 victory at Madison Square Garden over the Rangers on April 9, their 16th straight win to break the New York Islanders' previous mark of 15 straight set 11 years earlier.

Lemieux scored five goals in that game, which remains arguably the highest point ever reached by a Penguins team: they were two-time defending Cup champions, already the best team in the 1992–93 season and now owners of the longest winning streak the league had ever witnessed. The April 23, 1993, issue of *The Hockey News* included this headline on the cover: "The Unbeatable Foe, Pittsburgh Prohibitive Favorite to Win Cup."

But after a first-round win over New Jersey, the Penguins were shocked in the second round by the New York Islanders, who played virtually the entire series without their best player, injured Pierre Turgeon, and received terrific Game 7 goaltending from Glenn Healy. David Volek's overtime goal in Game 7 at the Civic Arena won the series after dramatic goals 2:47 apart by Francis and Tocchet had tied the game in the final four minutes of regulation.

"I'm not a handyman per se, but my dad was in town for those playoffs and he is, and for about three days after I just hammered nails in building a swing set for my kids, because I had so much frustration I had to get out," remembered Francis. "The best team in Pittsburgh I ever played on was the '93 team."

Theories abounded the Penguins had used too much energy focusing on their late winning streak, which didn't change their playoff positioning, but Stevens doesn't buy that. "We just ran into a tough series," said Stevens, who left Game 7 on a stretcher with frightening injuries to his face when he struck the ice after being knocked cold by a collision with defenseman Rich Pilon. "We couldn't get through it. That was by far the best team we had. Game 6, it was 4–4 in their place and they come back to beat us (7–5). That was the game we needed to win. We needed to win the sixth game so we wouldn't get to a seventh game where Healy could play his brains out and beat us."

Murphy, who later won two more Cups with Detroit, still calls Game 7 "the most disappointing loss of my career, by far. To this day," he said, "it still rubs me the wrong way. We were winning at the end of the season, but we were...developing bad habits. It was just coming too easy, so to speak. We were loosey-goosey. We just lulled ourselves into a sense of complacency. Everybody worked hard, but our mindset was what hurt us at the end.

"It wasn't our commitment. I think it sat in the back of our head that, you know, it's a bit of an exaggeration, but we're just so good we just have to show up. I think that (win streak) was the worst thing that could have happened to us. We would have been much better off if things were a lot rougher for us going into the playoffs. That finish came back to bite us at the end of it all."

16

Youth Is Served, 2009

In the fall of 2008, the Penguins had every reason to be optimistic about the season ahead of them. They had reached the Stanley Cup Final months earlier, falling to the Detroit Red Wings in six games with a young core of talent driving their playoff success under third-year coach Michel Therrien: Marc-André Fleury in goal and Sidney Crosby, Evgeni Malkin and Jordan Staal down the middle, with defensemen Ryan Whitney and Kris Letang showing real promise. The prospect of another long playoff run was nothing if not reasonable, despite some of their off-season losses.

Forwards Ryan Malone, Gary Roberts and Adam Hall all signed as free agents with Tampa Bay, and winger Jarkko Ruutu signed as a free agent with Ottawa. General manager Ray Shero's focus had been on using his salary cap space to sign free agent winger Marián Hossa, whom he had acquired at the 2008 trade deadline from Atlanta and who rocked the 2008 playoffs with 12 goals playing alongside Sidney Crosby—at the time, the most playoff goals ever scored by a deadline day acquisition in the ensuing post-season.

"But I couldn't really get them to engage," Shero said of his efforts discussing a contract with Hossa and his agent. "We offered him five years at $7 million. When it came out he had signed a one-year deal to go to Detroit (for $7.45 million)...that was a tough one." Hossa told the *Detroit Free Press,* "I wanted to have the best chance to win the Stanley Cup. I think the team in Detroit is something special."

While Hossa rejected the Penguins, there were plenty of other veteran players who did not. In the first six days of free agency, Shero signed wingers Miroslav Šatan (34), Matt Cooke (30), Ruslan Fedotenko (29) and Eric Godard (28), and it was just the start of Shero surrounding his young stars with older forwards whose experience could make a difference in the playoffs. He already had some veterans on defense, including Sergei Gonchar, Hal Gill, Rob Scuderi, Mark Eaton and Brooks Orpik, the latter having gained a measure of notoriety for a shift in Game 3 in the 2008 Final when he delivered four hits in the span of 15 seconds in his own zone to Kris Draper, Dallas Drake (twice) and Dan Cleary.

The Penguins' depth on defense was tested early in the season, as Whitney remained out until Christmas while recovering from foot surgery, and Gonchar suffered a shoulder separation in his first preseason game and was lost until mid-February. His injury was so bad, said Gonchar, that one doctor suggested bone replacement, which would have required a year and a half of rehabilitation.

Pittsburgh began the regular season in Stockholm, Sweden, splitting a pair of games with Ottawa as part of the NHL's

Premiere Series played in Europe, and shortly after returning to North America the Penguins went on a 9–2–1 run that gave them the league's fourth-best record. Included in that run was a memorable game in Detroit whose date—it was played on 11/11—seemed later to take on a karmic significance. Staal, the Penguins' No. 11, scored twice in the final five minutes to complete a hat trick, his third goal coming with 23 seconds left, and then set up Fedotenko's goal at 3:49 of overtime for a stunning 7–6 victory in a game the Wings led by three goals with 14 minutes left. It was the first meeting of the teams since they played for the Cup five months earlier.

By mid-November, Malkin was leading the league in scoring and Crosby was fourth. But then Fleury suffered a groin injury and missed the next 12 games, and it was the start of a 26-game stretch in which the Penguins lost 17 times. Gill (shoulder) and Tyler Kennedy (knee) also missed significant time during this stretch with injuries, and the Penguins sat three points out of a playoff spot in the second week of January. It was not where the team was expected to be, injuries notwithstanding, and when they went into Toronto on Feb. 14 and were shelled, 6–2, the Penguins fell five points out of a playoff spot.

Shero had seen enough. He fired Therrien and replaced him with Dan Bylsma, who had started the season as their AHL coach in Wilkes-Barre/Scranton. If there was risk involved, Shero wasn't thinking about it. "It was probably risky not to do something as well," he said. "You make a decision like that, you don't know if it's best. It's not easy. That was a difficult thing. To see how the team responded...never in my wildest dreams did I think that probably would happen."

What happened was the Penguins finished the regular season by going 18–3–4 in the remaining 25 games under Bylsma, including a 10–1–1 mark at home to finish second in the Atlantic Division. By earning 40 of a possible 50 points in this stretch, these Penguins had matched what the 1992–93 Penguins did by going 19–4–2 over their last 25 games—which included an 18-game unbeaten streak and a league-record 17-game winning streak.

But the roster that was turning things around was also different. Gonchar's first game back in the lineup was Therrien's last as coach, and Shero in late February sent Whitney to Anaheim for veteran winger Chris Kunitz, 29, and young winger Eric Tangradi, and then at the deadline acquired 38-year-old winger Bill Guerin from the New York Islanders and claimed 31-year-old center Craig Adams off waivers from Chicago. It was a continuation of Shero's summer moves to add experience to his forward group.

An undrafted native of Regina, Sask., Kunitz had already won a Stanley Cup with Anaheim in 2007, but only after he remade himself as a committed NHL player. A star at Ferris State, he was signed as a free agent by Anaheim in April 2003. But coming out of the lockout, he was put on waivers and claimed by Atlanta in early October 2005, then waived by the Thrashers two weeks later and reclaimed by the Ducks.

"I had made a point that summer of 2005, 'I've got to make this (Anaheim) team,'" remembered Kunitz, but he didn't. He played a preseason game for the Ducks in San Jose in late September, flew to Atlanta after being claimed on waivers, traveled with the Thrashers to Washington but was scratched, returned to Atlanta and made his Thrashers' debut against Montreal, was scratched for a home game against Toronto and then flew to New York for his final game with the Thrashers before returning to Atlanta and being waived again. The Ducks immediately assigned him to their new minor-league affiliate in Portland, Me.

"I was like touching all of the U.S. Not knowing what you know now, I needed to figure something out," Kunitz said. "I needed to get a little bit more professional. I had to be a little bit more serious. It wasn't just playing hockey that you were used to. It just took me a long time to figure that out. I didn't know that what it takes now was a lot more than I was giving. I needed those bumps in the road to be able to figure it out.

"Then getting picked back up by Anaheim…I remember going to Chicago, where my girlfriend was, I got my stuff and was driving out to Portland, and I picked up a buddy in Detroit and I was like, 'Man, I think I might have to get a job. This sucks.' After Portland…I figured out that even if I had to go hit Rob Blake, that made more sense than him hitting me for no reason. So then it kind of just clicked and things worked out. I got to make my career from there."

Kunitz played only five games in Portland—the last minor-league games of his career—and was recalled by Anaheim in late October. He had 19 goals in 67 games with the Ducks that season, then scored 25 the following season, playing in 13 playoff games as the Ducks beat Ottawa to win their first Cup. By February 2009, Kunitz had also represented Canada at the 2008 World Championships and felt ensconced in Anaheim, where he had developed a reputation as a terrific forechecker, a player who could play both ends of the ice and get you 20 goals.

"I always liked being in on the forecheck, I didn't mind being the first guy back on the backcheck," Kunitz said. "I liked to run into things. I didn't need the puck a whole lot to have success. I learned that in Anaheim by playing with Andy McDonald and (Teemu) Selänne. I didn't have the skillset to be a dangler or a pure shooter. I figured out what's going to get me on the ice—that's being the net-front guy, that's being the forecheck guy, that's getting the puck and getting it to the player who was paid really well."

Then came the trade to Pittsburgh.

"It was kind of crushing," Kunitz said. "I had signed a four-year deal, we bought a house, my wife was pregnant, we were in Boston and I got traded on her birthday. Ended up scoring in that first game, and it kind of kept growing from there. I had a personal relationship with Bylsma, he was an assistant coach of mine in the minors (in Cincinnati). I knew him, I felt comfortable with him. I liked him. He and (assistant general manager) Chuck Fletcher knew how I played the game and it kind of put me in a good scenario to excel in that area. That was something they were missing. It was a good fit."

Guerin, who had won the Stanley Cup with New Jersey in 1994–95, eliminating the Penguins in the second round along the way, was also a perfect fit in the Pittsburgh dressing room. "It was awesome," Guerin said. "So many young guys around and that youthful energy did a lot for me. They were young guys, but young guys who were elite players. They were great to be around."

Two of those elite players, Crosby and Malkin, had goals in a 4–1 Game 1 victory over Philadelphia to open the playoffs, and Guerin was the hero of Game 2, his second goal of the game winning it at 18:29 of overtime, 3–2. Simon Gagné had a pair of goals, including the winner, in a 6–3 Flyers' victory in Game 3 back in Philadelphia, but the Penguins took Game 4 there, 3–1, by killing all eight Flyers' power plays. When Martin Biron stopped 28 shots in a 3–0 Philadelphia win back in Pittsburgh for Game 5, however, the Flyers were right back in the series and going home.

Game 6 will forever be a favorite of Pittsburgh fans, not only because of the result but also because of the emotional way in which it was achieved. Penguin-killer Mike Knuble and Joffrey Lupul scored goals 51 seconds apart late in the first period for a 2–0 Philadelphia lead, and Daniel Brière added a power-play goal early in the second period for a 3–0 lead, leaving a Game 7 looking like a certainty.

Pittsburgh winger Max Talbot at that point decided to try and turn things around himself. Talbot had already proved himself a playoff difference-maker by scoring an extra-attacker goal with 35 seconds to play in Game 5 of the 2008 Cup Final at Detroit, setting the stage for Petr Sýkora's triple overtime winner (which Sykora had predicted in the dressing room), but Talbot wouldn't be using his stick this time.

"It felt like the momentum was switching in some way," he recalled. "I remember messing up on the first goal against, it was definitely my turnover at the blue line and it gets back in our net. I know I can't score three goals in a game. So what can I do? My first thought is to ask someone to fight. I knew Dan (Carcillo) pretty well, and he's the guy who doesn't back out from a fight, so I took a chance and asked him. I was pretty lucky he said yes."

The rugged Carcillo, originally drafted by Pittsburgh in 2003, had been suspended for one game for striking Talbot on the back of the helmet with his stick at the end of Game 1, although Carcillo maintained he hit Talbot with his hand, not his stick. At any rate, he seemed a logical candidate for Talbot as he tried to engage in a fight to lift the spirits of his team.

"Obviously, I didn't win the fight," Talbot said. "I remember looking out of the corner of my eye and I see Carcillo pumping the crowd, lifting his hands in the air. I was thinking the opposite of that was to quiet the crowd." So Talbot put his index finger to his lips to encourage the Philadelphia crowd to quiet down, but that functionally futile gesture was about to become a famous image for Pittsburgh fans.

Fedotenko scored 29 seconds later, and unlikely candidate Mark Eaton followed 1:57 after that to quickly make it 3–2 game. Crosby scored late in the period, and the Flyers' three-goal lead was gone heading to the third period. "That first goal, you're happy in the box, and then the second goal and the third goal, like, this is amazing," Talbot said. "I remember looking across the ice, I see all my bench pointing at me in the box. That was a pretty special moment for the team and for me. I spoke to (Carcillo) afterwards, and at that time it was his role. He thought it was going to give energy to the crowd, which it did, but I feel like my bench got more energy in that sequence for sure."

Gonchar scored early in the third period to give the Penguins their first lead, and Crosby added an empty-netter as Pittsburgh held the Flyers to just five shots in the final period of a series-clinching 5–3 victory. The Penguins, who had beaten the Flyers in five games in the 2008 Eastern Conference Final, had now eliminated their cross-state rivals in consecutive seasons by winning eight of 11 playoff games against them.

Now the Penguins moved from one rival to the next, facing the Washington Capitals in the second round. It was the first post-season matchup for Crosby and Alexander Ovechkin, so the hype surrounding the series was huge, both locally and nationally. The Capitals, who had lost six of their previous seven playoff series against Pittsburgh, had finished with the league's fourth-best record and had home-ice advantage; only the Sharks that season had been beaten fewer times at home than Washington.

Crosby and Ovechkin both had goals in the opening period of Game 1, but Tomáš Fleischmann's third-period goal was the difference in a 3–2 Capitals' victory. Two nights later, both stars recorded the first playoff hat tricks of their careers in a 4–3 Washington victory, giving Crosby six of the Penguins' last eight playoff goals. It was a dream start to the series from an NHL marketing viewpoint, which now needed the Penguins to recover from their 0–2 hole and ensure this series could be available on television screens for as long as possible.

Gonchar said being down in a playoff series wasn't as big a deal for the Penguins because of what they had to push themselves to do once the coaching change was made late in the regular season.

"Overall, we had a spirit of fighting. We were approaching every game like it was the last one for us," he said. "We had to win so much, so that playoff approach, that fighting mentality, started early for us. Since we were into that mode, we were fighting pretty much every game before the playoffs started just to make the playoffs. Even though we were down in the series, guys weren't worried about it too much. Everybody was focusing on their task."

The Penguins rallied. Ovechkin scored again in Game 3, giving him five goals in three games, but the Penguins earned a 3–2 overtime victory at home on a goal at 11:23 by Letang after Pittsburgh blew a 2–1 lead in the final minutes of regulation. Crosby and Guerin both had a goal and an assist in a 5–3 Game 4 victory, and the series was now even heading back to Washington. Defenseman Rob Scuderi credited his teammates for "not panicking when you seem to be down and out."

Pittsburgh was, however, hurt by an injury to Gonchar's knee suffered late in the first period of Game 4 after he was hit by Ovechkin in the Pittsburgh zone. Ovechkin said he had tried a shoulder check before Gonchar moved, but Orpik told the *Pittsburgh Post-Gazette* "it definitely looked like (Ovechkin) stuck his leg out...we got the feeling that he's really trying to hurt guys at times."

Gonchar was an important player for the Penguins, a veteran who was playing up to 26 minutes a night while providing a critical complementary alternative to the team's skilled forwards on the power play. He had superb mobility at the point, able to not only distribute the puck but get off big shots from the blue line that could beat goaltenders or set the stage for tips and rebounds. During his five seasons with the Penguins, he ranked second among all NHL defensemen in points per game and first in power-play points. His time in Pittsburgh included consecutive seasons of 65 or more points, the only time in his 21-year career he accomplished this.

Gonchar missed the next two games and was forced to wear a brace for the remainder of the playoffs. "It damaged my knee ligaments, it limited my mobility and it took me some time to adjust," said Gonchar, who had points in eight of the 10 playoff games before the hit and just three of his last 12 playoff games after the hit.

Ovechkin scored twice in Game 5, but it was Malkin's goal at 3:28 of overtime that won the game for Pittsburgh, 4–3, to give the Penguins their first lead of the series. It involved some serious puck luck, as Malkin beat Sergei Fedorov wide on the right wing before his pass for a streaking Crosby hit the stick of Capitals' defenseman Tom Poti and slid past goaltender Semyon Varlamov for a power-play goal off the rush. Penguins' fans at the Verizon Center in Washington erupted, and it was back in that timeframe traveling Pittsburgh fans commonly gathered on the steps of the National Portrait Center across the street from the arena to celebrate after Pittsburgh wins.

Guerin believes that goal was a catalyst for Malkin, who was in the process of putting together one of the greatest playoff seasons in NHL history. "He got that goal against Washington, that moment right there, and then Geno went to a different level," Guerin said.

Malkin had three assists in Game 6, but this time it was Pittsburgh finding the late tying goal, by Crosby, and Washington finding the overtime winner from David Steckel at 6:22 for a 5–4 win that forced a Game 7. Pittsburgh controlled most of the play in the series, in which it outshot the Capitals by an average of more than 10 shots per game, but nevertheless it was down to 60 final minutes.

If there was a game in this series that displayed how much the Penguins had learned from their run to the 2008 Stanley Cup Final, it was Game 7 in Washington. Pittsburgh limited the Capitals, a dominant home team during the regular season, to just 19 shots and didn't take a single penalty. The Penguins outshot Washington 16–5 in an impressive first period that saw Crosby and Adams score eight seconds apart, but the tone for the game was set not by the scorers but by Fleury.

Ovechkin was on his second shift of the game when the Penguins lost the puck in the Capitals' zone, and when the puck came to center Nicklas Bäckström, Ovechkin flew the zone past Scuderi on the left wing because he knew his centerman would get him the puck, which he did. Ovechkin swooped in on a breakaway against Fleury. As Scuderi dove to reach for the puck, Ovechkin elected to skate farther toward his right before shooting, and Fleury snatched the puck out of the air, preventing an early 1–0 deficit at the 3:00 mark. Years later Fleury told The Athletic he noticed Ovechkin taking the very same approach in similar situations during a highlight reel of Ovechkin goals displayed on the Verizon Center video board before the game.

It was yet another example of the Penguins' young stars not being overwhelmed by the pressure of a moment. "Sometimes when you're younger, there's less stress, there's less pressure," Fleury said. "It was like, just go play. You try to win that one, and if not, you try to win the next one. You don't overthink stuff."

The Penguins ripped off three more goals in the opening 12 minutes of the second period, chasing Varlamov, and Crosby added a goal in the third period of a 6–2 victory. Ovechkin finished the series with eight goals and 14 points, Crosby eight goals and 13 points, Malkin two goals and 10 points. But Pittsburgh at this point in the playoffs was also getting huge contributions up and down the lineup, from Fleury to the third line of Staal, Cooke and Kennedy.

"It's vital to have each line be a part of that grinding down you need to have in the playoffs," Bylsma said. "Staal's line is probably our best line at playing in the offensive zone, getting prolonged shifts, grinding teams down. Habits make a big difference. There are certain things we talk about and try to instill in our players and when you have those habits you give yourself a better chance to have time, space and room. It's not a 'Well, we don't have a chance to make a play, get rid of it in the corner' type of situation. We practice those habits, and when you do those things you have a chance to have more space, more time and give yourself a chance to get more separation and have a scoring chance."

Carolina was up next in the Conference Final, and for the second consecutive spring the Penguins eased through the third round, this time sweeping the Hurricanes. This was the Malkin Show, as he figured in on nine of the 16 goals scored by Pittsburgh in the opening three games, 3–2 and 7–4 home wins and a 6–2 drubbing in Carolina. Of his six goals in that span, none was prettier than his unassisted hat trick goal in Game 2, arguably the most breathtaking goal he scored in any Penguins' Cup run.

Malkin won an offensive zone faceoff forward in the left circle against Matt Cullen, then beat defenseman Dennis Seidenberg to it in the left corner and took off behind the net. He emerged on the other side to cut up toward the slot, with Seidenberg behind him, before unexpectantly turning to his backhand to unleash a shot that beat goaltender Cam Ward over the left shoulder.

"We had kind of run out of gas. We had two series that went to seven games and we kind of just hit a wall against a team that was rested and ready to go and playing at a super high level," remembered Cullen. "At that point, Geno was an unstoppable player. It was pick your poison a little bit. If Geno didn't do it, it was going to be Sid. Too much firepower."

By closing out the Carolina series with a 4–1 win in Game 4, the Penguins earned a rematch in the Cup Final with Detroit, the first time the same teams had met in consecutive Finals since Edmonton and the New York Islanders in 1983 and 1984. The Red Wings again had home-ice advantage and again took a 2–0 series lead, this time with a pair of 3–1 victories in which Pittsburgh outshot Detroit in both games and had an edge in special teams play as well.

Game 2 closed with Malkin's ever-present emotions firing up and he dropped the gloves with Henrik Zetterberg. Malkin had set up the Penguins' lone goal in Game 1 and scored their only goal in Game 2. He was frustrated, but the Penguins had dropped the opening two games of the 2008 Cup Final in Detroit by a cumulative score of 7–0, which explained why they had a different feeling about emerging with the same series deficit.

"The ability of those guys to rebound, to come back, the resiliency of their mindset...the Detroit series, we're in the Finals, and we go down in the first two games," remembered Bylsma, "and players after the game are saying and telling me, and telling the group, 'We're going to win this. It's different this time.' That's a testament to everybody in that room. We had great players and we had great leadership from a lot of guys in that room."

Added Talbot, "Yes, we lost, but it was a different vibe in the room. We had so much character in that room."

The Penguins were also a driven group that didn't really consider their youth the biggest factor in their favor.

"We were young, but we were really hungry," Crosby said. "For the guys that were young, they were quick to learn, quick to adapt, had high expectations, weren't happy with just being young in the league and establishing themselves. They wanted to have an impact on the team and on winning games, and the older players surrounding us were great players in their own right but also were very supportive in helping us and teaching us and making sure we were on the right track. It was a good mix. We pushed each other, whether you were a younger guy or an older guy. Everybody understood and valued everybody's role."

Their character was on display in Game 3 back in Pittsburgh, because the Red Wings responded to an early Talbot goal with goals from Zetterberg and Johan Franzén for a 2–1 lead. But Letang tied the game before the first period was over on the power play, and Malkin earned his third assist of the game when Gonchar put Pittsburgh ahead on the power play midway through the third period of what turned out to be a 4–2 victory. Malkin had figured in on each of the first five goals scored by the Penguins in the series.

After Malkin gave the Penguins an early lead in Game 4, the Wings got goals less than two and a half minutes apart from Darren Helm and Brad Stuart for the lead, then went on the power play for nearly four minutes after consecutive penalties to Malkin and Orpik. With Orpik still in the box, however, Staal scored a massive shorthanded goal to tie the game. Taking a pass from Talbot, Staal powered through the neutral zone one-on-one against defenseman Brian Rafalski, beat him going to his right, lowering his shoulder and going from his backhand to his forehand for a shot that sailed past goaltender Chris Osgood.

That changed everything. Crosby scored less than two minutes later for a 3–2 lead, and Kennedy followed with another as the Penguins scored three times in less than six minutes for a 4–2 victory that tied the series.

The defending champs answered in a big way in Game 5 at home, scoring four goals in less than 14 minutes in the second period for a 5–0 victory in which Pittsburgh managed only 22 shots. The last three goals all came on the power play for the Red Wings, who took advantage of Pittsburgh's lack of discipline to create nine power-play chances during the game. Detroit had also been bolstered for Game 5 by the return of center Pavel Datsyuk, who had two assists after missing more than two weeks with a foot injury suffered in the Western Conference Final against Chicago.

It was a bad and unexpected stumble for the Penguins, and for the second time in two seasons, Detroit was heading to Pittsburgh for a Game 6 with the Stanley Cup in the house. But the Penguins pushed back. Kennedy set up another Staal goal early in the second period and then scored one of his own early in the third period of a 2–1 victory that evened the series. Scuderi helped preserve that lead during a net-front scramble when he went down on his knees in the Pittsburgh crease to stop a pair of attempts by Franzén with 16 seconds to play.

The entire season was down to one game, but the Penguins had won three of their last four playoff games when facing elimination going back to 2008. And they had someone in their corner who knew something about playoff resiliency and decided to let his digital voice be heard the morning of Game 7. Just days after the Final concluded, *Pittsburgh Post-Gazette* columnist Ron Cook wrote owner Mario Lemieux had sent a text to every member of the team the morning of Game 7: "This is a chance of a lifetime to realize your childhood dream to win a Stanley Cup. Play without fear and you will be successful! See you at center ice."

"That," said Gonchar, "helped big-time."

After a scoreless first period, Talbot bumped Stuart on the forecheck behind the Detroit net, and Stuart then threw a pass that went off the skate of the forechecking Malkin and right onto the stick of Talbot. Talbot avoided a stick-check from defenseman Niklas Kronwall and zipped the puck past Osgood from the bottom of the right circle for a 1–0 lead.

The Penguins limited the Wings to just six shots over the first 25 minutes of the game, but they suffered a major blow five and a half minutes into the second period when a Franzén check in the neutral zone pinned Crosby's left knee to the boards and injured him. He went to the dressing room and played only one more shift that night, midway through the third period, but he simply couldn't recover and Staal took his place centering the top line.

After killing the second of two penalties early in the period, the Penguins got another big scoring chance when Kunitz took a puck off the wall in his own zone despite the efforts of a pressuring Stuart and slid a little pass to Talbot just outside the

Pittsburgh blue line. This created a two-on-one chance against Kronwall, with Talbot skating down the left wing with Kennedy on his right. Talbot had enough time to see Osgood was off his line.

"(Kronwall) is giving me time and space, but I look at Osgood, there was a hole there. I feel like he's not in the middle of the net," remembered Talbot. "This is a shot I've taken in a lot of practices, a shot I've scored some goals on in the NHL, which is weird to shoot on the far side coming down the left as a lefty, but I knew I had that shot in my toolbox. I had one thought right before I shot, it was about Marty Brodeur, and it came into my mind quick. Marty Brodeur is good at giving (space) and then taking it away. I wondered, is Osgood doing that? But I still gotta take my best shot. Luckily, no, that was not his strategy. He was just giving it."

Talbot whipped a wrist shot past Osgood's glove for a 2–0 lead at 10:07, his eighth goal of the 2009 playoffs—he had scored just three goals in his previous 22 playoff games. Unlikely heroes are a story as old as the Stanley Cup playoffs, and Talbot was writing one of his own. He scored twice as many goals in the series (four) than anyone else on either team.

The Penguins managed only two shots over the final 29-plus minutes of the game. Jonathan Ericsson ended Fleury's shutout bid with 6:07 to play, but Fleury stopped everything else the Wings threw at him. That included, off the game's last faceoff in the Pittsburgh zone, a sneaky shot through traffic from Zetterberg in the right circle and then defenseman Nicklas Lidström's last-second shot off the resulting rebound from the bottom of the left circle—after Fleury had quickly pushed off to get to his right. "The save in the Finals against Lidström, it was unorthodox but it was just his athletic ability and competitiveness getting over there," Guerin said.

Fleury had played two Game 7s in the 2009 playoffs and delivered saves in both that are now firmly part of Penguins' lore. The stop on Lidström, his most famous save, was a particularly fitting symbolization of how quickly the Penguins had gone from promising young team to champions—just one year earlier, an emotional Fleury, racing out of the dressing room at Joe Louis Arena to take the ice for his first Stanley Cup Final game, had stumbled and fallen; now he was stopping a future Hall of Famer at the heights of Game 7 Cup drama on the same ice.

"I'm fortunate I got to live it," he said. "To learn the hard way, with all those losses and the hard times. We had good veterans along the way to help us out. It meant a lot to go to the Finals and win that one, because we started from just being young guys and losing a lot and then becoming a good team."

The Cup victory put a bow on an incredible season for Malkin, who finished the playoffs with 36 points, a single-season level surpassed by only four players in NHL history through 2025: Wayne Gretzky, Lemieux, Connor McDavid and Paul Coffey. He won the Conn Smythe Trophy as playoff MVP after winning the Art Ross Trophy as the league scoring champion.

Thus Hossa, who would later win three Cups with Chicago, was on the losing end of the Stanley Cup Final for two consecutive seasons. The player he had come to Pittsburgh with from Atlanta more than a year earlier, popular and effective winger Pascal Dupuis, remained with the Penguins and was in the Pittsburgh lineup for Game 7—after which he met Lemieux at center ice.

17
Speed Merchants, 2016

The 2014–15 season was a time of transition for the Penguins. It was general manager Jim Rutherford's first season with the team as he replaced Ray Shero, and his first move was to fire coach Dan Bylsma, who had been behind the Pittsburgh bench for 401 regular-season games, at that point the longest continuous stretch of any coach in team history. It wasn't a smooth transition on the ice, as Pittsburgh didn't qualify for the playoffs until the final night of the season and then was eliminated in just five first-round games against the New York Rangers. If they had regained some of their swagger by reaching the Eastern Conference Final two years earlier, even though they were swept by Boston, the Penguins had lost it again.

So Rutherford set about making even bolder changes for the 2015–16 season, in which more than half of the 39 players used by the team made their Penguins debuts. The team walked away from a dozen players during the summer, most of whom had played more than half the previous season with them, and Rutherford's active summer began a process which ultimately would see eight everyday players join the team via free agency or trades, including forwards Matt Cullen, Eric Fehr, Conor Sheary, Phil Kessel, Nick Bonino and Carl Hagelin and defensemen Trevor Daley and Justin Schultz. Second-year coach Mike Johnston remained in place, but the pressure on his position wasn't exactly eased when former Bruins' coach Mike Sullivan was hired to coach the Penguins' AHL affiliate in Wilkes-Barre/Scranton.

Cullen was 38 that summer and had just concluded a two-season stay with Nashville, his seventh NHL team. He had won the Stanley Cup with Carolina in 2005–06 when Rutherford was the Hurricanes' general manager, and after he left the Hurricanes to sign as a free agent with the Rangers, Rutherford re-acquired him in Carolina in the summer of 2007. So when the Penguins' GM called him again in 2015, Cullen listened.

"It was later in my career, and I was kind of uncertain if I was going to keep playing," he said. "A big part of it was Jim. I had such a good couple of experiences with him in Carolina, and he called with the opportunity. It was a chance to play for Jim and also to play in a market like Pittsburgh where it was all hockey—and you had some first-ballot Hall of Famers. It was super appealing and a really good opportunity, and I thought, 'Man I can't pass this up.' The conversation was a lot about (Rutherford saying) it feels like we're close as a team, and just helping with that leadership piece was part of it."

The Penguins scored only 11 goals in their first seven games, losing four of them, before responding with a six-game win streak, but as the early portion of the season wore on it was obvious Pittsburgh, while playing well defensively, simply could not produce goals with any consistency. On top of that, the Penguins suffered a blow in early December when winger Pascal Dupuis, who had averaged 18 goals over his first five full seasons with the team, announced his retirement.

Dupuis came to Pittsburgh with Marián Hossa in a 2008 trade deadline deal with the Atlanta Thrashers, and while Hossa was the primary focus of the deal from Pittsburgh's viewpoint, Dupuis proved to be a marvelous addition, becoming a regular linemate of Chris Kunitz and Sidney Crosby in the 2010–11 season and subsequently enjoying the best production of his NHL career. Over the last 17 games of the 2011–12 season, Dupuis put together a memorable 17-game points streak that made him the NHL's third-leading scorer in that span behind only Crosby and Evgeni Malkin.

Dupuis was a popular teammate and an important player in the Penguins' dressing room, but he then encountered some poor injury luck. He was limited to just 39 games in 2013–14 because of a knee injury and then just 16 games in 2014–15 because of a serious blood clotting issue. Dupuis tried to rebound in 2015–16 while on blood thinners but could play only 18 games before retiring.

When the Penguins approached mid-December having lost nine of their last 15 games and sitting one point out of a playoff spot, Rutherford replaced Johnston with Sullivan. "I believe he gives a little more freedom on the offensive side of the game," Rutherford said of Sullivan, who was about to become the fourth Penguins' coach to win the Stanley Cup in his first season behind their bench.

The hiring of Sullivan the previous summer to coach the Penguins' AHL affiliate in Wilkes-Barre/Scranton, technically done by associate general manager Jason Botterill, had foreseen the possibility of a coaching change in Pittsburgh. "There was some question in my mind where that was going to go," Rutherford said of Johnston's tenure. "When Jason met with me and was discussing some of the options, I told him someone having NHL experience and being capable of stepping into Pittsburgh would be a priority for us."

The Penguins were above .500 for the season at 15–10–3 when the coaching change was made, yet it didn't come as a surprise. "I went to Pittsburgh thinking we were close, and the first part of the season it sure didn't feel like we were close," said Cullen. "(Johnston) was a super-intelligent hockey mind… sometimes you can't always put your finger on why a certain coach works and a certain coach doesn't, but for whatever reason, it didn't work with that group." Bonino added that Johnston was "a great guy, but the room just wasn't responding."

Sullivan pushed the Penguins to play at a higher pace, emphasizing their forecheck, but he also realized along with Rutherford that the lineup needed some younger legs to get there. Over Sullivan's first three weeks as coach, the Penguins recalled four 23-year-old rookie forwards: Sheary, Scott Wilson, Tom Kühnhackl and Bryan Rust. Only Rust (19 games) and Wilson (one) had NHL experience among this group, and while an ankle injury in early March ended Wilson's season, the other three were all in the lineup when the Penguins won the Cup that June.

By mid-January, Rutherford had also dealt veteran forward David Perron to Anaheim for speedy winger Hagelin and sent Rob Scuderi to Chicago in a trade that brought Daley to Pittsburgh. Rutherford wasn't done, but the Penguins were changing and so were their results. They didn't get an immediate "bump" from the coaching change, losing each of their first four games under Sullivan, but the Penguins then earned points in nine of their next 11 games, one of their two regulation losses coming in Chicago against the defending Cup champion Blackhawks.

From Jan. 17 to the end of the regular season, the Penguins had the NHL's best record, winning 28 of 39 games. During this second-half surge, Crosby led all NHL scorers with 51 points while Kris Letang, in the midst of his best season, was tied for third with 39 points. Pittsburgh had seven different players contribute 10 or more goals over this stretch, which was important as Malkin missed 25 games with injuries and Bonino and Fehr also had significant injuries. Rutherford made his last trade in late February, acquiring Schultz from Edmonton for a third-round pick—an absolute steal.

That the Penguins' speed and conditioning was playing a critical role in their success by wearing down opponents was never more evident than a six-game stretch from late January through early February in which they three times won games late in which they had trailed by two goals. Down 2–0 at home to Philadelphia on Feb. 21, Pittsburgh earned a 4–3 win as Kessel scored twice; down 3–1 at home to Vancouver two nights later, the Penguins won, 5–4, behind a hat trick from Malkin and four third-period goals; and in Florida on Feb. 6, Pittsburgh trailed 2–0 with six minutes to play but won, 3–2 in overtime, thanks to two goals from Letang, including the game-winner at 1:27. There were more such comebacks on the near horizon, as the Penguins twice in eight days down the stretch overcame three-goal deficits to beat the Sabres and Senators.

But two other major developments unfolded beginning in late February that had major impacts on the Penguins' fate this season.

The first was the final recall of promising rookie goaltender Matt Murray from the AHL in late February. In his first full

AHL season in 2014–15, Murray had imprinted his name all over the AHL record book. He posted 12 shutouts, most ever by an AHL rookie; he set the AHL record for longest shutout sequence (304:11); and he won both Rookie of the Year and Goaltender of the Year post-season awards, having led the league in goals-against average (1.58) and save percentage (.941). Murray had started four games in late December while Marc-André Fleury was out with a concussion, but with this recall his time in Wilkes-Barre/Scranton was over.

"You knew he was a talented player coming in, but I would say it was impressive coming in right out of junior, the way that he played," recalled Wilkes-Barre/Scranton coach John Hynes. "He kind of took command of the net, and you saw the ability that he had. But his ability to make key saves at key times, to play well in big moments, that was something else. We just saw him get better and better, and when he got to the NHL, he was truly ready to play and performed at a high level."

Murray supplanted Jeff Zatkoff as Fleury's backup in late February and won three of his next four starts, and when Fleury went down with another concussion in early April, Murray started the last five games of the regular season, winning the first four and then leaving the regular-season finale with an upper-body injury. The goaltending depth which Murray and Fleury provided the team would soon turn out to be essential, and Murray had the ultimate teammate in Fleury.

"He was a huge role model for me," Murray said. "I tried to not talk his ear off too much, but just getting to watch him, the way he operates, the way he practices, the way he prepares himself, the way he conducts himself in the media interviews… it was just his professionalism, all the little intangible things that go along with being a pro."

Meanwhile, Sullivan had hit upon a forward combination that was about the give the Penguins the scoring depth so critical to playoff success. On March 13 in New York against the Rangers, with Malkin now out of the lineup for the rest of the regular season with an upper-body injury, Sullivan put Bonino in Malkin's place on a line with Hagelin on the left and Kessel on the right. The "HBK Line" as it would soon be known allowed Crosby to stay on a line with Chris Kunitz and Patric Hörnqvist, and when the playoffs arrived and Malkin returned to health, Sheary and Fehr also had top-six roles on the wings.

The HBK Line's chemistry emerged at a critical time, as the Penguins were holding just a two-point edge on Philadelphia for the final playoff spot in the Eastern Conference when Malkin was hurt. "A lot of the league had written us off: 'Alright, they're not going to make the playoffs.' We played some really, really good hockey just to get in," Cullen said. "Rusty stepped forward and played some big minutes, Conor Sheary stepped in and played really well. That last part of the year was some of the better hockey I've ever been part of on any team."

Together for the last 15 games, the HBK Line was easily one of the NHL's best over the last three weeks of the regular season, combining for 43 points and producing at least one goal in 10 of its last 13 games as Pittsburgh won 14 of its last 16 games. The line's offensive highlight came March 26 in Detroit, when it produced 12 points, including five each from Bonino and Kessel, in a 7–2 romp in Detroit.

"Never had points come as easy as they did then," said Bonino. "Phil had always put up points, and I always felt capable of it. Phil had speed and could finish, Haggy had speed and could finish, and I was just trying to be in right spot, make the right play, use my brain. That was a year that just everything seemed to go in, and we were playing the right way. It made our team just a matchup nightmare in the playoffs."

Pittsburgh's lights-out second half of the season landed it in second place in the Metropolitan Division, to which it had moved for the 2013–14 season, and fourth overall in the league. The team that was having problems scoring wound up as the NHL's third-highest scoring team and its sixth-best defensive team, and the Penguins as a forechecking dynamo also led the league in shots per game.

Fleury's concussion kept him out of the lineup for the entire month of April, and Murray's injury kept him out of the first two games of the opening round against the Rangers. That put the Penguins in the strange position of playing their third-string goaltender in the opening game of the post-season, but the 28-year-old Zatkoff produced a 35-save gem in Game 1, his first career playoff start. Hörnqvist delivered a hat trick, Kühnhackl a key shorthanded goal and Crosby a goal and two assists as the Penguins got a critical 5–2 win.

Malkin was finally back in the lineup as the Rangers took Game 2, 4–2, but Murray returned to make his Stanley Cup debut at Madison Square Garden in a 3–1 Pittsburgh victory in Game 3 and followed that with a 31-save shutout in Game 4 for a 5–0 victory that put the Penguins in position to win the series at home. Crosby had two assists to push his points total for the series to eight, and Rust scored twice in a 6–3 Game 5 victory that eliminated the Rangers and turned out to be an omen for Rust performances in series-deciding games.

Winning his first three playoff starts, after concluding the regular season by winning each of his last seven decisions, gave Murray's confidence a big boost.

"I just felt very fortunate to be on such a good team," he said. "For me personally, it just solidified or gave me more of a lasting impression that maybe I did have what it takes to make the NHL and stay there. The reason I got called up was a bit of a fluke, because of injuries, so I didn't necessarily feel I had earned my spot there. It was just kind of the luck of the draw, so I kind of felt I didn't quite belong, and having that success early on gave me the impression that I could stick around for a while."

Next up were the Presidents' Trophy winners, the Washington Capitals, who again held home-ice advantage over the Penguins for their first playoff meeting since 2009, when Pittsburgh had to win Game 7 on the road to beat them in the second round. For the eighth time in their nine playoff meetings, the Capitals took Game 1, this time with a 4–3 victory supplied by T.J. Oshie, whose third goal of the game came at 9:33 of overtime.

Murray took a shutout into the third period of Game 2, but it took a goal from former Washington winger Fehr with 4:28 to play to give the Penguins a 2–1 victory and even the series. Fleury returned from his concussion to serve as the backup for Game 3, but there was no question Murray was holding on to his net. He was brilliant, stopping 47 shots in a 3–2 victory that saw Pittsburgh take a 3–0 lead and then hold on under a barrage of 21 third-period shots from Washington. The HBK Line produced what turned out to be the game-winning goal from Hagelin late in the second period.

Hörnqvist won Game 4 for the Penguins, 3–2, with an overtime goal at 2:34 for a 3–1 series lead, but the Capitals took Game 5, 3–1, to keep their season alive. The Penguins jumped out to a 3–0 lead early in the second period of Game 6, with Kessel scoring twice and Hagelin once, but Washington mounted a crazy rally to tie the game, starting with a late second-period power-play goal from Oshie. Justin Williams made it 3–2 early in the third period, and the Penguins then looked to be self-destructing by taking three delay-of-game penalties in the span of 2:02. Pittsburgh killed a :54 five-on-three power play for the Capitals before John Carlson's five-on-three goal made it a 3–3 game with 6:59 to play.

This was a series in which neither Crosby nor Malkin helped much with production, managing only two points each, and fittingly it was the HBK Line that ended it at 6:32 of overtime. Kessel took a puck off the boards in the left corner behind the Washington net and sent a pass into the slot for Hagelin, who skated around the outstretched stick of defenseman Taylor Chorney to get off a wrist shot that Holtby stopped with his right pad. But Bonino stopped in front of the net, behind defenseman Matt Niskanen, and backhanded the rebound home for a 4–3, series-clinching victory.

"That series was so intense, all the stars, about as evenly matched a series as you could get," remembered Cullen. "Washington was in our minds the whole second half of the season; everyone knew it was going to go through them in the East."

The HBK Line combined for 18 points and two game-winning goals in the series, including seven points from Hagelin and six from Kessel, and was a difference-maker for the Penguins when they needed it most. Through 2025, the Penguins had won only six playoff games when both Crosby and Malkin were kept off the scoresheet, and two of them came in this series in Game 3 and Game 6. "We were built, at that point, to win," said Bonino.

Returning to the Conference Final for the second time in four seasons, the Penguins faced a Tampa Bay team that had needed just five games to eliminate both Detroit and the New York Islanders, and Lightning goaltender Ben Bishop was delivering arguably the best performances of his playoff career—after leading Tampa Bay to the Cup Final the previous season. But Bishop, a finalist for the Vezina Trophy, injured his left leg 13 minutes into the opening game, leaving the ice on a stretcher. The Lightning were already missing star Steven Stamkos, who had missed the entire playoffs to that point with a blood clotting issue and managed to play only the final game of the Pittsburgh series.

But Andrei Vasilevskiy came on in relief of Bishop and stopped 34 shots to help Tampa Bay to a 3–1 victory in Game 1 in Pittsburgh. Crosby scored the first overtime goal of his Stanley Cup playoff career just 40 seconds into the extra period of Game 2 for a crucial 3–2 victory that evened the series, and Crosby also produced the winning goal in a 4–2 Game 3 victory in Tampa. But the Lightning raced to a 4–0 lead after two periods of Game 4, chasing Murray. Fleury made his 2016 playoff debut and stopped all seven shots he faced in the third period, which saw the Penguins rally before falling, 4–3, and Sullivan was now faced with a serious question: Who was his starter for the critical Game 5?

This would not be the last significant playoff goaltending decision Sullivan encountered as coach of the team. He chose Fleury, who had missed more than six weeks with his concussion but had also won eight of his last nine regular-season starts before being injured. The Penguins weren't exactly bringing in a backup. Pittsburgh allowed only 13 shots through two periods, although Tampa Bay scored goals 1:10 apart late in the second period to cut the Penguins' lead to 3–2. But Nikita Kucherov scored with just 3:16 left to tie the game, and Tyler Johnson's goal 53 seconds into overtime gave the Lightning a 4–3 victory and put them in the driver's seat with a 3–2 series lead as they returned home to try and end it.

Not surprisingly, Sullivan gave Murray the start in Game 6, citing his "calming effect" on the team, an interesting comment about a goaltender who was only three months removed from his last AHL game. The Lightning scored on their first shot 5:12 into the game, as Jonathan Drouin finished a pass from Ondřej Palát, but Pittsburgh video coordinator Andy Saucier believed Drouin had been offside. He communicated his feelings to the bench and the Penguins challenged the goal, which was overturned—a moment that had the potential to boost the Penguins. And it did. Kessel then scored late in the period for a 1–0 lead, and Letang and Crosby added goals for a 3–0 lead after two periods, Crosby's turning out to be his third straight game-winner. The Lightning rallied to within a goal later in the third period, but a goal by Rust cemented a 5–2 victory in which Murray made 28 saves.

A Notre Dame graduate who played primarily on the right wing, Rust was becoming an important supporting member of the Penguins' cast in his first exposure to the Stanley Cup playoffs. Drafted six years earlier in the third round, the Pontiac, Mich., native brought very good speed and a no-nonsense approach with the puck, going straight to the net with it when given the chance. His forechecking ability played precisely into the game Sullivan was espousing, and while he was not expected to be a prodigious goal-scorer, he was making noticeable contributions as his finishing ability improved surrounded by talented players.

Rust scored two goals and added an assist in the series-clinching Game 5 of the first round against the New York Rangers, and he now reprised that role in a much bigger setting—Game 7 with a trip to the Cup Final on the line. Catching the Lightning on a line change, Rust took a pass from Kunitz and whipped a 35-foot wrist shot past Vasilevskiy's glove for the game's first goal early in the second period, then whacked the puck past Vasilevskiy's glove just over eight minutes later after Ben Lovejoy banked a pass off the back boards toward the Tampa Bay net. His second goal came 30 seconds after Drouin tied the game and stood as the game- and series-winning goal in a tense 2–1 victory.

During the 2016 and 2017 Cup runs by the Penguins, Rust scored seven goals in deciding games, more than any other teammate. Three of those came in Game 7s, tying the franchise record for career Game 7 goals shared by Lemieux and Kunitz. "It pretty much allowed me to believe that if I brought my game and played well and consistently, I could contribute at this level and I could contribute not only on the fourth line but be a guy who could chip in some offense and help the team win games," Rust said.

That put Pittsburgh into the Cup Final against the San Jose Sharks, a playoff meeting that felt like it was bound to happen eventually. The Penguins and Sharks had been the NHL's best teams over the previous 10 regular seasons, compiling remarkably similar records—Pittsburgh had won 464 games, the Sharks 457. The Sharks, who were making their first Cup Final appearance, boasted the top four playoff scorers in Logan Couture, Joe Pavelski, Brent Burns and Joe Thornton—with the red-hot Pavelski scoring 13 goals over 18 games. They also owned the Penguins in San Jose, where just six months earlier the Penguins had won for the first time in more than 18 years.

Rust scored the opening goal of Game 1, giving him four of the Penguins' last five goals, and Sheary added another 1:02 later in the first period before the Sharks scored twice in the second to forge a tie. Pittsburgh, however, dominated the third period and Bonino again contributed a vital goal by converting a superb pass from the right ring corner by Letang with just 2:33 left to give the Penguins a 3–2 victory.

"In the playoffs, I felt like I was always pretty good in those moments," said Bonino, who led the Penguins in playoff assists that season as a No. 3 center. "The biggest thing was I was emotionally...I'm very even keel on the ice. You're not seeing me get too down on myself, not seeing me get too high. Never with teammates, just staying even keel. It just allows you to play the same game you always play."

The goal took on a permanent place in the memory of hockey fans everywhere, however, after the call of the goal by Harnarayan Singh on *Hockey Night in Canada*'s Punjabi broadcast went viral. "Bonino Bonino Bonino Bonino Bonino... Nick Bah-KNEE-Nooooooo," Singh shouted, and it became such a rallying cry for the Penguins they invited Singh and his broadcast partners to Pittsburgh for the team's Stanley Cup celebration.

Murray took a shutout deep into Game 2 before Justin Braun tied the game, 1–1, with just 4:05 to play, but it simply set the stage for more of what was becoming typical late-game heroics from the Penguins. Nine of their first 14 playoff victories in 2016 came via winning goals in the third period or overtime, and seven of those nine came in the final half of the third period or later. Sheary added to that list at 2:35 of overtime, becoming the first rookie to score a Stanley Cup Final overtime goal in 30 years.

Crosby, putting a memorable ending on a dominant night in the circle that saw him win 17 of 24 faceoffs, told Sheary to alter his pre-faceoff positioning by moving to the left wing boards and then drifting to the middle of the ice after the draw. Crosby won the draw cleanly on the backhand from Joel Ward back to Letang, who waited for Sheary to find his spot at the top of the left circle. Letang shoveled a pass to him, and Sheary slid just inside the top of the circle and beat goaltender Martin Jones with a wrist shot that also benefited from a Hörnqvist screen.

Pittsburgh did a superb job limiting the Sharks' chances in Game 3, allowing only 15 shots through two periods while building a 2–1 lead. But Ward tied it midway through the third period and Joonas Donskoi won it for San Jose at 12:18 of overtime, but Malkin had a goal and assist and Kessel two assists in a 3–1 Game 4 victory that gave the Penguins a chance to do something they had never done—win the Cup on home ice.

Consol Energy Center was a nervous madhouse leading up to Game 5, and thousands of fans jammed Washington Place adjacent to the arena to watch the game on a big screen in anticipation of a party. The Sharks, who had never led in the series, scored on two of their first three shots to take a 2–0 lead before Malkin and Hagelin scored 22 seconds apart to tie it—the teams producing four goals in the opening five minutes, a wacky start to a Cup Final game. But Melker Karlsson's late first-period goal restored San Jose's lead, and Pavelski added his only goal of the series into an empty net as Jones made 44 saves for a 4–2 San Jose win. "We had a slow start and couldn't make up for it," Murray said.

Back in San Jose for Game 6, Sullivan concluded his pregame remarks to his team by saying, "Let's get this thing done here. Enough is enough."

Defenseman Brian Dumoulin played an important, but unusual, role early in the first period. He drew a penalty to give Pittsburgh the first power play of the game, but with the Crosby line having just finished a shift, Sullivan decided not to employ his first power-play unit. Thus Dumoulin got a rare chance for some ice time with the extra man, and he scored his first and—through 2026—only career playoff power-play goal for a 1–0 lead at 8:16. It was another example of the Penguins getting contributions from unlikely sources, a staple for Stanley Cup champions.

Couture tied the game for San Jose in the second period, but the Penguins again answered quickly, scoring 1:19 later when Letang converted a shot from the bottom of the right circle after taking a pass from Crosby behind the net.

The Penguins, who had allowed just four shots in the opening period, did not allow a shot for a 15:29 stretch of the third period while protecting their lead. Coming on the road against a team whose season and dreams were on the line, it was an absolute clinic. "We totally shut it down that game," said Murray, who completed his first season in the NHL by winning an astounding 22 of his last 28 starts. "It was one of the best all-around games I've been part of. It was pretty impressive to watch from back where I was."

And in a case of the first overall pick in 2005 setting up the last overall pick in 2005, Crosby blocked a Marc-Édouard Vlasic shot in the game's dying moments and fed Hörnqvist for the empty-net goal that finished a 3–1 win and brought the Cup back to Pittsburgh. Only Kessel (10) scored more goals for the Penguins than Hörnqvist (nine) during the 2016 playoffs, during which Kessel also led Pittsburgh with 22 points.

The Penguins had been widely expected to make several serious runs at another Cup after winning in 2009, but they never got closer than eight victories away before it finally happened in 2016. That seven-year wait had been marked by various setbacks: the absence of both Crosby and Malkin due to injury in 2011; upsets by Jaroslav Halák and the Canadiens in 2010 and the Flyers in 2012; and a blown 3–1 series lead against the Rangers in 2014. But this spring they heeded Sullivan's mantra to tune out distractions and frustrations and "just play." And they weren't done.

18

American Accent, 2017

THAT THE DEFENDING STANLEY CUP CHAMPION PENGUINS were feeling confident about the state of their roster in the summer of 2016 was highlighted by a relative dearth of activity from general manager Jim Rutherford. The team lost backup goaltender Jeff Zatkoff and defenseman Ben Lovejoy to free agency, but Rutherford's only significant moves were the re-signing of free agents Matt Cullen and Justin Schultz. While he certainly was limited by a payroll already smashed up against salary cap limits, Rutherford knew how to create financial space if he felt the need.

The return of Cullen, a fourth-line center, and Schultz, a bottom-pairing defenseman, was a reflection of the comfort those two found in their roles as first-year players in Pittsburgh. Schultz emphasized that comfort by taking a pay cut of $2.5 million to sign a one-year deal, telling the *Pittsburgh Post-*

Gazette, "I love my teammates. I love the coaches. The city...I don't know if I had had that much fun ever playing hockey." He was clearly betting on himself and banking on the team's ability to win again in 2017, and so was everyone else in the organization.

Schultz's return turned out to be a critical factor for the Penguins, not only because he responded with the best season of his 11-year NHL career but because the 2016–17 season was about to become a very bumpy ride for a Pittsburgh defense decimated by injuries and forced to use 14 different players—the second-highest single-season total in team history. But the season began with a worrisome injury to the forward ranks.

Sidney Crosby was injured in practice in early October and a few days later was diagnosed with another concussion. Given the concussion that had cost Crosby 61 games over the 2010–11 and 2011–12 seasons, and the subsequent soft-tissue neck injury that cost him another 40 games just two weeks after returning, the Penguins had every right to be nervous. Fortunately for Pittsburgh, he missed only the first six games, and the team won 17 of its next 24 with him in the lineup.

His second Stanley Cup in hand, and coming off captaining Canada to the World Cup of Hockey title after leading the September tournament in scoring, Crosby scored 14 goals in his first 14 games of the season to take over the league lead. He kept it, too, finishing with a league-high 44 goals, the second-highest total of his career to win a second Maurice "Rocket" Richard Trophy. Crosby's 14-goal explosion helped put the Penguins fourth in the league's overall standings and, by Thanksgiving, they also seemed to have discovered a new offensive weapon.

Twenty-three-year-old winger Jake Guentzel was the first Nebraska native to reach the NHL after being drafted. He played high school hockey in Minnesota before playing junior hockey in Sioux City, Iowa and attending the University of Nebraska–Omaha. He didn't draw a typical geographic line to the NHL, but he wasn't a typical prospect, either. The 5-11 left shot, the son of a hockey coach, didn't overpower defenders with size or speed but beat them with a sharp hockey IQ and slick hands. He was a born finisher around the net, and when he made his NHL debut with the Penguins in late November, he proved it quickly.

Guentzel scored 1:02 into a home game against the Rangers, the quickest goal ever scored by a Pittsburgh player making his NHL debut. Before the game was 14 minutes old, he had two goals, at that point joining Bobby Simpson, John Chabot and Rob Brown as the only Penguins players to score multiple goals in their team debuts. He added another goal three games later and, after a return to the AHL, came back to the NHL in mid-January to stay.

"His whole life, it's been like, 'Well, can you do that at the next level?' He's not overly impressive physically, not overly impressive with his speed. But yeah, 'Can he do it at the next level?'" remembered Cullen. "He's heard that from high school to college to pro. Then he starts out with a great game, pops a couple, and it's like, 'Can you do it the whole season?'"

Guentzel could, scoring 30 goals five times in his first eight full NHL seasons and hitting 40 goals three times.

At that point, when coach Mike Sullivan had a healthy lineup to work with, Pittsburgh's top nine forwards were a scary group: Crosby playing with Conor Sheary on the left and Bryan Rust on the right; Malkin playing with Guentzel on the left and Patric Hörnqvist on the right; and the HBK Line of Carl Hagelin, Nick Bonino and Phil Kessel. In their NHL careers, eight of those nine scored at least 20 goals in a season; six of them at least 30 goals; and three of them at least 40 goals.

Upon Guentzel's return, the Penguins won 10 of their next 14 games despite Sheary, Malkin, Rust, Hagelin and Cullen missing some time with injuries, Rust 20 games with an elbow injury. By mid-February, however, the injury situation was much worse on defense.

Just three weeks after Brian Dumoulin returned from a 10-game absence with a broken jaw, Olli Määttä suffered a broken hand that knocked him out of the lineup for 25 games. One week later, two more injuries hit at the same time: Trevor Daley suffered a knee injury that cost him 20 games, and Kris Letang was lost for the entire season with a herniated disc in his neck that required surgery—a massive blow to the Penguins, who initially expected him back and then in early April announced his surgery. When he left the lineup, Letang had already missed 18 games earlier in the season with upper-body, lower-body and knee injuries, and he wound up playing only 41 games in 2016–17 coming off arguably the best season of his career.

Two days after Letang played what turned out to be his final game of the season in late February, Rutherford acquired veteran defenseman Ron Hainsey, 35, from Carolina. Joining his sixth NHL team, the Bolton, Conn., native had played almost 900 NHL games when he arrived in Pittsburgh, but he had never played a single playoff game. But with the Penguins just five points off the top spot in the league's overall standings, that was about to change, and Hainsey would replace Letang beside Dumoulin and have himself a memorable first post-season experience.

One player who didn't present an injury challenge for the Penguins was right wing Kessel, who would become the first player in NHL history to play 1,000 or more consecutive games (1,064)—still the league record. The 5-11 native of Madison,

Wisc., was one of Rutherford's most outstanding additions during his time as the Penguins' GM, coming in a trade from the Toronto Maple Leafs in the summer of 2015 that involved nine assets and sent youngsters Kasperi Kapanen and Scott Harrington and a first-round pick to the Leafs.

There weren't any physical elements to his game, but Kessel possessed great speed and a lightning-quick release. He was already a five-time 30-goal scorer when he came to Pittsburgh, and he scored 26 goals in his first season with the Penguins, the vast majority coming five-on-five, and led the team in playoff scoring. During the Penguins' Cup victories in 2016 and 2017, only Crosby and Malkin (46 each) had more points than Kessel (45), who was also a singular personality in the dressing room and a huge fan favorite.

"Phil was awesome," said Bonino. "At the same time the grumpiest and the happiest person. Like a funny grumpy with Phil. I don't know if I ever asked him how he was doing and he said good. It was like, 'My hand's bugging me,' or 'I'm tired,' and he said it with a smile. Everyone enjoyed him."

Added goaltender Matt Murray, "He brought a lot of levity and lightness in those heavy, tense moments. He was a guy a lot of guys looked to for a little laugh, he would always have a funny moment when we needed it, just to loosen the tension a bit. That goes a long way...helps the team bonding, and when you loosen up like that, it gives you a boost of energy. And everything he brought on the ice, he was obviously a critical part of that team. We don't get it done without him. A massive, massive part of that team."

The Penguins were not only having success because of their speed, scoring ability and forechecking prowess but also because of the way they swarmed the puck whenever they lost it in the neutral or attacking zones. Backchecking had never been as consistent a factor for the Penguins than it was under Sullivan.

"Our coaching staff was using our team to what we were: a forechecking kind of team that would play with pace and get on top of you and force you to do things you didn't want to do," remembered Kunitz. "It was a team buy-in: this is how we're going to play if we're going to have success. We're going to backcheck really hard, make sure we force pucks, we're going to forecheck, we're going to flip pucks out and hunt, put teams under pressure."

Pittsburgh's first game without both Letang and Daley also saw them missing Rust, Sheary and Määttä: an NHL Stadium Series game at Pittsburgh's Heinz Field against the Flyers. Guentzel had two assists and Virginia, Minn., native Cullen scored the game-winner early in the third period of a 4–2 victory that started a stretch of 13 games in which the Penguins won nine times. Late in that stretch Malkin left the lineup with an upper-body injury that kept him out for the rest of the regular season, and Guentzel and Kunitz also missed time.

The Penguins finished second to Washington in the stacked Metropolitan Division, which featured three of the league's top four teams (including third-place Columbus) and four of the league's top nine teams (including the fourth-place Rangers). Just getting out of the division promised to be no picnic, even for a Pittsburgh team that had amassed 111 points in the standings—the second-highest total in team history.

Daley and Määttä returned late in the regular season, although both Hagelin and Kunitz would miss the entire first round of the playoffs. Murray had missed the first six games of the season with a thumb injury, but Sullivan had essentially split the goaltending chores between he and Marc-

André Fleury in the first half of the season. But Murray got the majority of starts in the second half, when he won nine of his last 12 decisions. So there was no question that Murray would start the playoffs in goal—until the warmups for Game 1 against Columbus.

"I probably was hanging on by a thread for a while, I had been dealing with a lot of soreness around my hamstring, and I felt it pop on me in warmups," Murray said. "Thankfully we had a guy like Flower there to step in and take us a long, long way, because without Flower we wouldn't have been in that scenario. A very, very disappointing moment for me. I was feeling very dejected at that moment, like I let everybody down."

Fleury had a so-so end to his regular season, although he didn't benefit from starting just seven of the team's last 26 games. But he stepped in and allowed just a single goal in each of the opening two games, 3–1 and 4–1 home wins for Pittsburgh. Guentzel then delivered a hat trick to rally the Penguins from a 3–1 Game 3 deficit in Columbus to a 5–4 victory, scoring the game-winner at 13:10 of overtime. The Blue Jackets jumped to a 3–0 lead and held on for a 5–4 win in Game 4, but it was the Penguins who got to a 3–0 lead in Game 5 and won, 5–2, to end the series.

Rust scored twice in the final first-round game, giving him a pair of goals in three of the five deciding playoff games in which he had played to that point in his career. Malkin, who had been out of the lineup since mid-March but returned for the start of the playoffs, had three assists in Game 5 and ended the series with 11 points to lead all league scorers in the opening round.

This brought yet another matchup with the Capitals, who had eliminated Toronto in the first round. Crosby scored goals 52 seconds apart early in the second period of Game

1 for a 2–0 lead, but the Capitals rallied to tie the game before Bonino—the Hartford, Conn., native whose goal had eliminated Washington the previous spring—delivered another game-winning goal with 7:24 left for a 3–2 Pittsburgh victory as Fleury made 33 saves.

Guentzel and Kessel each had two goals and three points in Game 2, a 6–2 Pittsburgh win in which five of their goals came from Americans. The Penguins this season used 15 American-born players, the second-highest number in team history and more than all but New Jersey, Boston and Los Angeles that season. Coached by a Marshfield, Mass., native in Sullivan, the Penguins in the 2017 playoffs got 11 of their 16 game-winning goals from American-born players, including five from Guentzel, and their 15 former NCAA players were most by a Cup champion through 2025.

Back home in Pittsburgh for Game 3, the Penguins stunned Washington by scoring twice in 48 seconds with less than two minutes to play to force overtime, the latter goal coming from Schultz with 1:05 left, but the Capitals' Kevin Shattenkirk scored on the power play in overtime for a 3–2 Washington victory. In Game 4, the Capitals rallied from a two-goal deficit to forge a tie before Schultz again came through with a huge power-play goal, the game-winner in a 3–2 victory in which the Penguins managed only 18 shots but Fleury stopped 36 in a spectacular performance. "You need a goalie to steal you a game, especially in those (Washington) series, and we got that each year," remembered Dumoulin.

Pittsburgh seemed destined to finish the series in Game 5 at Washington, taking a 2–1 lead into the third period, but the Capitals scored three times in less than five minutes early in the period for a 4–2 victory, then followed it up with a convincing 5–2 win in Pittsburgh in Game 6 to tie the series. Murray was now able to dress as the backup for Game 7, and it surprised no one to watch Rust break a tense scoreless tie with a goal just before the midway point. Fleury delivered 29 saves for a 2–0 shutout, including a superb blocker stop on an Ovechkin one-timer from the slot late in the second period in a 1–0 game that caused Ovechkin to begin raising his arms in celebration until he understood what looked like a sure goal had been stopped.

The Penguins were now 6–0 all-time when a Game 7 was played on the road, with three of those coming at Washington as Pittsburgh continued to torture its longtime division rivals. For the second time in as many seasons, the Capitals had compiled the league's best regular-season record and been eliminated by the Penguins in the second round of the playoffs. When Pittsburgh went on to win the Cup, it meant the Penguins had eliminated the Capitals on their way to each of their five Stanley Cups.

Next up were the Ottawa Senators, the team the Penguins' stars had cut their playoff teeth against, losing in five games in 2007 as Ottawa eventually reached the Stanley Cup Final and then sweeping the Senators the following season on their way to the Stanley Cup Final. Now their roles were reversed, as the Penguins were proven playoff performers and the Senators had entered the 2017 playoffs with just one series win in nine years before dispatching Boston and the New York Rangers.

A late goal from Malkin forged a 1–1 tie in Game 1 at Pittsburgh, but Bobby Ryan's early overtime goal gave the Senators a 2–1 Game 1 victory, and Hörnqvist suffered a lower-body injury that knocked him out of the series. Fleury responded with his second shutout in three games, making 23 saves in a 1–0 win as Kessel scored with 6:55 to play, using his quick release to zip his own rebound past Craig Anderson. Pittsburgh had evened the series but also lost Rust for two games with an upper-body injury, and including the previous loss of Letang, the Penguins were now without three important players.

Back in Ottawa to host their first Conference Final game in 10 years, the Senators poured four goals past Fleury in the opening 13 minutes of Game 3 on the way to a 5–1 victory, with Murray playing the final 47 minutes and stopping 19 of 20 shots in his first action of the 2017 playoffs. It turned out to be the final playoff appearance in a Penguins' sweater for Fleury, the franchise's all-time leader in playoff games played (115), wins (62) and shutouts (10).

In Game 4, defensemen Määttä and Dumoulin scored goals and Crosby had his second power-play goal in as many games to go with an assist as the Penguins built a 3–0 lead and held on for a 3–2 victory. When the Penguins took a penalty for too many men on the ice in the final minute, Murray made two critical stops while Dumoulin and Bonino blocked shots to ensure the win.

Murray made 25 saves in a 7–0 Pittsburgh victory in Game 5, as Rust returned to the lineup with a goal and an assist while Malkin had three assists and the Penguins' power play, stagnant at the start of the series, converted all three of its chances. The Penguins chased Anderson with four first-period goals and had control of the series, 3–2. But Anderson rebounded in a big way in Game 6, stopping 45 shots as the Senators claimed a 2–1 win that sent the series to a Game 7.

Kunitz had been playing on both Crosby's line and Malkin's line at various times in the series, but he began this game on the fourth line with Cullen and Sheary, which was unusual. But that line opened the scoring when Kunitz delivered his first goal of the playoffs—and first in 34 games going back to the regular season—midway through the second period. Kunitz and Sheary got more shifts with Crosby later in the second period and then throughout the rest of the game, which saw Kunitz pick up a power-play assist on a Schultz goal that put Pittsburgh ahead, 2–1, with less than nine minutes to play. But Ottawa tied the game again three minutes later, making it just the second Game 7 for the Penguins to reach overtime on home ice.

Pittsburgh then dictated most of the play, as the Senators didn't have a single shot in the opening 11 minutes and just two in a scoreless first overtime. When it came to playing in overtime of a Game 7, Murray said there "is no playbook on how to approach something like that. It was so high stress you kind of go into blackout mode and you're just trying to get through it, take one thing at a time."

Early in the second overtime, Schultz threw a pass for Crosby at the bottom of the left circle that went off the back boards and was recovered by Crosby as he turned away from defenseman Chris Wideman. Kunitz had drifted to open space at the top of the left circle and took a pass from Crosby, and his ensuing shot fluttered past forward Jean-Gabriel Pageau and over the right shoulder of Anderson at 5:09 to win the series—the last goal he ever scored for Pittsburgh.

"I hadn't been having a great season up until that game... for whatever reason, in a team sport, somebody ends up having an unbelievable game, like Max Talbot in 2009. It was just my time, I guess," Kunitz said. "That made it one of the best games for me ever to be part of. It makes it fun to rewatch that goal, see that crowd reaction, how much Pittsburgh meant to you. It was a lot of fun to help out. I hadn't always been that kind of go-to player that I got to be that day."

The first multiple-overtime playoff game ever won by the Penguins on home ice touched off a raucous celebration at PPG

Paints Arena, as the team had won consecutive Game 7s to advance to the Cup Final again. "I don't have strong memories of anything in that game other than the Kunitz winner, the relief, the jubilation," Murray said. "It was probably the most intense game I've ever been a part of."

The Stanley Cup Final was familiar territory for the Penguins, but it was new to an 18-year-old Nashville franchise that was the No. 8 seed in the Western Conference before sweeping Chicago and eliminating St. Louis and Anaheim in six games each. Pittsburgh welcomed back to its lineup Hörnqvist, who had spent the first six seasons of his NHL career with the Predators before being traded to the Penguins in the summer of 2014—the first trade made by Rutherford after joining the Penguins.

Pittsburgh scored on three of its eight shots against veteran goaltender Pekka Rinne in the first period, all in the final four and a half minutes, setting the tone for an unusual Game 1 in Pittsburgh. The Predators got on the board midway through the second period and then scored twice in three and a half minutes of the third period to tie the game, and by then Pittsburgh's silenced home crowd must have believed another Penguins goal was out of the question. Pittsburgh had been held without a shot in the second period, the first time that had ever happened to the Penguins in a playoff period, and all told the Penguins went 37 minutes without a shot, twice missing the net and 11 times having shot attempts blocked by the Predators.

Guentzel would have been among the most unlikely to produce a go-ahead goal, as he had gone eight games without a goal. But when Nashville lost the puck in the neutral zone, it came to Cullen, who fed Guentzel into the Nashville zone. Going one-on-one against defenseman Ryan Ellis, Guentzel beat Rinne with just 3:17 to play, and Bonino added an empty-net goal for a crazy 5–3 victory in which the Penguins had played almost the equivalent of two full periods without a shot. Rinne allowed four goals on 11 shots.

That game got Guentzel going, as he scored twice in Game 2 to help the Penguins to a 4–1 victory, with Murray stopping 37 shots. But Pittsburgh paid a price for the victory. Bonino blocked a power-play shot by P.K. Subban midway through the first period, limped off the ice and then returned to play one more shift late in the period. He had suffered a non-displaced broken leg, but he returned to start the second period and played 19 more shifts and 11:52 over the final 40 minutes anyway.

"I took a shot of some numbing, it wasn't even a question that I wouldn't play. You're in the Cup Final," he said. "I took the shot and it felt amazing. I went out and played the second and third periods, left the game in a walking boot. I told my family and friends, 'Yes it's broken, but, like, I feel amazing.' Then in middle of the night, I woke up to go to the bathroom and I stepped out of bed and I just crumpled."

Bonino missed Game 3 but, amazingly, tried to come back for Game 4, taking another shot from doctors. "I could go forwards OK but I couldn't turn that well," he remembered. "I took warmups for Game 4 but I just couldn't do it. I said, 'I could give you some minutes, but it could displace and it would leave you without a forward. It could hurt you.'"

Nashville was far from done. Feeding off the wild atmosphere in Bridgestone Arena, the Predators responded to an early Guentzel goal by scoring the game's final five goals. Rinne stopped 27 shots, then stopped 23 more in Game 4 for a 4–1 victory. After taking a commanding 2–0 series lead, Pittsburgh had been outscored, 9–2, in two games at Nashville and the series was up for grabs.

The Penguins remained confident despite the consecutive losses, and they showed it in Game 5 back in Pittsburgh, scoring three times in the opening period to chase Rinne on the way to a 6–0 victory. Crosby had three assists and Kessel added a goal and two assists in the game, which Hainsey finished off with a spectacular goal, avoiding a check before skating out of his own zone with the puck, dishing it to Kessel and going to the net to finish off a pass from Malkin. It was the second and final playoff goal of his career.

Game 6 was a dynamic battle between Rinne and Murray, with the Predators unable to cash in on four power plays, including a :32 five-on-three midway through the final period. Ian Cole and Dumoulin came up with blocks during the two power plays, and with time running out, the Penguins created something from nothing. Kunitz controlled the puck along the right wing boards and sent it out to Schultz at center point, and his shot went through traffic, off the back boards and then bounded off the side of the net to Rinne's left, where Hörnqvist banked it off the goaltender and into the net with 1:35 to play. Hagelin added an empty-net goal and the Penguins' 2–0 win made them the first team in the salary cap era to win consecutive Stanley Cups.

"We never really gave them a chance," said Murray, who stopped all 51 shots he faced over the final two games of the series to become just the third NHL goaltender in 65 years to record consecutive shutouts in the Cup Final, joining Martin Brodeur and Chris Osgood. "We had a lot of big blocked shots that game, a three-on-five, a textbook example of a team sacrificing to win and we were ultimately rewarded for it."

Guentzel, who was an AHL player in late November, wound up leading all goal-scorers in the 2017 Stanley Cup playoffs with 13 goals, including five game-winners—matching

Mario Lemieux's single-season team record set in 1992. Just as Murray had done the previous spring, Guentzel in 2017 gave the Penguins a young player performing at a level that wasn't foreseen this quickly in his career. Malkin led the team in scoring with 28 points and Crosby had 27 points while winning his second consecutive Conn Smythe Trophy.

While their goal-scoring prowess often got the attention, the Penguins had recorded five of their final nine victories in the 2017 playoffs by shutout, two by Fleury and three by Murray. Fleury won nine games that spring and Murray seven, becoming the first duo in NHL history to each record seven or more wins in one playoff year. Fleury's competitiveness was an integral part of his success, but it was also part of Murray's makeup as he became the first goaltender in NHL history to win two Stanley Cups as a rookie.

"Such a calm, poised and confident young guy. He was technically sound, ultra competitive," remembered Cullen. "He was hard to play against in practice. He hated getting scored on and he'd slash guys in front of the net, a super-competitive guy. You know, it's not an easy spot to step into when you're filling in for one of the most beloved players in the history of the NHL. Matt had a different calm, a poise about him that allowed him to step in and handle that. It was super impressive what he was able to do. He never seemed like he was out of position, and it translated into a little bit of a calming effect on the team. He had a way of making big saves seem easy."

Said Kunitz, "Matt Murray was amazing. Probably didn't get enough credit." Added Rutherford, "Look, we wouldn't have won in 2017 without Fleury. But it's accurate to say (Murray) deserves a lot of credit, probably more credit than he's received."

The Penguins went on to win a first-round series against Philadelphia in the 2018 playoffs, equaling the team record for consecutive playoff series victories with nine. But they lost in the second round to eventual Cup champion Washington and, through 2026, hadn't won another playoff series. The Penguins' during these back-to-back Cup runs, however, had displayed a combination of elements proven to have worked for NHL teams for decades: established stars providing expected contributions, goaltending excellence, veterans supplying dependable depth, young players playing outsized roles and a management team that worked together to find and deploy players who could execute an established strategy.

PART 5

THE BUILDERS

19

Creating a Winner

Eddie Johnston's 16-year career as a National Hockey League goaltender was hardly generic. A Montreal native playing most of that career with the Canadiens' rival Boston Bruins, he was the last goaltender to play in every game of a season, staying on the ice for all but 23 seconds of the 1963–64 season with the last-place Bruins, pulled for an extra attacker in a November game in Chicago. He was severely injured in October 1968 when a pre-game warmup shot by Bobby Orr went off Johnston's stick and struck him in the temple, precipitating a long stay in a Detroit hospital.

He won Stanley Cups with Boston in 1970 and 1972, in the latter season splitting playoff starts with Gerry Cheevers and outperforming Cheevers as part of the Big, Bad Bruins team led by stars Orr and Phil Esposito. After time in Toronto, St. Louis and Chicago, he retired and went directly behind the bench, coaching the Black Hawks' farm team in New Brunswick, N.S., in 1978–79 before being promoted to coach the Hawks the following season.

When Chicago fired him after one season despite reaching the second round of the playoffs, Johnston took over as coach of the Penguins, a career move he calls "the best thing that ever happened to me." In a pair of best-of-five, first-round playoff series, his underdog Penguins pushed both the Blues (1981) and New York Islanders (1982) to overtime before falling in Game 5 defeats, and in those seasons Johnston turned the Penguins into a power-play machine. Pittsburgh set an NHL record for power-play goals in a season with 99 in 1981–82, the result of Johnston's system of using picks that had grown out of his many discussions with Celtics' coach Tommy Heinsohn during his Boston days.

"In basketball, you face the guy, but in hockey we would turn away from him to block a guy without getting a penalty. If their high forwards moved out, we picked the defenseman down low, and one guy would be open in the slot. We ran a lot of practices with it, so we got it down to a science," said Johnston. Only Hall of Famers Mike Bossy and Marcel Dionne had more power-play goals from 1980 to 1982 than the Penguins' Paul Gardner and Rick Kehoe.

Johnston loved coaching "because things change in a matter of a minute or two, you see something the other team is not doing, or something you can do, and if you execute you can change the game up a little bit. I enjoyed that. You're right on the spot. You have to be sharp right away."

But he was promoted to be the Penguins' general manager after Baz Bastien's death in 1983, and Johnston immediately set out to keep as many draft choices as possible and stop a maddening practice of Pittsburgh management—trading away high picks. Through 2024–25, the Penguins had made only four trades in their history in which they acquired a first-round pick without sending one back, and Johnston made the first two of those within 10 months of being named GM.

Those trades landed Doug Bodger and Roger Belanger in the first round of the 1984 Entry Draft to follow Johnston's choice of Mario Lemieux with the first overall pick, and Bodger was the major asset sent to Buffalo four years later by GM Tony Esposito to acquire goaltender Tom Barrasso, who backstopped Pittsburgh's first two Stanley Cups. In total, Johnston drafted eight players who later won a Cup with the Penguins (six of whom were drafted in the third round or later) and drafted five others who were traded for players that won the Cup in Pittsburgh.

Johnston also had a fair amount of success in the trade market as Pittsburgh's GM, acquiring four players who would go one to score 30 or more goals for the Penguins in Kevin Stevens, Dan Quinn, Randy Cunneyworth and Paul Coffey. The acquisition of Stevens, a future 50-goal scorer, from Los Angeles came just months after the Kings had drafted him in the sixth round and was the second trade Johnston made and certainly one of his best. His last trade of significance was also his biggest, acquiring Coffey, Dave Hunter and Wayne Van Dorp from the Oilers for Dave Hannan, Moe Mantha, Craig Simpson and Chris Joseph—the latter two first-round picks by Johnston.

The reshaping of the Penguins' draft philosophy didn't bring Johnston's teams quick results on the ice, however, and he was fired after they failed to reach the playoffs in his first five seasons at the helm. He spent three seasons as general manager of the Hartford Whalers before returning in 1993–94 to begin a nearly four-year stint as coach of the Penguins, taking the team to within one victory of reaching the Stanley Cup Final in the spring of 1996. That team was sparked by a first-round, four-overtime Game 4 victory at Washington on a goal by Petr Nedvěd, but it was doomed when a foot injury to Ron Francis kept him out of the Eastern Conference Final against Florida, leading to a Game 7 loss.

Johnston had coached 516 games behind the Pittsburgh bench when he was replaced near the end of the 1996–97 season, a team record that lasted 25 years before being broken by Mike Sullivan. Affectionately known simply as "EJ" around Pittsburgh, Johnston stayed with the team for another 12 years as assistant general manager and senior advisor to hockey operations.

Tony Esposito lasted just over a year and a half as Johnston's successor, one of the shortest stints for a GM in Pittsburgh history, but the man who replaced him, Craig Patrick, spent more than 16 years in the position—still the longest tenure of any Penguins' GM. A Detroit native, Patrick played 401 NHL games for California, St. Louis, Kansas City and Washington and is part of one of hockey's most famous families.

His father, Lynn, won the Stanley Cup as a player with the New York Rangers in 1940; coached the Rangers and Bruins to the Cup Final; and was GM of the expansion St. Louis Blues when they reached the Cup Final in 1968. After a long playing career as a defenseman in the National Hockey Association and Pacific Coast Hockey Association, among other leagues, Craig's grandfather Lester Patrick coached the Rangers to the Cup in 1928 and 1933, famously playing goal at the age of 44 in an emergency during the 1928 playoffs. He was general manager of the Rangers for their 1940 championship and in 1974 had his name given to an NHL division, the one to which his grandson's team now belonged. Lester and his brother Frank founded the Pacific Coast Hockey Association, opened up the game with numerous rule changes and built Canada's first artificial ice rinks. Both Lynn and Lester are in the Hockey Hall of Fame as players, and Frank was inducted as a builder.

"I can remember when I was just a kid in kindergarten," Patrick said, "the teacher sending notes home to my parents asking, 'Can't we get him to draw something other than a hockey rink?' I always pictured myself in hockey, all my life."

The season after his playing career ended, Craig Patrick gained fame as Herb Brooks' assistant coach for the 1980 U.S. Men's Olympic Team, whose Miracle on Ice at Lake Placid brought hockey a visibility it had never had in the United States. Patrick then joined the Rangers management and in 1981 became the youngest GM in their history. He was serving as athletic director at the University of Denver, where he won NCAA championships as a player in 1968 and 1969, when Penguins' vice president Paul Martha offered him their GM position in December 1989. "I've had other offers and turned them down," Patrick said. "But I couldn't turn this one down. This is too good of an opportunity."

Instead of hiring a coach, he also stepped behind the Pittsburgh bench to replace Gene Ubriaco for the rest of the season, which ended without a playoff berth but taught Patrick a lot.

"He wanted to see exactly what we had, not only on the ice, but what was on the bench, what was being said, how guys respond to certain situations," remembered defenseman Randy Hillier, who later worked under Patrick as an assistant coach. "He wanted to know exactly what he had and, more importantly, what he needed. He was observing more than he was coaching, taking it all in. I thought that was interesting. What he saw the remainder of the year led him to what he ultimately did in the off-season."

What Patrick did in the nine months from June 1990 through March 1991 was nothing short of amazing. He drafted Jaromír Jágr and immediately got him to Pittsburgh after the four teams ahead of the Penguins in the 1990 draft passed on him; hired Scotty Bowman as director of player development and "Badger" Bob Johnson as coach; signed Bryan Trottier as a free agent; and traded for Joe Mullen, Ron Francis, Larry Murphy, Gordie Roberts and Scott Young. All of these players, coaches and administrators are in either the Hockey Hall of Fame or the United States Hockey Hall of Fame with the exception of Jágr, a lock for induction into the Hockey Hall of Fame once he decides to retire.

Francis, who after retiring as a player became a general manager in both Carolina and Seattle, could appreciate the hiring of Bowman and Johnson setting the tone for a franchise about to evolve into a champion.

"A lot of people don't want to bring in other people around them, because they may want to be the smartest guy in the room," Francis said. "Craig had no ego in that regard, he brought good people in, smart people in, and ultimately that made the whole organization and him look smarter and better. A lot of smart hockey minds help you when you get into those tough situations. I was impressed with the cast he assembled. I learned a lot from watching that group."

The trade for Francis in 1991 was an illustration of the fact Patrick had a trait critical for successful general managers: the confidence to make difficult decisions. He understood trades which made sense from an on-ice perspective might also risk upsetting the chemistry in the dressing room, and he had to weigh those considerations with moving John Cullen in 1991 and Mark Recchi in 1992.

"That's the definition of an architect: identify what the weak link is in the house, and go out to get the next piece of lumber that's needed to get this house to the next level," said Phil Bourque, who played on the 1991 and 1992 Cup teams. "It's one thing when you talk about the players he traded, but it's another thing when you talk about the importance of those players in the locker room as far as how loved they were, to know what those people, both Recchs and Cully, meant to us."

The acquisition of Rick Tocchet, Kjell Samuelsson and Ken Wregget in 1992 meant not only losing Recchi but Paul Coffey. "He traded two Hall of Famers," recalled assistant coach Pierre McGuire. Winger Bob Errey said the 1992 Cup "wouldn't have happened if we didn't make that trade for those three players. Craig was never afraid to take that shot."

Later in his time with the Penguins, Patrick acquired goaltender Johan Hedberg, defenseman Darius Kasparaitis and forwards Petr Nedvěd and Alexei Kovalev, all of whom were very productive in their time with Pittsburgh and played for the Penguins in the Conference Finals. He also missed on trades, in 1996 sending Markus Näslund to Vancouver for Alek Stojanov and then failing to get any productive prospects in the 2001 Jaromír Jágr trade, necessitated by finances and other factors. But that happens to all longtime GMs, and no Pittsburgh GM has ever acquired more players who won the Cup with the team.

Patrick also took the Pittsburgh drafting philosophy into new territory. In the 10 drafts from 1990 through 1999, the Penguins spent eight of their first-round picks on European-born players (seven of those skilled forwards, including Näslund) and picked more players who had skated for European teams in their draft year than any other NHL team. In the 1990, 1991 and 1992 drafts, the Penguins were the only NHL team not to draft a single player from the Ontario Hockey League, historically the most-utilized breeding ground for NHL players, while also going heavy on drafting American prep and college players.

Despite the uncertain health of Mario Lemieux after their two Cup victories, Patrick kept the Penguins in the Stanley Cup conversation. After their shocking 1993 playoff loss to the New York Islanders, the Penguins finished the labor-shortened 1994–95 season with the league's third-best record and reached the Conference Final in both 1996 and 2001. The Penguins' run of qualifying for the playoffs in 11 straight seasons, then a team record, ended in 2002 and the following season Patrick played the long game when trading for the No. 1 overall pick in the 2003 draft and selecting goaltender Marc-André Fleury, who won three Stanley Cups with the Penguins.

"In meetings, he was very cerebral, quiet, takes it all in, makes decisions," remembered Hillier, who said the coaching staff got to the 2003 draft concerned about their future depth at center. "(Eric) Staal would have looked pretty good for us, but to Craig's credit, he said, 'You can't win a championship without a goalie.'"

At least four players on all five Pittsburgh Cup-winning teams were brought to the organization by Patrick, a claim no other Penguins' GM can make. Patrick was inducted into the United States Hockey Hall of Fame in 1996 and the Hockey Hall of Fame as a builder in 2001.

Patrick made nine coaching hires in more than 16 years with the team, but he never made a more impactful one than bringing Johnson to Pittsburgh in the summer of 1990. "Badger" won three NCAA titles during his 15 seasons as the University of Wisconsin and also built an international reputation, coaching the U.S. National Team for four years, guiding Team

USA in the 1981 and 1984 Canada Cup tournaments and also coaching the U.S. Olympic Team in 1976.

During his five-year stint as coach of the Calgary Flames from 1982–87, Johnson took the team to its first Stanley Cup Final in 1986, where the Flames lost to Montreal. But after three years as executive director of USA Hockey, Johnson was ready for another chance in the NHL and came to Pittsburgh, where his son Mark, one of the stars of the 1980 U.S. Olympic Team, had played for parts of three seasons after winning the gold medal.

"I guess I've always referred to myself as a career coach. Where was Bob Johnson the happiest? As I look into the 1990s, obviously I was happiest in coaching," said Johnson, who had contacted Patrick shortly after Patrick had been named the Penguins' general manager to let him know about his desire to return to coaching. "So it was a simple decision. You'll find Bob Johnson very positive, very enthusiastic, a guy that enjoys going to the rink, enjoys his work. I think that's important."

That's why any day was always a chance for Johnson to tell players, reporters and others, "It's a great day for hockey."

New Penguins' right wing Joe Mullen had played for Johnson in Calgary. "When I got (to Pittsburgh), everybody asked me about him, and I said, 'Well, he's a little different type of coach than you're used to. But he knows his stuff,'" remembered Mullen.

Johnson's optimism and positivity took many of the Penguins by surprise. His style was to develop honest relationships with his players and to emphasize the good things they were doing, no matter how difficult the times. And the 1990–91 Penguins had some of those, given the absence of the injured Mario Lemieux for the first 50 games and the amount of turnover on the playing roster. Through mid-December, they had lost 16 of their first 31 games and were next-to-last in the Patrick Division.

"Thank God we had him," said winger Bob Errey, for whom Johnson was the sixth coach in eight seasons. "I remember when Gilly (Randy Gilhen) first came in, Bob was out on the ice with him. He was saying, 'Give me a little hop. I'm going to get a little more hop out of you, an extra stride out of you, Gilhen.' Gilly's going around in circles in the neutral zone. Bob is behind him going, 'That's it, that's it, Gilly. I'm going to get another stride out of you.' He was so positive, you could be down 8–1 and he'd come in there and talk about something positive. He was the first guy I really know who was able to form those relationships with every player."

Recalled Mark Recchi, "Badger was always just himself. There were times in the course of the season we struggled, maybe got beat the night before handily, and he came to practice the next day and he was the same person. This went on, you didn't think it was real at first, then by January and February, you're like, this guy's not changing. Not changing at all. It's a calming feeling.

"And he always communicated well. I remember one time, working on the power play, we had a terrible practice, I think we had a team party the night before was probably the reason...he comes in and says, 'Golfers, you know, they have to practice every day and be good every day.' It was a different way to send a message, that we had to be better, but it was pretty funny."

Johnson had a simple philosophy about the way he interacted with his players. "I'm a great believer that we should allow the players to do the things they do best," he said. "You don't find a complete hockey player, and slowly and surely you try to improve on his deficiencies. But let's not be critical of the players. Let's let them do the things they do best and take it from there."

And the Penguins got better, and Johnson kept it all top of mind with the help of the ever-present steno notebooks he had behind the bench. To say he was a student of the game would be a massive understatement; he kept every notebook for every game back to start of his Wisconsin career, and he also had notebooks in which he took notes from other teams' practices or planned his own. "It's not what you know," he said. "It's what you teach on the ice."

Said Mullen, "He never left that notebook and pen at home. You'd get on an elevator with him and he would pull it out, and say, 'We've got to start doing things like this,' and he's drawing things up...he always had hockey on his mind."

Paul Coffey was a member of the 1986 Edmonton team Johnson and the Flames had upset on the way to the Final, and he remembered Johnson "put an incredible system together" to do it. "He was ahead of his time," Coffey said. "He was always drawing stuff. He was a motivator, a tactician."

Johnson would find a way to get his message delivered, no matter where he was. In the Penguins' dressing room he had a huge rink taped onto the floor and pucks with every player's face on them, and he would use a stick to move them around as his team watched.

"He played a soft lock, and he was not so much run through the guy but make sure you maintain body position," said Bryan Trottier. "He had a forecheck system in the offensive zone, a neutral zone forecheck, defensive zone positioning. He was very deliberate in how he approached it, and clear on where he wanted the first, second and third forechecker, when he wanted D to pinch down the wall, when to step up in the neutral zone. He was very patient."

Larry Murphy remembered one afternoon in Boston "we practiced the power play breakout in the ballroom. He arranged the chairs, had a net, we're all in street clothes, and we'd circle around the net how he wanted the breakout to go."

The Penguins began to take off in mid-December and won more games than all but the Kings and Blues the rest of the way, getting Lemieux back in late January and taking the first division title in team history. And Johnson's repetitive messaging and practices built a foundation the team relied on in the playoffs.

"He taught us about details. If you do the details, you're going to win consistently, you'll win the right way in the regular season that will help you win in the playoffs," Phil Bourque said. "It was the way we practiced. We'd do Hockey 101 things, making 10-foot passes to each other, then he'd blow the whistle and we'd do stationary passing, then he'd tell us to get on the backhand. We're looking at each other and saying, 'I used to do this stuff in hockey school.'"

That the Penguins got to the head of the class by late May, winning their first Stanley Cup, was a function of the team Patrick had assembled and Johnson had nurtured into a winner. When the news broke in late August 1991 that Johnson had been diagnosed with a brain tumor and rushed to Mercy Hospital, it turned the Penguins' world upside down. Bourque called Patrick and was told Johnson wasn't seeing visitors.

"I was sitting at home, it was later at night, I was like, 'I'm going to go down.' I talked my way in," remembered Bourque, who saw his coach before surgery to remove the tumor. "It was right after I got married, he grabbed my hand and squeezed my hand, 'Heard you got married.' I said, yes, I got married a week ago. And he was like, 'It's going to be good for you.' He was really happy to hear that news. Nothing to do with hockey.

That's him in a nutshell, that's how he connected with players: something personal, and then it easily segued into hockey."

Johnson died of brain cancer on Nov. 26, 1991, at his home in Colorado Springs. He was inducted into the United States Hockey Hall of Fame that same year and the Hockey Hall of Fame in 1992.

The winningest coach in hockey history, Bowman was officially named the Penguins' interim coach three days before the start of the 1991–92 season. "I really didn't feel I was in any position to say no," Bowman said. "I felt for the team, too. I know what these players endured last year to win the Stanley Cup. I want to contribute in the best way the organization thinks I can."

Bowman, who had coached Montreal to five Stanley Cups in the 1970s, had served as both general manager and coach of the Buffalo Sabres in the 1980s, but less than a month after he relinquished his coaching duties in Buffalo in 1986 to concentrate solely on his GM position, he was fired by the Sabres. He received interest from other NHL teams during three years as an analyst with *Hockey Night in Canada,* but Patrick's offer of a position as director of player development in the summer of 1990 fit for Bowman because he could largely work from home.

"I wanted to get back in, but I had three kids going to high school," Bowman said. "I wasn't that interested in moving the family. Craig said, 'You won't have to move.' That was the appealing part of the job. It made a good fit."

Now he was back behind the bench and spending more time away from his family, but Bowman made it clear he wasn't planning to stay. "The job is interim, and with me it's very interim," he said. "We want to try to preserve everything that (Johnson) did for this team. They don't know me as a coach.

But they know what Bob wants, and a lot of our positions are the same. I told them the things that make me tick. I don't like to lose. Bob didn't like to lose, either."

Bowman's style was not conducive to building relationships with players, and he would sometimes embrace unusual tactics. In 1984, unhappy with the Sabres' play, he briefly demoted star goaltender Tom Barrasso to the AHL; he used two-time Norris Trophy winner Paul Coffey as a forward in Pittsburgh; and in the final and meaningless regular-season game of the 1991–92 season at Madison Square Garden, he decided to regularly rotate goaltenders Ken Wregget and Wendell Young, changing them nine times during stoppages in play. It was too inviting for both of them, who decided to change on the fly in the third period.

But Bowman's superb hockey mind and ability to understand the way any 60-minute game was evolving and use it to inform his deployment of players was legendary. On a game night, Bowman running your bench was the best you could ever hope to do.

"Scotty is more of an old-school, you know, 'You better show up every day.' It's not going to be rah-rah to get you going," said Barrasso upon Bowman replacing Johnson. "Behind the bench, he's the best coach I've ever seen in my life. I think that's the most important thing. That's what's really going to get us through—his ability behind the bench."

Bryan Trottier said when he listened to Bowman, he heard the familiar echo of coach Al Arbour, who had played for Bowman in St. Louis in the late 1960s before later leading Trottier and the New York Islanders to four straight Cups.

"I saw where Al Arbour got a lot of his sayings and coaching philosophies," Trottier said. "During the year, Scotty was just trying things, and I think he frustrated a lot of players. A lot of it was not having the flow of practice. Scotty would stop and explain, stop and explain...but in one-on-one meetings, and I had a few with him, he explained what his strategy was and I said, 'All right, I think that's a good one.' He wasn't confrontational. He was just matter of fact.

"Scotty is a strategist. He's got a great feel for the bench, probably the best I've had. He knew what he could get from the players and when he could get it. He utilized his bench very, very well. Scotty was never rattled. Always had the same tone in the locker room, on the bench. He gained a lot of respect here in Pittsburgh. It was a wonderful experience in the sense that we found a way. There was a lot of transition that year from the players' perspective to the coach and vice versa. It wasn't easy, but it's not supposed to be, because that's how you win championships. You learn a lot about yourself."

Even after their late-season trade to acquire Rick Tocchet, Kjell Samuelsson and Wregget, the Penguins were barely hanging on to the last playoff spot in the Patrick Division. But they lost only 10 of their final 39 games that season, playoffs included, and Bowman had his sixth Cup.

Given that ending, it was less surprising to see Bowman stay for the following season, too. The Penguins won the only Presidents' Trophy in team history and established an NHL record with 17 consecutive wins in 1992–93 before falling in the second round of the playoffs to the New York Islanders. Bowman, who went on to win Stanley Cups as Detroit's coach in 1997, 1998 and 2002, was inducted into the Hockey Hall of Fame in 1991.

20
Tied Together

THE LOCKOUT OF 2004–05 WAS A BITTER PILL FOR THE NHL to swallow, but optimism abounded when the league finally returned to play in the fall of 2005 with a salary cap in place that, according to *Forbes* magazine, helped increase by almost 50 percent the average value of a team over the next six seasons. New rules encouraged more scoring, and the introduction of the shootout became quickly popular with fans.

Pittsburgh fans also had the start of the Sidney Crosby era to cheer them up after three consecutive bottom-five finishes in the standings, and while he had a spectacular rookie season, the team was a mess on the ice. Despite some high-profile roster additions designed to take advantage of the new scoring environment, the Penguins lost their first nine games and were the worst defensive team in the league, and the fourth-weakest scoring team, when coach Ed Olczyk was fired in mid-December.

General manager Craig Patrick hired coaching veteran Michel Therrien to replace Olczyk—the first of six consecutive head coaches of the Penguins' AHL affiliate in Wilkes-Barre/ Scranton to later win NHL head coaching positions, followed by Todd Richards, Dan Bylsma, Todd Reirden, John Hynes and Mike Sullivan. In his first six weeks, things didn't get much better for Therrien, who had coached the Montreal Canadiens for parts of three seasons earlier in the decade. Mario Lemieux played his last game, sidelined by heart irregularities; veterans Lyle Odelein and Ryan VandenBussche and 26-year-old Matt Murley were lost for the season with injuries; and skilled winger Ziggy Pálffy, despite averaging a point per game, walked away from $11 million by retiring "for personal reasons."

Pittsburgh lost 22 of its first 26 games under Therrien, but he was the man for the job at hand. After his 11th game behind the bench, a fairly typical 3–1 home loss to Edmonton in early January, he went on a steadily delivered post-game rant that went well beyond the ordinary, describing his defense with an adjective that is the biggest insult you can give a hockey player.

"Not impressed," he said. "It's a pathetic performance. Half the team doesn't care. Are we going to be happy to play eight minutes?...That defensive squad, I really am starting to believe their goal is to be the worst defensive squad in the league. And they're doing such a great job...they turn the puck over, they have no vision, they're soft...I've never seen a bunch of defensemen soft like this...they pretend to care, but I know they don't care."

Therrien's rant changed nothing immediately, as the Penguins lost their next seven games, starting with a 6–1 blowout in Columbus 24 hours later. But defenseman Brooks Orpik, who was injured and did not play in the loss to Edmonton, understood that some of the young players on the team—nine of the 20 players dressed against the Oilers were

24 or younger, four of them 22 or younger—needed something more than encouragement.

"With where the organization was at the time, I think his hiring was necessary to come in and install a lot of discipline and habits to replace bad habits that had become acceptable," said Orpik, who was in his first full NHL season in 2005–06 and later won Stanley Cups with both the Penguins and Capitals. "They were definitely not habits conducive to having a winning culture. At the time, that type of coach was definitely needed. I probably didn't agree with everything he did, but he did a lot of good things. He obviously wanted the defensive structure, and some of the defensive habits we all learned from him, they became so ingrained in us that they became part of your game for the rest of your career."

Added Max Talbot, "Without what we went through with Therrien, we would never have won. Lot of props to him."

After finishing with the league's second-worst record, the Penguins over the next two seasons added Evgeni Malkin, Jordan Staal, Marián Hossa, Kris Letang, Hal Gill, Petr Sýkora, Gary Roberts, Pascal Dupuis and Tyler Kennedy, among others, and quickly turned things around. They came within two victories of the Stanley Cup in 2008, which included a dramatic triple-overtime Game 5 win in Detroit made possible by Talbot's goal with 35 seconds to play after Therrien sent him on the ice to replace Fleury. "Mike was so good at feeling guys on the bench and trying always to create something," Talbot said. "That's exactly what he did for that game. There was a lot of talent on the bench. He pushed on my shoulder, and I kinda looked back like, 'Really, you sure you want to send me?' It was a feeling he had."

But Pittsburgh did not build on that finish over the first four and a half months of the 2008–09 season. The Penguins suffered a dismal 6–2 loss in Toronto on Feb. 14, losing a 2–0 lead and allowing five goals in the third period—their own version of a Valentine's Day Massacre, which left them five points out of a playoff spot. That was the end for Therrien, who had lasted almost two seasons under general manager Ray Shero, who hadn't hired him—always a factor weighing against coaches in that situation.

"I wanted to give Michel an opportunity," Shero said. "I had a really good relationship with Michel, I respected him a lot. He's a very loyal guy. He had structure, he had discipline. We had a young team that wanted to learn, and he was really good to work with."

Therrien had simply been unable to sustain results, and the end of that story was somewhat predictable. "You look at the NHL, it's just kind of the way it works," said Orpik. "It kind of seems like coaches' expiration dates are a lot shorter in the NHL compared to other leagues. When he got replaced, we probably wouldn't have won it if he was still there."

The new coach coming from Wilkes-Barre was Bylsma, a checker who had played 429 games in the NHL with Los Angeles and Anaheim, his Ducks team losing to New Jersey in Game 7 of the 2003 Stanley Cup Final. He had led his AHL team to the league's fourth-best record at that point in the season, and he brought a different approach to his first NHL head coaching job, signing a contract handwritten by Shero.

"At that point in the season, it was just such a lack of fun surrounding the team. We had a great team, but the guys' confidence was starting to get shot," remembered Orpik. "There was a lack of joy and fun going to the rink. When Dan came in, his personality and his coaching style was kind of perfect for turning around what we were in at the time. Everybody started having fun again. Systems were a little different, but not much. I think guys were genuinely excited to come to the rink again."

The effect of the change was dramatic, with the Penguins suffering one regulation loss in their first 16 games under Bylsma—they had eight regulation losses in their last 16 games under Therrien. They finished the regular season 18–3–4 under Bylsma. The lineup had been bolstered by the return of defenseman Sergei Gonchar, who had missed the entire season with a shoulder injury until returning for that fateful game in Toronto, and the addition of veteran forwards Bill Guerin, Chris Kunitz and Craig Adams, but the mood around the team had been lifted.

"It just gave us air, in a way," Talbot said. "Every time you change a coach, you kind of go for the opposite type of coach, and teams that have a players' coach will change for a tough coach, and for us it was different. When Dan got there, it was like, 'Let's go, let's play hockey.' We changed a couple of things in the neutral zone. He had 'Moustache Boy' after practice. These were the fun games Dan would bring, going on a two-on-one drill, he would go down and block shots without equipment, just being that ex-player who just wanted to have fun."

As part of a regular program of practicing shootouts, Bylsma soon implemented an end-of-practice routine once a month in which all players participated in a shootout drill, the last player who failed to score being required to grow a moustache over the next month. It was a lighthearted way to practice what became an important part of the game for the Penguins, who became a shootout-winning machine with Fleury in goal and a talented group of forwards who obviously benefited from the practice. During Bylsma's time behind the Penguins' bench, they led the NHL in shootout winning percentage by a significant margin.

But there was more to what Bylsma was accomplishing.

"(Assistant GM) Chuck Fletcher knew Dan from Anaheim, and the thing you noticed right away...he played 10 years in the NHL, and had played with star players, and Dan right away had a real good command of the room in terms of a presence," said Shero, for whom that presence was an important consideration. Just days after winning the 2009 Stanley Cup, Shero had reminded everyone that coaching a very talented team is not as easy as it looks.

"When you have so many young guys, and they're talented players...I go back to the Montreal Canadiens and Scotty Bowman," he said. "Everybody thought, when they were losing eight games a year, that it was so easy for Scotty Bowman. I know my father (Cup-winning Flyers' coach Fred Shero) was coaching against him and he said Scotty probably had the hardest job trying to satisfy the players in terms of their roles and ice time. It's the same thing with us.

"To satisfy these players...some of these guys are top offensive guys; they want to be in certain roles or need to be in certain roles. You have to manage that and have to manage their expectations and let them realize this is a team game."

Bylsma today still points mostly to the player additions made by Shero as the biggest force in driving the Penguins to their third Cup. "A lot of changes happened in that time period at the end of February, and it gave the team an opportunity to reach their potential," he said. "Without Guerin and Kunitz and Gonchar...fortunately for me coming in late February we had success, and with all those changes we built momentum toward the end of the season. Those changes are a huge reason why we went on to win the Stanley Cup."

Bylsma went on to spend 401 regular-season games behind the Penguins' bench, at the time the most consecutive games in team history. But he could not take them to another championship, the biggest misses coming in a first-round loss to the Flyers in 2012 and a Conference Final sweep at the hands of the Bruins in 2013, a series in which Pittsburgh scored only twice. He was fired in early June 2014, not long after losing a 3–1 series lead in the second round against the Rangers and just weeks after Shero was replaced by Jim Rutherford.

Bylsma and Shero spent five years and three months together, the longest stretch in team history for a general manager and a coach, and during that time the Penguins had the NHL's best record to go along with one Stanley Cup. "I think we should have won more than one," Shero said, "but you see how hard it is to win one."

Thinking back to his time running the Penguins, Shero couldn't help but reflect on the Pittsburgh careers of Crosby, Malkin and Letang, who played their 20th season together in 2025–26.

"When they won in 2016 and 2017, maybe that was a better way to do it," he said. "What they went through, on and off the ice as players—concussions, MCL tears, a lot of falling short—they went through the hard times, and I think they would appreciate that more, without even knowing it, than if they had just won again in, say, 2011 and 2012. If they had won three Cups but won them early...I think their legacy is better having won them this way."

Shero, who passed away in 2025, had a profound impact on the Penguins' championship history. Of the 87 players whose names are engraved on the Stanley Cup as Pittsburgh champions, 24 of them were acquired by Shero—only Craig Patrick, who was in the job for twice as long, had more (27). Shero acquired 15 of the players who won in 2009 and nine others who won for the first time in either 2016 or 2017, although some of those players saw limited playoff action.

"He did a really good job," Crosby said of Shero. "First, just instilling a lot of confidence and belief in us. It was more from a cultural standpoint. We wanted to win, we wanted it so bad, but there's steps you have to go through, and there's things I think organizationally he did...just the way, whether it was free agents or guys traded to the team, the way he treated them, and the ways things were run. He really believed in that culture, and just making this a place people wanted to come to. We had some great results because of it."

If any Cup-winning general manager had put in his time preparing for success, it was Shero. Before succeeding Patrick as Pittsburgh GM in the summer of 2006, Shero spent six years as an assistant GM in Ottawa and then eight more as an assistant GM in Nashville, where his AHL affiliate Milwaukee Admirals won the Calder Cup in 2004 and lost in the Calder Cup Final in 2006.

A native of St. Paul, Minn., Shero played at St. Lawrence University and was drafted by the Los Angeles Kings in 1982, although he began working as a player agent upon graduation. It was hardly a surprising career path for Shero, whose father, Fred, coached the Flyers to Stanley Cup titles in 1974 and 1975 and later coached the New York Rangers, taking six of his 10 NHL teams to the third round of the playoffs or further.

The Penguins went from 58 points in the standings in 2005–06 to 105 points in Shero's first season as their GM, with Malkin and Staal making huge impacts in their rookie seasons. "I was like, 'It can't be this easy.' But it was a lot of growing together as a group," he said.

And when the group needed another push in future seasons, he went through all channels to provide it, signing free agents Petr Sýkora and Darryl Sydor, promoting Tyler Kennedy from the AHL and acquiring Marián Hossa, Pascal Dupuis and Hal Gill via trades. He followed in 2008–09 by signing free agents Matt Cooke, Ruslan Fedotenko and Miroslav Šatan, acquiring Guerin and Kunitz through trades and landing Craig Adams on waivers. Like Patrick before him, Shero had made moves in consecutive seasons that got his team to the Stanley Cup Final in both.

What Shero had inherited and built upon featured the stability of Fleury in goal and depth at center no other NHL team could match: Crosby, Malkin and Staal. But with Staal entering the final year of his contract in 2012–13, Shero had a challenge negotiating an extension as rumors persisted Jordan—the first player Shero drafted as GM of the Penguins—wanted to play with his brother Eric in Carolina.

"(Carolina GM) Jim Rutherford gave me the head's up, basically," remembered Shero, "that if he's not signed a year from now, 'I just want to let you know we're going to come after Jordan hard. Just want to give you a head's up.' Which was really good of him. I really wanted one more try with these three centers.

"(Jordan) never asked for a trade. We offered him 10 years at $5.75 (million). It took a lot for Jordan to turn down that kind of money. I think it was more of getting out of that shadow (of Crosby and Malkin) and obviously, the opportunity of playing with Eric might have been another thing. We talked a lot. He had my word that even if he did sign, if for some reason he wasn't happy, I'd trade him where he wanted to go. Everything was up front.

"He said, 'I probably need some more time to think about it. I'm getting married.' I told him the draft is in a couple weeks, and if we don't have a deal, I can't make any promises. He was leaving my office, we shook hands and he turned around and he goes, 'You wouldn't trade me on my wedding day, would you?' It wasn't like I was trying to trade him on his wedding day."

But that's exactly what happened at the draft, which was held in Pittsburgh. Staal went to the Hurricanes for center Brandon Sutter, defenseman Brian Dumoulin and a first-round pick that turned out to be defenseman Derrick Pouliot. Staal signed an extension with Carolina at $6 million for 10 years, while Dumoulin became a regular on both the 2016 and 2017 Cup teams as the partner for No. 1 defenseman Letang. Shero said he had been given the option of taking a draft pick or Dumoulin and chose the latter.

Shero also surprised the hockey world at the 2013 trade deadline by acquiring Jarome Iginla from Calgary for a Penguins team that became the third under Shero to reach at least the Eastern Conference Final. Also at that deadline, he completed a deal with Dallas that brought him the third-round pick he used that summer to draft Jake Guentzel, who won the Cup with Pittsburgh in 2017.

His legacy in Pittsburgh was also highlighted by the opportunities he gave to other future NHL general managers, including Fletcher, Guerin, Tom Fitzgerald, Jason Botterill and Patrik Allvin, whom he hired as a scout. Shero later spent four and a half seasons as GM of the New Jersey Devils before becoming a senior advisor with the Minnesota Wild, the post he held at the time of his death. Shero in 2025 was awarded the Lester Patrick Trophy for outstanding service to hockey in the United States.

21
Making History

After spending 13 seasons as an NHL goaltender, including parts of three with the Penguins in the early 1970s, Jim Rutherford began a considerably longer career in NHL management when he was named president and chief operating officer of the Hartford Whalers in the summer of 1994. He took over the general manager's duties weeks later and served in the NHL as an interim GM or GM for each of the next 28 seasons.

Even when he finally stepped down as interim GM of the Vancouver Canucks in January 2022, he was still the man in charge in Vancouver, retaining his post as president of hockey operations—a title he was still holding in the 2025–26 season at the age of 76. For the man who moved with the Whalers to Raleigh, N.C., and won a Stanley Cup there in 2006, getting out of the game just wasn't in his genes.

Maybe it shouldn't have been surprising that Rutherford, while resigning as GM of the Carolina Hurricanes in April 2014 while retaining his post as their president, hinted that day he might not be done staying in or very close to managing an NHL team. "Today I feel very good about it," he told the *Raleigh News and Observer*. "But I think when you get to three months from now or four or six months from now, will that itch be there? Because I competed all my life, as a player, as a manager...we'll see what the next chapter brings."

The next chapter started some six weeks later when the Penguins hired him in June 2014 to replace Ray Shero, becoming the first former Pittsburgh player to serve the Penguins as general manager. Two years later, he became the first modern-day GM to win Cups with two different franchises as the Penguins reached the first of two consecutive titles under his direction, becoming the first team to go back-to-back in the NHL's salary cap era. In winning Cups with two different teams, Rutherford followed the footsteps of Tommy Gorman, who won Cups as the GM with Ottawa, Chicago, the Montreal Maroons and Montreal Canadiens in the 1930s and 1940s.

It wasn't simply a case of good timing on his part, either. "I don't think we have all the pieces here to get back to where the Penguins were (in 2009). But with some changes—they don't have to be sweeping changes—we can do this in the very near future," Rutherford said at the press conference welcoming him back to Pittsburgh.

But it did, in fact, take sweeping changes to put the Penguins in position to lift the 2016 Cup, in the process earning Rutherford 2016 honors as General Manager of the Year. Nearly 72 percent of the players who had skated for the team Rutherford inherited in 2014 were gone, as well as all four coaches, when he got his hands on his second Cup. Mostly via trades, Rutherford brought in 12 new players in his first season with Pittsburgh, which ended with a quiet first-round playoff exit against the New York Rangers. Many of those players were gone for the 2015–16 season, for which Rutherford added another 16 new players through trades and free agency, and nine of those saw their names engraved on the Cup.

"Jim is a deal-maker. The best advice Jim ever gave me is, 'Don't ever try to win a trade, because if you try to win a trade, you're never going to make it because you're too busy trying to win. And if you win one, you're probably going to screw the other guy over and he's never going to make another trade with you again.' It's a good philosophy," says Bill Guerin, who became GM of the Minnesota Wild after moving up the management ranks under Shero and Rutherford in Pittsburgh.

"That's what allowed him the ability to make some of the critical trades he did make. Both Ray and Jim, they had the courage to make big trades, to put their neck on the line, and sometimes it didn't work. And you know what? They just fixed it."

Rutherford added forward Patric Hörnqvist and defenseman Ian Cole in 2014–15, and then before or during the following season signed free agents Matt Cullen, Eric Fehr and Connor Sheary and traded for Nick Bonino, Phil Kessel, Trevor Daley, Carl Hagelin and Justin Schultz. These were all regulars who, with the exception of Fehr, went on to win two Cups with the Penguins.

"If you didn't fit the system, he wasn't afraid to make a bold move, wasn't afraid to trade a draft pick," said defenseman Brian Dumoulin. "He had such a vision of how he wanted the team to play, had such a good relationship with Sully (coach Mike Sullivan), and those two were together on it. When you create that line of communication throughout your organization, the expectation of how you're going to play, it simplifies everything. But it also creates a pressure where you have to go out and perform. You can't just be knowing your job is going to be there, everything is fine and dandy and he's not going to trade guys. As soon as you see guys (getting traded), it's like, 'OK, let's go.' He's trying to spark something in our group.

"I always remember when we played badly or had a bad stretch of games, Jim would just walk through the room. He wouldn't talk to anybody on game days. He was very quiet. After a bad stretch of games, he would just walk through one entrance of the locker room and then out the other entrance. He was just walking slowly, staring at the floor, and just exit the other side. As a group, we knew what that meant. We had to get going. It was so intimidating.

"He was showing that he cares about the group and he wants to win, and he's willing to make a change to do what's best to try to win," Dumoulin said. "As a player, you want your GM to give your team the best chance to win...we're not going to sell guys, we're not going to trade guys for draft picks. The guys we are going to trade for are players that are going to help us now. Which is all you can ask for."

Rutherford's first deal, made three weeks after he was hired, was a big one, sending 40-goal scorer James Neal to Nashville for Hörnqvist, who didn't score quite as much as Neal but played hard and was a major nuisance in front of the net, an element Pittsburgh was missing. Rutherford traded Brandon Sutter, the player he had dealt to Pittsburgh for Jordan Staal in 2012 as GM of the Hurricanes, for Bonino, who became a critical part of the Cup teams. Arguably his signature move was the acquisition of Kessel, who Rutherford theorized would take his game to a new level once out from under the pressure of being the focal point of Toronto's attack—which was exactly what happened.

"My comment came true about him getting some of that pressure off from being the go-to guy, but it was two-fold. It took some of the pressure off our go-to guys, Sid and Geno and Tanger and Kunitz and all of them, they didn't have to do it every night," Rutherford said. "There was another guy that was a game-changer that could help take the pressure off them, too. He was critical, played a big part in big games we won in the regular season and playoffs."

Rutherford missed on deals acquiring and then trading Ryan Reaves, who played only 58 games in Pittsburgh, giving up Oscar Sundqvist, Filip Gustavsson and first-round picks in both deals. But on balance he made mostly profitable trades for Pittsburgh and also an astute hire in the summer of 2015 to name Sullivan as coach of the Penguins' AHL affiliate in Wilkes-Barre/Scranton. The Penguins had been good but lacked spark in their first season under Mike Johnston, and Rutherford understood when hiring Sullivan that he might be landing the Penguins' future coach.

At the time of his hiring, Sullivan, who played more than 700 NHL games as a checking forward, had already spent two seasons coaching the Boston Bruins and six seasons as an assistant coach under John Tortorella in Tampa Bay, New York and Vancouver. So when Rutherford fired Johnston in mid-December 2015, Sullivan came to Pittsburgh with a good understanding of the young players skating in the AHL, and his direction to his new team was to play fast. Every night.

"We didn't necessarily know what that meant, but he kept harping on it and he kept showing it: this is what playing fast is. It spoke to our group," Dumoulin said. "We had lot of fast players, and even players that weren't fast knew how to play fast. It was D-to-D (defensemen passing), center and the puck was going north. When I went D-to-D, I could start up the weak side and support the rush because I knew the puck was going north and not coming back to me. Sid could get so much speed in the neutral zone because the puck was coming—either to that winger or to him, so he could fly and know where the puck was going to go."

Sullivan brought more than just a different pace of play; he also brought a different demeanor to the job. "Sully was just a confident guy, speaks his mind, held everyone accountable," said Bonino. "That was a big change that season, where Mike Johnston was more 'just let the guys play.' Sully was a breath of fresh air the team needed."

Sullivan pushed the Penguins, and his interactions hit the mark with his new team—right from the start.

"His messaging the very first day...he came in and held a meeting: this is what we need to do," remembered Chris Kunitz. "The first day was a video of Sid and Geno doing something wrong. That kind of makes everybody else align. His messaging was, 'Guys, if we fix this, it will put us in good areas.' It was him showing our big guys doing something wrong, (knowing) they'll fix it, and now everybody else will fall in order."

Sullivan augmented what the Penguins already had by adding Bryan Rust, Connor Sheary, Scott Wilson and Tom Kühnhackl from Wilkes-Barre/Scranton, and Rutherford traded for veteran speedster Carl Hagelin as Pittsburgh's forechecking game wore down opponents. Sullivan's approach also applied to playing without the puck, as the Penguins began to swarm opponents if they lost it.

"We really worked together as five-man units. That was fun," remembered Crosby. "There wasn't a lot of thinking, just being on your toes, aggressive, and it lent itself to forechecking but then reloading on the other side of the puck. Everybody understood how we needed to play and it really played to the strengths of our group."

Cullen was 39 and 40 years of age when he played on the Penguins' back-to-back Cup teams, and he was impressed with what he saw from Sullivan.

"I've never been around a better coach than Sully," Cullen said. "He fit our team perfectly, had a clarity of message that fit our team perfectly. Sully probably doesn't get enough credit for kind of pushing the game forward. The way he taught the game, the way we played, then combine it with the personnel we had and he brought in...we played the game at a higher pace than anybody else that season, and I remember thinking it was some of the best hockey I've ever been a part of.

"We were able to overwhelm teams because we skated so well, played at such a high pace, and even guys who weren't fast were smart guys who could put pucks in areas where we could use our speed. When we had the puck, we were coming at teams and when we didn't, we were pressuring the puck everywhere. Sully was so good at teaching that."

When the Penguins repeated as Cup champions in 2017, Sullivan became the first American-born coach to win two Cups and joined Montreal's Toe Blake (1956–60) and Ottawa's Pete Green (1920, 1921) as the only coaches to win championships for their NHL teams in their first two years on the job.

Sullivan later said he tried to be a role model while providing an atmosphere conducive to winning. "I'm cast in a leadership role and I take that responsibility very seriously," he said. "You try to lead by example. I try to walk the walk and not just talk the talk. I look at it as trying to create an environment where people are inspired and empowered to do what they do. That's the art of coaching. And for me, that's the most challenging, but it's also the most rewarding. It's a humbling experience. And it's a privilege to be cast in that role."

Goaltender Matt Murray, who played under Sullivan for five seasons, credited him for understanding how to adapt his approach to coaching all the personalities in his dressing room at any given time.

"You hear the term, 'He had his finger on the pulse of the room,' and he was able to have that. He was really good at coaching different players in different ways; he wasn't a one-size-fits-all kind of guy," Murray said. "He recognized that some guys need different things than others. He was also good at delegating a lot of different things, like the way (assistant coach Rick) Tocchet was kind of the Phil Kessel whisperer. When certain guys maybe didn't want to hear from Sully, he understood that and let other guys do the talking. He had a high emotional intelligence, I would say. He understands how people operate, and he's able to pick up on that and act on it. I think that's what really helped us in those two Cup runs."

Rutherford agreed, saying Sullivan was "well-prepared, a great communicator and could read the team on a daily basis on what the needs and adjustments were."

But the Penguins never again came close to replicating their phenomenal initial success under Sullivan. They were eliminated by eventual champion Washington in the second round of the 2018 playoffs and never won another round under Sullivan, hurt by goaltending inconsistency, defensive deficiencies and an aging team that wasn't being infused with younger talent, Pittsburgh having traded many of its draft picks while in its customary win-now mode.

The Penguins' playoff defeats ran the gamut: a surprising sweep at the hands of the New York Islanders in 2019 in which they scored only six goals; a shocking qualifying-round loss in 2020 to Montreal, a team that finished 15 points below the Penguins in the standings; and losses to the Islanders (2021) and New York Rangers (2022) in which they held 2–1 and 3–1 series leads, respectively. The Penguins moved on from Sullivan in April 2025 after the team had failed to qualify for the playoffs in three straight seasons, snapping a franchise-record string of 16 consecutive playoff qualifications. Sullivan left the Penguins as their greatest coach by any metric; he coached them longer and won more games and more Stanley Cups than any of his predecessors.

Rutherford didn't last as long. He stunned the team by resigning in early January 2021, just seven games into the COVID-truncated 2020–21 season for personal reasons. Rutherford was in the last year of his contract when he resigned, and he was hired 10 and a half months later as Vancouver's president of hockey operations—the title he said he had expressed interest in to the Penguins during his last seasons with the team.

Late in the summer of 2022, Rutherford told the *Pittsburgh Post-Gazette* his resignation was related to his struggles with working in the COVID environment of the time. "I wasn't as mentally strong as I should have been to be myself and continue to do that job," he said. "I was starting to react to things differently than I normally would, which led to where I got to." Both he and team president David Morehouse denied speculation there was friction between them.

Together, however, Rutherford and Sullivan had instantly created some real magic in Pittsburgh. Looking back, Cullen said simply, "We were really a hard team to play against."

Acknowledgments

I'D LIKE TO THANK BILL AMES FOR BRINGING THIS FANTASTIC opportunity to me, Michelle Bruton and Adam Motin at Triumph Books for their wisdom and guidance, Phil Bourque for writing the foreword in his inimitable style and Cindy Himes, the Penguins' director of community/alumni relations, for helping connect me to so many former players.

Many thanks to Dan Potash and Jay Caufield of SportsNet Pittsburgh, Penguins Communication Specialist Paul Steigerwald, Nancy Angus of the Mario Lemieux Foundation, Kelli Wilson of Power Forward, Vince Comunale for his information on local amateur hockey history and Mindy Lascheid for her input on her father's team song. Thanks to the many PR professionals around hockey who helped set up interviews: Evan Schall of the Penguins, Dylan Daniel of the Wild, Chase Pyke of the Capitals, Justin Cummings of the Kings, Joe Siville of the Flyers, Craig MacEwen of the Canucks, Kyle Shohara of the Kraken, Jay Burnham at UMass and Kelly Masse at the Hockey Hall of Fame.

A special thanks to all the players, coaches, managers, broadcasters and other media members who took the time to chat with me.

Books:
Jagr: An Autobiography. Jaromír Jágr with Jan Smid. Warwick Publishing Group, 1997.

Newspapers and Periodicals:
Pittsburgh Press
Pittsburgh Post-Gazette
Pittsburgh Tribune-Review
Ottawa Citizen

Websites:
The Athletic
Forbes.com
Newspapers.com
NHL.com
Pittsburghpenguins.com
Sportsnet Stats
USA Hockey.com